Shakespeare
in 100 Objects

Shakespeare *in* 100 OBJECTS

Treasures from the
Victoria and Albert Museum

NICK HERN BOOKS
London
www.nickhernbooks.co.uk

A Nick Hern Book

Shakespeare in 100 Objects
first published in Great Britain in 2014
by Nick Hern Books Limited,
The Glasshouse, 49a Goldhawk Road, London W12 8QP
in association with the Victoria and Albert Museum, London

© Victoria and Albert Museum, London

Designed and typeset by Nick Hern Books, London
Printed and bound in Great Britain by
Ashford Colour Press Ltd, Gosport, Hampshire

A CIP catalogue record for this book is available from the British Library

ISBN 978 1 84842 361 9

Contents

Histories

Tragedies

For the Victoria and Albert Museum

General Editor	Janet Birkett
Contributors	Sarah Belanger, Janet Birkett, Kate Dorney, James Fowler, Catherine Haill, Beverley Hart, Claire Hudson, Veronica Isaac, Jane Pritchard and Sophie Reynolds
Thanks	David Caamano, Neil Carleton, Vanessa Eyles, Amy King, Geoffrey Marsh and Simon Sladen

For Nick Hern Books

Publisher	Nick Hern
Consultant Editor	Nick de Somogyi
Commissioning Editor	Matt Applewhite
Production Editor	Jodi Gray

66 …Your gallery
Have we pass'd through, not without much content
In many singularities… **99**
The Winter's Tale (5.3)

Introduction

The Victoria and Albert Museum is the world's leading art and design museum. Founded in 1852 as the Museum of Manufactures, its purpose was threefold – to make works of art available to everyone, to educate, and to inspire designers, craftspeople and commercial manufacturers. Those principles have not changed.

The museum moved to its present site in 1857, becoming the South Kensington Museum. Then in 1899, when Queen Victoria laid the foundation stone for a new frontage and entrance hall, it was renamed the Victoria and Albert Museum to commemorate both the Queen and her late husband, who had been an enthusiastic supporter of the original museum. As the building expanded so did its collections. Today they encompass paintings, prints and drawings, photographs, textiles, woodwork and metalwork, ceramics and sculpture, glass and plastic, mixing the contemporary with the historic in displays in the permanent galleries and in a continuing programme of exhibitions. Archive collections and a public reference library, the National Art Library, are available to researchers, and a website gives access to images and information.

An art and design museum may not seem the natural place to find objects relating to Shakespeare and his plays. Yet within the collections is a wealth of material with links to the playwright and his work. Some of those links are direct. The generosity of three of the museum's nineteenth-century patrons – Alexander Dyce, John Forster and John Jones – gave the National Art Library copies of the First Folio, as well as Second and Third Folios and quarto editions of many of the plays. Amongst the V&A's sixteenth- and seventeenth-century treasures, of a style and type that Shakespeare would have recognised, is one which he certainly knew by repute – the Great Bed of Ware, mentioned in *Twelfth Night*, which now has pride of place in the V&A's British Galleries. But the V&A's Shakespearean connections are not limited to the playwright's own time, and anyone interested in the plays and how they have been acted, interpreted and costumed down the centuries, will find scenes and characters represented in paint, in sculpture and ceramic, and in any number of engraved prints and etchings, drawings and watercolours. Some are the product of an artist's imagination, some record actual stage productions. The production process is represented in designs and costumes from stagings of the plays and from reinterpretations of the stories as dance, musicals, opera and cabaret. There are the posters and playbills that advertised them, and the photographs that have captured the performers and preserved their performances.

This book contains a selection of one hundred objects chosen by curators in the Theatre and Performance Department from across the museum, and is intended as an introduction to the range of material that relates to Shakespeare and his plays. The majority of items come from the collections of the Theatre and Performance Department. The department owes its origins to devoted theatre enthusiast Gabrielle Enthoven (1868–1950), who amassed a vast collection of playbills, programmes and newspaper cuttings, along with prints, designs, photographs and all manner of theatrical ephemera, which she donated to the V&A in 1924. In 1974, her collection became the core of the V&A's Theatre Museum which, from 1987 until 2007, was housed in the old Flower Market building in Covent Garden. The Theatre Museum amalgamated Mrs Enthoven's gift with those of the British Theatre Museum Association and the Friends of the Museum of the Performing Arts, two privately run organisations whose founders had long campaigned for a Theatre Museum to be opened in London. These were augmented by donations, large and small, from a host of organisations and private individuals. Now renamed the Theatre and Performance Department, with galleries at the V&A and a reading room at Blythe House, Kensington Olympia, the collections continue to develop, with an ever-growing number of archives relating to theatres and theatre people, many of which provide information about the staging of Shakespeare. The department is also the home of the National Video Archive of Performance which, as its name implies, makes archival quality recordings of live stage performance, available to view by appointment, and currently holds over thirty Shakespeare productions, recorded in London and Stratford-upon-Avon.

Choosing a hundred objects for the book was not easy. The Droeshout engraved portrait that appears as the frontispiece of the First Folio has been reproduced countless times in countless forms, and the engravings from the first illustrated edition of the plays, published by Nicholas Rowe in 1709, are well known, but these are of such significance that the book would be incomplete without them. The engraved prints and etchings of theatres, actors and performances, are, by their nature, not unique, though many are rare and deserve a wider audience, as do the images from the department's extensive photographic archives. Many objects cannot be found elsewhere – there are set and costume designs for productions in London and Stratford, costumes worn by famous names of the British theatre, paintings of great Shakespearean actors in the roles which revealed their skill and versatility. We have included artists' representations of actors as Shakespeare's characters – the first great black actor, Ira Aldridge, as Othello; Richard Burton as an Old Vic Henry V – along with Hester Booth, an acclaimed eighteenth-century Cordelia who began her career as a dancer and female harlequin, and Edmund Kean, who dominated the nineteenth-century stage, is represented in engraved prints in his most famous role of Richard III, but also as Giles Overreach in an oil sketch by George Clint that brings the performer to life, capturing the volatility and passion that led Coleridge to liken Kean's performances to 'reading Shakespeare by flashes of lightning'. The esteem in which Kean was held can be gauged by the richly decorated presentation sword, given to him by the Edinburgh admirers of his 1819 Macbeth.

Other objects have unexpected Shakespearean links. There is an engraved print of Nell Gwyn who, as the mistress of King Charles II, had her theatre-going, including four visits to see *The Tempest* in one year, paid for by the Royal Exchequer. There is the illustration from an early edition of Charles Dickens's *The Old Curiosity Shop*, which shows the horse-drawn caravan containing Mrs Jarley's waxworks, a Dickensian invention given an afterlife by two nineteenth-century authors in a series of playtexts which enabled amateur actors to impersonate movable wax figures of the great, good and not-so-good, including a range of Shakespearean characters. Shakespeare himself is portrayed by the eighteenth-century sculptors Roubiliac and Rysbrack as a noble, romantic figure, but he also appears in more down-to-earth guise as the advertising logo for the Stratford brewery, Flowers, to whose generosity we owe the existence of the Royal Shakespeare Theatre. Some surprising Shakespearean connections are provided by the costume design for a 1970s nightclub floor show, which manages to convey the essentials of

Antony and Cleopatra using the minimal of covering, and the costume designs for a *Hamlet*-inspired revue, drawn by artist Ronald Searle while a prisoner of war in 1944, for which Berowne's query, 'To move wild laughter in the throat of death? / It cannot be: it is impossible', becomes horribly appropriate (*LLL*. 5.2.843–4).

Beginning with the Folio itself and a view of Bankside as Shakespeare would have known it, the book echoes the sequence of Shakespeare's First Folio, grouping together the Comedies, Histories and Tragedies, but interspersed with objects which portray buildings, events, and the playwright himself. Virtually every play is represented, and many feature more than once. *A Midsummer Night's Dream* is represented by objects from three influential twentieth-century productions, by Harley Granville-Barker, Tyrone Guthrie and Peter Brook, by two ballets and by Rowe's 1709 illustration which portrays the eighteenth-century operatic adaptation. *Love's Labour's Lost*, photographed at the Old Vic in a traditional setting, also provides the inspiration for *The Big Life*, a twenty-first-century musical about Caribbean immigrants arriving in Britain on MV *Empire Windrush*. Works by Shakespeare which were omitted by the First Folio's compilers are also included. As well as *Pericles*, we have represented the 'lost' *Cardenio* by a still from the V&A's video recording of the Royal Shakespeare Company's 2011 production, and *Vortigern*, which eighteenth-century hoaxer William Ireland attempted to pass off as a rediscovered Shakespearean work, features in a satirical print.

All Shakespeare quotations are taken from the Complete Works, edited by Peter Alexander. Appropriate quotations have been added to each short essay, selected by Consultant Editor Nick de Somogyi, who also suggested the book's structure. Full details of each object are supplied in an Appendix. Unlike the outlaws in *The Two Gentlemen of Verona*, we have been unable to 'show thee all the treasure we have got' (4.1), but this book will give an idea of how much Shakespearean treasure can be found in the V&A.

MR. WILLIAM

SHAKESPEARES

COMEDIES,
HISTORIES, &
TRAGEDIES.

Published according to the True Originall Copies.

Martin Droeshout sculpsit London.

LONDON

Printed by Iſaac Iaggard, and Ed. Blount. 1623.

1

"Devise, wit; write, pen; for I am for whole volumes in folio.**"**
Love's Labour's Lost (1.2)

The Shakespeare First Folio (1623)

At the Frankfurt Book Fair in 1622, a list of forthcoming English publications advertised: 'Playes, written by M. William Shakespeare, all in one volume printed by Isaack Iaggard, in fol.'[1] Shakespeare had already been dead for seven years by the time the First Folio appeared in 1623. John Heminge and Henry Condell, actors in Shakespeare's company, the King's Men (previously the Lord Chamberlain's Men), demonstrated their devotion to the memory of their friend and colleague by producing a volume of indisputable cultural (and ultimately financial) value.

Ben Jonson had published his *Workes* in Folio in 1616 to much mockery for his presumed bumptiousness in an age when the reputation of playwrights, though upwardly mobile, was far from secure. The Folio format relates to a large sheet of paper folded once to create two leaves, or four pages, and is therefore usually large (at least fifteen inches (38cm) in height) and impressive. At the time it was not a natural choice for playtexts, which were considered insufficiently respectable to warrant a handsome style of book usually reserved for Bibles and other important works.

The volume cost approximately one pound, probably less for an unbound copy, and was clearly something of a trophy for an affluent bibliophile. Past estimates of the print run have ranged from 250 to a thousand copies, with the consensus hovering at around 750. Roughly a third of the surviving copies are in the Folger Shakespeare Library, Washington DC, while the V&A holds three copies. Half the thirty-six plays it includes would be lost to us but for the efforts of Heminge and Condell and their publishers. Although many of Shakespeare's plays had been available individually in inexpensive quartos, plays such as *Macbeth*, *Antony and Cleopatra*, *Julius Caesar*, *Twelfth Night* and *The Tempest* had never appeared in print before. *Pericles* is omitted (and was not included until the second impression of the Third Folio in 1664).

6

The volume is dedicated to the brother Earls of Pembroke and Montgomery, William and Philip Herbert. William Herbert had been Lord Chamberlain, responsible for regulating the professional stage, including supervision of the Master of the Revels, who licensed plays and theatres. The preliminary pages of early modern plays teem with commendatory verses and prefaces that tend to flattery and floweriness, but Heminge and Condell's epistle to their Lordships has a touching simplicity:

> We have but collected them, and done an office to the dead, to procure
> his Orphanes, Guardians; without ambition either of selfe-profit, or
> fame, onely to keepe the memory of so worthy a Friend & Fellow alive
> as was our SHAKESPEARE.

Eulogies were contributed by Ben Jonson, and the poets Hugh Holland, Leonard Digges, and his friend and fellow translator, James Mabbe.

The editors have also endowed us with one of the few authenticated likenesses of the poet: the engraved head-and-shoulders portrait by Martin Droeshout that is endlessly reproduced and parodied. There are no such images of the two men who put together the First Folio. Their memorial stands in the former churchyard of St Mary Aldermanbury in the City of London, the parish in which they both lived and raised families. The church on the site was destroyed twice, once by the Great Fire in 1666, and again during the Blitz in 1940. Their names are inscribed beneath a bust of the man who left them both money in his will to purchase mourning rings, and whom they in turn would help to immortalise.

The V&A's copies of the First Folio were all bequeathed to the museum by nineteenth-century collectors. The copy illustrated belonged to John Jones (1799–1882), a wealthy tailor and army clothier, whose bequest also included a Second Folio (1632), a Third Folio (1664), and over a hundred paintings. The scholar and editor of Shakespeare, the Reverend Alexander Dyce (1798–1869), and the literary historian John Forster (1812–1876) also bequeathed First and Second Folios to the museum, along with extensive libraries and collections of paintings. Forster's First Folio lacks the famous title page, while the title page of Dyce's copy has been remounted.

1. W.W. Greg, *The Shakespeare First Folio*, p. 3.

2

Bankside, London, *c.* 1600 (1638)

This map, published in 1638, shows the South Bank of London as it was in 1600. The Globe is the furthest to the east of the playhouses depicted, close to the smaller Rose, with the Bearbaiting house (the Hope playhouse from 1613) to the west, and the Swan towards the western edge of the map. Acquired by the museum in 1982, the map is based on earlier views of London published by J.C. Visscher in 1616 and the engraving *Civitas Londini* by John Norden of 1600. Each theatre is marked by a flag and is shown to be polygonal in shape. The detail of the cupola surmounting the Globe, and its tiled roof, seems to be a later addition to reflect the appearance of the Second Globe, rebuilt after the First Globe burned down in 1613, ignited by wadding from a cannon fired during a production of Shakespeare and Fletcher's *Henry VIII*:

> Now, King Henry, making a masque at the Cardinal Wolsey's house, and certain chambers being shot off at his entry, some of the paper... did light on the thatch... it kindled inwardly, and ran round like a train, consuming within less than an hour the whole house to the very grounds... one man had his breeches set on fire, that would perhaps have broiled him, if he had not by the benefit of a provident wit put it out with bottle ale.[1]

The First Globe was built on the South Bank in 1599 for the Lord Chamberlain's Men, reusing the timbers from the company's original theatre in Shoreditch, which was dismantled after the expiry of the lease and rebuilt in the new location. One of the first recorded productions at the Globe was Shakespeare's *Julius Caesar*, which a Swiss tourist, Thomas Platter, saw in the year of the theatre's opening:

> After dinner on the 21st of September, at about two o'clock, I went with my companions over the water, and in the strewn roof-house saw the tragedy of the first Emperor Julius with at least fifteen characters very well acted. At the end of the comedy they danced according to their custom with extreme elegance. Two in men's clothes and two in women's gave this performance, in wonderful combination with each other.[2]

Shakespeare's plays were also performed at the indoor Blackfriars Theatre from 1609, and at the Second Globe Theatre from 1614, until the theatre was bought by a developer in 1644, who used the site to build tenements. Accounts from local residents suggest that the remains of the Globe survived among the tenements for a further century and Samuel Johnson's friend Mrs Thrale became convinced that, when her husband's brewery acquired land in 1732 fronting on Globe Alley, it had bought land formerly occupied by the Globe Theatre:

> For a long time, then – or I thought it such – my fate was bound up with the old Globe Theatre, upon the Bankside, Southwark; the alley it had occupied having been purchased and thrown down by Mr Thrale to make an opening before the windows of our dwelling house. When it lay desolate in a black heap of rubbish, my Mother, one day, in a joke, called it the Ruins of Palmyra; and after that they laid it down in a grass-plot. Palmyra was the name it went by, I suppose, among the clerks and servants of the brewhouse… But there were really curious remains of the old Globe Playhouse, which though hexagonal in form without, was round within.[3]

An attempt had been made by William Poel in 1900 to find a site to rebuild the Globe and a half-size model was built by Sir Edward Lutyens for an exhibition at Earls Court in 1912, but replicas of the Globe had been built in San Diego, California; Odessa, Texas; Ashland, Oregon; Cleveland, Ohio; Cedar City, Utah; the Folger Library, Washington; and Tokyo, Japan – before Shakespeare's rebuilt Globe opened for performance close to the site of the original theatre on London's South Bank in 1997.[4] That the project happened at all was due to the American actor Sam Wanamaker, who, inspired by the model of the Globe he saw at the Chicago World Fair in 1933–4, worked tirelessly to raise funds for the project, which thanks to his efforts and those of his dedicated assistants, was safely on the way to completion by the time of his death in 1993. Opening with a production of *Henry V* starring Artistic Director Mark Rylance, the Globe has mounted an extensive repertoire of plays by Shakespeare and his contemporaries, and has been joined by an indoor Jacobean theatre, named after Wanamaker, which opened in January 2014.

1. E.K. Chambers, *The Elizabethan Stage*, vol. 2, pp. 419–20.

2. *Ibid.*, p. 365.

3. *Ibid.*, p. 428.

4. Barry Day, *This Wooden 'O'*, pp. 18–20.

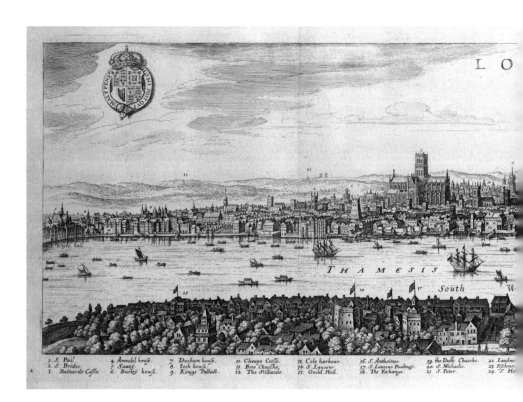

LO

White hall

THAMESIS

South

1. S. Paul.	4. Arondel howse.	7. Durham howse.	10. Cheape Crosse.
2. S. Brides.	5. Sauoy.	8. Iock howse.	11. Bow Churche.
3. Barnards Castle	6. Burley howse.	9. Kongs Pallast.	12. The Stilliarde.

13. Cole harbour.	16. S.Anthoines.	19. the Duth Churche.	22. Leadne
14. S. Laurens.	17. S. Laurens Poultney.	20. S. Michaelis.	23. Fishmo
15. Guild Hall.	18. The Exhange.	21. S. Peter.	24. S. He

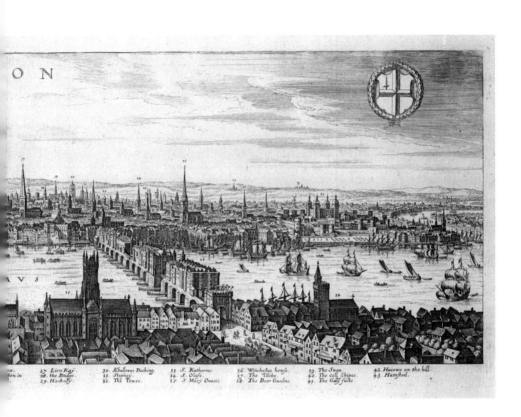

ON

AVS

Comedies

François Boitard, illustration of the opening scene of *The Tempest* (1709)

This vibrant image by François Boitard (*c.* 1667–1719) is the earliest published illustration of a scene from Shakespeare: the opening scene of *The Tempest*, the initial play in the first illustrated edition of Shakespeare's works, edited in 1709 by playwright and Poet Laureate, Nicholas Rowe (1674–1718). There had been four large-format Folio editions of Shakespeare's works in the seventeenth century, in addition to a series of compact quarto editions of individual plays, but surprisingly, with the exception of the engraved portrait of Shakespeare on the title page of the First Folio (and reproduced in its subsequent editions), none of these contained illustrations. Rowe's edition cost thirty shillings, placing it beyond the purse of most playgoers, who knew Shakespeare primarily in the form presented on stage, which for the most part was heavily adapted to appeal to popular taste. The adaptation by Dryden and Davenant of *The Tempest*, subtitled *The Enchanted Island*, rapidly became one of the most popular works on the Restoration stage. Charles II had specified, when re-establishing the theatre after its closure during the Commonwealth, that plays should make full use of music and special effects, and allow women to play female roles for the first time on the public stage. Davenant's adaptation augmented the opportunity for singing, dancing, and spectacle afforded by Shakespeare's text, and Dryden wrote an introduction to the adaptation, lavishly praising Davenant's changes, especially his counterpoint to the scene in which Miranda sets eyes upon a man for the first time: 'he design'd the Counter-part to Shakespear's Plot, namely, that of a Man who had never seen a Woman; that by this means those two Characters of Innocence and Love might the more illustrate and commend each other.'[1] The fashion for symmetry leads Davenant to give Miranda a sister called Dorinda, and Caliban a sister called Sycorax.

A leading playwright in his own right, and author of the historical play *Jane Shore*, which remained in the repertory for well over a century, Rowe uses an illustration of the storm scene that appears to closely parallel the description of the storm in the stage direction thirty years earlier in *The Enchanted Island*, which details

> a thick Cloudy Sky, a very Rocky Coast, and a Tempestuous Sea in perpetual Agitation. This Tempest (suppos'd to be rais'd by Magick) has many dreadfull Objects in it, as several Spirits in horrid shapes flying down amongst the Sailers, then rising and crossing in the air. And when the Ship is sinking, the whole House is darken'd, and a shower of Fire falls upon 'em. This is accompanied with Lightning, and several Claps of Thunder, to the end of the Storm.[2]

Pepys records in his diary seeing *The Tempest* eight times, finding the play 'so full of variety' that he did not tire of it, saying 'this day I took pleasure to learn the [tune of the] Seamans dance – which I have much desired to be perfect in, and have made myself so.'[3] The authors of the satirical play *The Rehearsal* were less complimentary, when dancers are berated by a disgruntled author: 'you dance worse than the Angels in *Harry* the Eight, or the fat Spirits in *The Tempest*'.[4] Shakespeare's *The Tempest* was still being adapted in musical form as recently as the 1980s, when Bob Carlton's rock musical *Return to the Forbidden Planet*, combining Shakespeare's play with the plot of a science-fiction film, was marketed as 'Shakespeare's forgotten rock-and-roll masterpiece'. The musical is set in outer space, with rock music from the 1950s. Considerable liberties are taken with Shakespeare's plot, with the teenage Miranda falling for the commander of the spaceship, Captain Tempest, against the wishes of her father, Doctor Prospero. Shakespearean language from different plays occurs at random in the script, such as 'Beware the Ides of March' and 'There are more things in Heaven and Earth than are dreamt of in my laboratory'. The musical won the Olivier Award for Best Musical in 1989 and 1990, toured Australia in the 1990s, was revived in a touring version in the UK in 2006, and performed by the Stratford Musical Theatre Company at the RSC Courtyard Theatre in Stratford-upon-Avon in 2011.[5]

1. William Shakespeare and William Davenant, *The Tempest, or, The Enchanted Island* (1676), Preface, sig. [A3].

2. *Ibid.*, p. 1.

3. *Diary of Samuel Pepys*, vol. 9, p. 48.

4. George Villiers, *The Rehearsal*, ed. Edward Arber (1919), Act Two, Scene Five, lines 15–17 (p. 63).

5. David Ward, *Transformation*, p. 124.

Loudon Sainthill, preliminary set design for *Pericles* (1958)

If the title page of the 1609 Quarto edition of *Pericles* is to be believed, the play was 'diuers and sundry times acted by his Maiesties Servants, at the Globe on the Banck-side'. It remained popular until the closure of the theatres by Parliament in 1642, and can claim to be the first of Shakespeare's plays to have been acted when the theatres reopened in 1660. However, its early popularity waned. A plot that hinges on an incestuous relationship and features scenes in a brothel was not likely to find favour in the nineteenth century, and doubts on the authorship, coupled with the problems of staging a play that sends its characters journeying round the Mediterranean, did not encourage revivals. There were only three productions at Stratford before the founding of the Royal Shakespeare Company in 1961, and, to date, the RSC has only given six productions, and only two in its main house at Stratford. The others were staged in its smaller auditoria and one was a site-specific collaboration with Cardboard Citizens.

Pericles may not be a crowd-pleaser, but the third Stratford staging, in 1958, at what was then called the Shakespeare Memorial Theatre, was one of the most spectacular presentations it has ever been given. Its director, Tony Richardson (1928–1991), is usually associated with contemporary drama – particularly the plays of John Osborne at the Royal Court Theatre. *Pericles* was his first Shakespeare production, and was very different from the 'kitchen sink' drama that made his name. It featured a cast of thirty-nine, with Richard Johnson as Pericles and Geraldine McEwan as his daughter, Marina. There was a chorus of singing mariners, and Greek- and Byzantine-inspired designs by artist Loudon Sainthill.

Tasmanian-born Sainthill (1918–1969) came to England in 1949. He had designed for the stage in Australia but it was in Britain that his theatrical career developed and flourished. His lavish sets and costumes for Michael Benthall's 1951 production of *The Tempest* at Stratford established him as a leading designer and he became associated with a flamboyant fantastical style, though he could also create everyday reality, as demonstrated by his interiors for the film version of Osborne's *Look Back in Anger* (1959).

The design for *Pericles* was Sainthill at his most opulent. He usually chose to work on black paper in pastel and gouache, and this gives his drawings an exotic, jewel-like quality. Richardson wanted to give unity to the play's wide-ranging action by imagining it as a shipman's tale brought to life. Edric Connor, the first black actor to appear at Stratford, played the narrator, Gower, who in the production became a sailor, amusing his fellow shipmates by relating Pericles's adventures. As he spoke, and sometimes sang, his lines, the action took place within a permanent setting in the form of a ship. The design shown here is so beautifully realised that it appears to be the finished product, but it is, in fact, Sainthill's initial drawing. The finished design is also held by the V&A Theatre and Performance Department, and this shows that, while the basic shape remained in the final design, it underwent some adaptation. The ship became more stylised – basically a high stern, and a hull on a raised platform at the rear of the stage, making more space for the actors. A view of the sea and rocks was introduced behind, the colours became stronger, and the 'waves', which block the access to the ship in the projected design, disappear in the final version, opening up the stage area and removing 'trip hazards' in the process.

66 The ship is under sail, and here she comes
amain…**99**
Love's Labour's Lost (5.2)

**Still from the National Video Archive of Performance
recording of *The Big Life*, by Paul Joseph and Paul Sirett,
based on *Love's Labour's Lost* (2005)**

The Big Life was a 'ska musical' interpretation of *Love's Labour's Lost*,
developed and produced by the Theatre Royal Stratford East in 2004. Set
in the 1950s, the show followed a group of Caribbean immigrants who
arrived in London on the MV *Empire Windrush*, in search of a better life.
As in Shakespeare's original, the plot centres on a group of ambitious
young men who swear an oath to scholarship, vowing to devote
themselves to work and study, and to abstain from alcohol and the
company of women for three years. Unsurprisingly, this vow proves far
harder to keep than expected, resulting in a series of struggles and comic
misadventures.

After two successful runs at Stratford East, the show transferred to the
West End in 2005, where it ran for four and a half months at the Apollo
Theatre, making history as the first West End show to depict the lives of
black Britons. As Jeremy Kingston pointed out in *The Times*, 'There have
been black musicals on Shaftesbury Avenue before, and black British
musicals set in exotic islands far away, but not till now a show in W1 that
presents the black experience of living on this island, here. That's a first
worth celebrating.'[1] The show was lauded for capturing the vibrant spirit
of the Caribbean, with music, dancing, and humour throughout. It also
dealt adroitly with such typically Shakespearean themes as love, educa-
tion, cunning, and trickery, and the exploration of the world. In the
opening number, the characters daydream happily about the better life
they believe is waiting for them in London. 'Wi mek it big in a Inglan,'
they sing – confident that success and fortune will fall into their laps as
soon as they arrive. Success, however, is not so easy to come by, and the
characters' optimism quickly deflates; indeed, as soon as they arrive on
the *Windrush* (shown here), the inclement British weather signals a down-
turn in their fortunes. Through the eyes of these characters, the show

offered a wry outsider's look at British politics, racial discrimination, and lack of opportunity, as symbolised by the grey British weather.

The show was subtitled '*The Ska Musical*', and featured songs composed by local reggae musician Paul Joseph, with lyrics by Paul Sirett. These numbers featured musical styles from across the West Indies, including traditional ska, calypso and gospel. With its bright, sunny harmonies and toe-tapping rhythms, the music offered an escape from the harshness of life for fifties immigrants, trapped as they were by rain, poverty, and racial discrimination.

As well as re-imagining the plot of *Love's Labour's Lost*, many of the show's production elements seemed distinctly Shakespearean. The band, for example, situated onstage and dressed in bright white suits and angels' wings, was highly visible throughout the show – a visual link to the musicians who regularly featured onstage, or in the musicians' gallery, in early modern theatres.

Another Shakespearean link was created by the atmosphere in the auditorium, which was informal and fun, with audience members talking to and interacting with the performers. The creation of this relaxed atmosphere was aided by an additional character, Mrs Aphrodite, who was positioned in a theatre box throughout the show, and provided a running commentary on the action in the style of a stand-up comedian. This enjoyably irreverent commentary broke down the barrier between the characters and the spectators, creating a 'groundling' atmosphere, reminiscent of that at Shakespeare's own theatre, the Globe.

On 22 June 2005 the V&A filmed this production for the National Video Archive of Performance (NVAP). Using three cameras located around the auditorium, the recording aimed to capture the spirit and ambience of the production, as well as the action onstage.

1. *The Times*, 25 May 2005.

The Dorset Garden Theatre, viewed from the River Thames (*c.* 1671)

Although not completed until three years after the death of William Davenant (1606–1668), the Dorset Garden Theatre, opening in 1671, was the culmination of his vision for a state-of-the-art English theatre to rival continental theatre for the latest scenery and stage machinery. Shakespeare's works were favoured by Davenant, even though, numerically speaking, the plays of Beaumont and Fletcher, and Ben Jonson, were more in vogue on the Restoration stage, and it was found necessary to adapt Shakespeare's works to suit Restoration taste. Davenant combined *Much Ado About Nothing* and *Measure for Measure* to make a new play, *The Law Against Lovers*, which failed to find favour, but his adaptations of *Hamlet*, *The Tempest* and *Macbeth* appealed to Restoration audiences.

Styling himself Shakespeare's godson, Davenant did not discourage gossip that he might have even been the older playwright's natural 'bastard' son. Starting out as a dramatist and author of court masques, Davenant's own career was interrupted by the Civil War and the Interregnum, during which the public theatres were officially closed, though this did not prevent him from staging *The Siege of Rhodes* (the first English opera) at the Cockpit Theatre in 1658. Masques and musical entertainments had continued to be performed at the Protector's court during the Commonwealth (Cromwell's regime might otherwise have lost prestige with visiting ambassadors), and so despite having been knighted by Charles I and imprisoned as a Royalist, Davenant laid himself open to the later charge of having served as 'Master of the Revels to "Oliver"'.[1]

One of Charles II's first acts on his return to the throne in 1660 was to reopen the public theatres, but he kept a tight rein on the theatre by limiting it to two companies, patronised by himself and his brother, the Duke of York, respectively managed by Thomas Killigrew and William Davenant. Patents were issued, giving each of these exclusive rights to stage spoken drama (a privilege not revoked until 1843). Davenant and

Killigrew divided the repertoire of pre-Restoration plays between them. We know from Pepys's Diary that he saw Killigrew's company (the King's Company) perform 'The Moor of Venice' – i.e. Othello – (twice), The Merry Wives of Windsor (three times), Henry IV (four times, though it is unclear which parts), and A Midsummer Night's Dream (once), as well as The Taming of the Shrew in an adapted form by John Lacey, entitled Sawney the Scot. At Davenant's riverside theatre (the Duke's Company), he saw Hamlet (five times), Twelfth Night (three times), Henry VIII (twice), Macbeth (nine times), Davenant's own The Law Against Lovers – see above – (once), Romeo and Juliet (once), and The Tempest (eight times). In addition, Thomas Betterton, who succeeded Davenant as manager of the Duke of York's company in 1668, records that Davenant laid claim to King Lear, and had sole rights to Pericles for two months.

Shakespeare's romantic comedies tended not to find favour with Pepys; he said of Twelfth Night that, though 'acted well… it be but a silly play and not relating at all to the name or day.'[2] The romantic theme of Romeo and Juliet also failed to impress: 'it is the play of itself the worst that ever I heard in my life'.[3] The play he saw most often (nine times) was Macbeth, which exploited the scenic potential of the witches' scenes and transformed them into spectacular displays of singing and dancing. He found Macbeth 'a most excellent play in all respects, but especially in divertisement, though it be a deep tragedy; which is a strange perfection in a tragedy, it being most proper here and suitable.'[4]

1. Philip Edwards (et al.), ed., The Revels History of English Drama, Vol. 4: 1613–1660, p. 299.

2. Diary of Samuel Pepys, vol. 4, p. 6.

3. Ibid., vol. 3, p. 39.

4. Ibid., vol. 8, p. 7.

The Dukes Theatre, in Dorset Gardens.

London Published for the Encyclopædia Londinensis, May 13. 1813.

'Measure for Measure'. Act II. Scene II.

7

> **"** Kneel down before him, hang upon his gown... **"**
> *Measure for Measure* (2.2)

William Poel's production of *Measure for Measure*, Royalty Theatre (1893)

A typical photograph of a nineteenth-century theatre production shows actors recreating a scene in a studio. The images of William Poel's productions in the V&A's collections are unusual: though posed for the camera, they are taken at the performance venues with the actors positioned onstage. This photograph shows *Measure for Measure* at the now demolished Royalty Theatre in Soho. Angelo, seated on the left and gesturing dramatically towards the kneeling Isabella, is the director William Poel (1852–1934). Poel began his career as a touring actor. Having appeared in productions where the stage picture was more important than the text, he became convinced that Shakespeare's plays should be performed on a bare platform stage in authentic period costume. His own productions pioneered Elizabethan staging at a time when this seemed novel and eccentric. Poel worked with amateur players, not all of them accomplished. He only gave plays for a handful of performances and had little commercial success. But he inspired many actors and directors, including Harley Granville-Barker, who took his ideas to a wider audience.

Measure for Measure was one of his earlier productions. In 1887, Poel became instructor to the Shakespeare Reading Society, which gave annual 'rehearsed' readings. At first evening dress was worn, but Poel introduced Elizabethan costume, and in 1893 tried a more radical experiment. The staging of *Measure for Measure* would, according to the publicity leaflet, 'test the Dramatic Effect of Acting an Elizabethan Play under Conditions the Play was written to fulfil'. Poel and his designer, R. Minton Taylor, were inspired by the 1600 builder's contract for the Fortune Theatre, held in the Edward Alleyn papers at Dulwich College, though they did not follow the contract to the letter. They had to recreate their stage within an existing theatre and alter all the proportions accordingly. What they devised was a thrust stage which extended over the Royalty's orchestra pit, with two 18-foot pillars to support the canopy which projected from a tiring house with a painted tiled roof. Canvas panels turned existing balconies into Elizabethan galleries. The original Fortune was a square building but Poel and Taylor angled their galleries to suggest a curving amphitheatre, similar to the one shown in the 1596 sketch of the Swan Theatre, known as 'the De Witt drawing', which was discovered in the Netherlands in 1880 but had only recently been published. The stage was designed to be easily deconstructed and rebuilt. It made regular appearances in later productions by the Elizabethan Stage Society, which Poel founded in 1894.

The photograph shows a crowded stage, which was another experiment in authentic staging. The seated actors and the ladies in the galleries represented the Elizabethan audience. This was not a success, as the moustachioed, pipe-smoking gallants distracted the real audience, and it was not repeated in later productions.

"Shape it. I would not have things cool...**"**
The Merry Wives of Windsor (4.2)

8

Agatha Walker, figurine of Dorothy Green as Mistress Ford in the 1923 Lyric Theatre, Hammersmith production of *The Merry Wives of Windsor* (1924)

Ceramic figurines of Shakespeare's characters and of famous players in Shakespearean roles were popular ornaments in the nineteenth century. Brightly coloured and often crudely modelled, they decorated the mantelpieces of people who might never have seen the actors but liked the subject matter. Though not as plentiful, wax figures were also produced. Wax was a good medium for portraits as it could be used to create fine detail. The figures were cast in moulds and painted to give them a lifelike appearance. The V&A has a wax model of Edmund Kean as Richard III, dating from the 1830s, which is a convincing three-dimensional representation of the print from which it is taken.[1]

In the 1920s, artist Agatha Walker (*c.* 1888–1980) revived the traditions of both wax modelling and theatrical figurines with a series of limited edition statuettes of performers in successful London productions. She sculpted her subjects from life, capturing the sitter's characteristic poses and expressions, and used the sculptures to make moulds from which she cast twelve-inch plaster figurines. These were coated with a fine layer of wax and then coloured. Walker created her own wax mixture and the exact ingredients have never been established, but it is likely that resin was added to the wax to harden it and give a translucency to the flesh tints.

Two of the figurines depict Mistress Ford and Mistress Page from the 1923 production of *The Merry Wives of Windsor* at the Lyric Theatre, Hammersmith. Staged as the Christmas show to fill a gap in the scheduling, the play delighted the critics – 'a brilliant revival', according to the *Daily Telegraph* – and was directed by W. Bridges-Adams (1889–1965), then director of the Shakespeare Memorial Theatre, and featured many of his Stratford actors, including Dorothy Green (1886–1961), who had played Mistress Ford there on more than one occasion.[2] Her Mistress Page was Edith Evans (1888–1976), whose subsequent fame has eclipsed that of her co-star. Green seldom appeared in West End hits and her name is no longer well known, but in a fifty-year stage career she acted at Stratford, first with Frank Benson's Shakespeare Company, then for Bridges-Adams in the 1920s, and her roles comprise a roster of Shakespeare's greatest female characters, including Cleopatra, Lady Macbeth, Viola, Desdemona, Imogen, Ophelia and Portia. By the time she appeared at Hammersmith, the *Morning Post* commented that her record of successes in Shakespeare was 'unapproached by any other actresses on the English stage'.[3] She went on to play further Shakespearean heroines at Stratford and also at the Old Vic, where, in the 1930–1 season, her roles ranged from Juno in *The Tempest* to Cleopatra, Beatrice and Goneril, all opposite John Gielgud. When she died in 1961, her *Times* obituary quoted Old Vic director Harcourt Williams, who called her 'a perfect example of the repertory "leading lady"'.[4]

1. S.1091–1996 (wax figurine of the actor Edmund Kean as Richard III, *c.* 1830).

2. *Daily Telegraph*, 23 December 1923.

3. *Morning Post*, 24 December 1923.

4. *The Times*, 16 January 1961.

> **❝** If it should come to the ear of the court how
> I have been transformed... **❞**
> *The Merry Wives of Windsor* (4.5)

David Scott, *Queen Elizabeth Viewing the Performance of 'The Merry Wives of Windsor' in the Globe Theatre* (1840)

This oil painting by David Scott (1806–1849), which was exhibited at the Royal Academy in 1840, coincides with an intense interest in history, reflected in historical novels and history paintings, which stimulated the desire to historically reconstruct the world of Shakespeare's plays. Scott's painting is one of the first attempts to imagine the interior of the first Globe theatre, prompted by the tradition recorded by Rowe in his 1709 edition of Shakespeare's works that Queen Elizabeth had 'commanded' a new Falstaff play 'to shew him in Love'.[1] The painting shows the Queen watching a public performance of *The Merry Wives of Windsor* at the Globe, although there is no evidence that she ever visited the public theatre; the first monarch known to have done so is Queen Henrietta Maria, wife of Charles I, who is recorded in the accounts for the Master of the Revels as a frequent visitor to the Blackfriars Theatre.[2] When Scott's painting was exhibited, it was accompanied by the following description:

> In the royal box, in attendance on the Queen, are the Earl of Leicester, in armour, the Earl of Essex, and Walsingham. Towards the foreground is Sir Walter Raleigh, in a light red dress, between whom and Shakespeare, who stands upon the landing-place at the end of the seats, are Spenser, his hands on his breast, the Earl of Southampton, Fletcher, and Beaumont. To the other side of Shakespeare are Ben Jonson, in a black doublet, Thomas Sackville, Earl of Dorset, and Dr Dee, who addresses a youth. The group behind the figure of Shakespeare represents Cecil, Lord Burleigh, Mildred, his wife, and a son and daughter. In the line of seats before these, but farther from the spectator, stands Sir Philip Sidney, and higher, towards the left, Francis Bacon and Drake, Massinger, and Harrington.[3]

The artist must have been aware that it was completely impossible for all the persons depicted to have been gathered together at the same time; Sir Philip Sidney, for example, had died in 1586, long before the Globe was built in 1599. These anachronisms may have contributed to the poor reception of the picture when it was first exhibited: 'It was not a success at the

1840 Royal Academy, ostensibly because of bad hanging but even in 1840 the promiscuous mixture of literary figures from Sir Philip Sidney to Beaumont and Fletcher must have seemed more than faintly ridiculous.'[4] In assembling the personages, Scott was imagining an ideal audience of the most prominent figures of the Elizabethan age. To depict these, he drew upon collections of engraved portraits, such as Edmund Lodge's *Portraits of Illustrious Personages of Great Britain* (1821–34) and *Granger's Biographical History of England* (1769–74), often adding his own variations to the standard engravings. Shakespeare's image is based on the Chandos portrait, but Scott omits his earring, and Queen Elizabeth's portrait is a composite one derived from various sources. The first image of a contemporary view of an interior of an Elizabethan theatre, De Witt's sketch of the stage at the Swan Theatre, was not published until 1888, almost fifty years after Scott's painting of the Globe. Scott's depiction is based upon written descriptions in Malone's edition and Collier's *History of English Dramatic Poetry* (1831), although in some respects Scott's auditorium more closely resembles early nineteenth-century theatres with a dress circle extending over the stalls rather than the vertical galleries of Elizabethan theatres.

The picture was painted in an era that strove towards greater authenticity in performing Shakespeare, with William Charles Macready restoring Shakespeare's text in his productions of *King Lear* and *The Tempest* at Covent Garden in 1838. Ludwig Tieck produced *A Midsummer Night's Dream* in Elizabethan style at the royal palace of Potsdam in 1843, inspiring James Robinson Planché's production of *The Taming of the Shrew* in authentic manner with original text at the Haymarket Theatre in 1844 and 1847. Planché's production drew upon the researches published in his *History of British Costume* (1834), which Scott was able to draw upon when researching the costumes for his painting.

1. Nicholas Rowe, *The Works of Mr. William Shakespear* (9 vols), (1709), vol. 1, pp. viii–ix.

2. Andrew Gurr, *Playgoing in Shakespeare's London*, p. 196.

3. James Fowler 'David Scott's *Queen Elizabeth Viewing the Performance of 'The Merry Wives of Windsor' in the Globe Theatre* (1840)', p. 29.

4. Geoffrey Ashton, *A Catalogue of Paintings in the Theatre Museum, London*, p. 49.

Interior of the Shakespeare Gallery, Pall Mall (1790)

At the beginning of the eighteenth century, there were practically no known illustrations of Shakespeare's plays; the now famous drawing of *Titus Andronicus* by Henry Peacham (*c.* 1578–1644) lay undiscovered in the library of the Marquess of Bath until 1907 and did not become generally known until 1925.[1] But by the end of the century, Shakespeare had a purpose-built gallery dedicated to paintings and prints of his works. Boydell's Shakespeare Gallery opened on 4 May 1789 with thirty-four paintings on view, and a further twenty-two were added the following year. It quickly became a magnet for fashionable society, as may be seen from the company depicted in this watercolour by Francis Wheatley (1747–1801), in which Alderman John Boydell is shown with his nephew Josiah in an illustrious company. The Dukes of York and Clarence stand in the centre of the picture with Sir Joshua Reynolds between them. Georgiana, Duchess of Devonshire, holds a catalogue and is in conversation with the playwright Sheridan, and the Countess of Jersey, in blue, stands on the far right. On either side of the arch are paintings of *The Merry Wives of Windsor* and *Much Ado About Nothing* by Matthew William Peters and above the arch can be seen the foot of Reynolds' vast canvas showing Macbeth in the cavern of the witches.

John Boydell (1720–1804) trained as an engraver and became a highly successful publisher of prints with a large export trade to the Continent. He became an Alderman of London in 1782, serving as Lord Mayor in 1790. The idea for the Shakespeare Gallery grew out of the discussion at a dinner held by Boydell's nephew Josiah (1752–1817), attended by artists including Benjamin West, George Romney, and Paul Sandby.[2] The Gallery aimed to establish an English school of painting through the illustration of Shakespeare's plays. It was planned to publish an edition of Shakespeare illustrated with engravings from the paintings commissioned for the Gallery, and this was accomplished in 1802. During the seventeen years of its existence between 1789 and 1805, Boydell's Gallery displayed 167 paintings by more than thirty contemporary artists. Boydell paid the market value for the works he commissioned:

Benjamin West was given 1,000 guineas for his 'King Lear in the Storm' and Reynolds the same for his 'Death of Cardinal Beaufort'. This was the highest fee; in lower brackets were Romney, who was given 600 guineas for his painting of a scene from *The Tempest*, and Joseph Wright of Derby, whose services were valued at 300 pounds.[3]

Boydell's project generated such interest that it quickly inspired rivals and imitators. In 1788 – the year before Boydell opened his doors – Thomas Macklin (c. 1753–1800) launched the Poets' Gallery in Fleet Street, featuring subjects taken from the work of the English poets, including Shakespeare. James Woodmason opened a rival Shakespeare gallery in Dublin in 1792 with works by Fuseli, Northcote, Opie, Wheatley and Peters. The failure of the enterprise in Dublin led Woodmason to move to London to a gallery opposite Boydell in Pall Mall, which survived until 1795. Many artists who painted for Boydell contributed works to Robert Bowyer's History Gallery which opened in Pall Mall in 1793, and the painter Henry Fuseli (1741–1825) opened a short-lived gallery devoted to the poet Milton in 1799.

Although the cartoonist James Gillray (1756–1815) had launched a savage attack upon Boydell, lampooning his Gallery in a caricature entitled 'Shakespeare Sacrificed, or, The Offering to Avarice', in fact the Gallery turned out to spell Boydell's financial ruin.[4] The outbreak of war with France in 1793 disrupted Boydell's foreign print trade and the huge outlay of the Shakespeare Gallery, eventually reaching more than £100,000, began to strain the finances of the firm. In 1804 the Gallery and its contents were offered for sale in a lottery to avoid bankruptcy. 22,000 tickets were sold at three guineas each and after John Boydell's death in December 1804, his nephew offered the lottery winner £10,000 for the paintings, with a view to keeping the collection together as a gift to the nation. Unfortunately the offer was rejected; the paintings were auctioned, making little more than £6,000, and the collection scattered. The location of many of the original paintings is now unknown, but they survive in engravings widely disseminated in Shakespeare editions during the nineteenth century.

1. R.A. Foakes, *Illustrations of the English Stage, 1580–1642*, pp. 48–9.

2. Robin Hamlyn, 'The Shakespeare Galleries of John Boydell and James Woodmason', p. 97.

3. *The Boydell Shakespeare Prints*, with an introduction by A.E. Santaniello, p. 7.

4. Gerd Unverfehrt, 'John Boydell's Shakespeare Gallery in Gillray's Caricatures', p. 163.

66 When he goes in his doublet and hose and
leaves off his wit...**99**
Much Ado About Nothing (5.1)

11

Henry Irving's doublet and hose as Benedick (1882)

This pale-blue silk doublet and trunk hose were worn by Sir Henry Irving (1838–1905) as Benedick in the 1882 Lyceum Theatre production of *Much Ado About Nothing*. It is part of a collection of over one hundred costumes and associated accessories used by the celebrated actor-manager in a career spanning five decades, which was acquired by the V&A's Theatre and Performance Department in 2010.

The surface of both the doublet and the paned trunk hose is covered with seed pearls, each carefully hand stitched to the silk beneath. Approximately 1,000 of these tiny pearls still remain, but recent conservation treatment revealed that this is probably only about twenty per cent of the quantity with which the costume was originally embellished. Equal care was devoted to the shoes, which were also part of this costume. The leather was dyed to match the blue of the main costume, and the high tongues of the uppers were 'slashed' to expose puffs of silk edged with gold braid. Illustrations show that the costume could be worn with or without a short shoulder cloak. Surviving costumes can reveal an unexpected level of detail about a production. For instance, the level of wear evident in tears and darned repairs often indicates that, as was the case with *Much Ado About Nothing*, the play remained in the repertoire of the company for a long period of time and was frequently revived. As a result, the conservation treatment needed to make such garments stable enough for display is often particularly complex and time-consuming: in the case of this costume, over 350 hours.

The costumes associated with Irving have a particularly interesting history as many of them were passed on to, and indeed worn by, his eldest son H.B. (Harry Brodribb) Irving (1870–1919), also an actor, after Sir Henry's death in 1905. It is therefore often possible to discover evidence of alterations which have been made to let out seams (Irving was notoriously thin and tall), modify surface decoration, or even to create new parts for existing costumes. The cuffs on the doublet of this costume are, for example, believed to be later replacements, but have been retained as they provide vital evidence about the complex history and various incarnations of the garment – rather in the same way that the Folio text of *Much Ado About Nothing* reflects the cuts and modifications of its early theatrical life.

Lavish sets and sumptuous costumes, such as this ensemble, were not unusual in Irving's productions; indeed, he was renowned for the scale and splendour of the plays staged at the Lyceum Theatre. This production was set in a reinterpretation of Elizabethan England, and Irving appeared opposite his onstage partner Ellen Terry as Beatrice, who was dressed in a pale-gold silk velvet gown with a high lace collar and strands of matching seed pearls entwined around the sleeves and across the bodice. The costumes would have complemented each other perfectly.

Though many critics, both at the time and since, have bemoaned the fact that Irving never gave Terry the chance to appear as Rosalind, finding no character of sufficient stature for himself in *As You Like It*, Irving did take on the part of Benedick, a role he is said to have disliked. This gave Terry the opportunity to shine as Beatrice, a part perfectly suited to her mercurial acting style, and the charm and quick wit for which she was so often praised. Terry seems to have been conscious of this sacrifice and found 'much to admire' in Irving's portrayal of Benedick, though she was also forced to acknowledge that while 'a great actor can do nothing badly', Irving's meticulous method made it close to impossible for her to find the pace and swiftness that she felt the role demanded.[1] Despite Terry's personal dissatisfaction, the 1882 production of *Much Ado About Nothing* proved a great success and its popularity was such that it became a longstanding part of the Lyceum Company's repertoire.

1. Ellen Terry, *The Story of My Life*, p. 162.

David Garrick as Benedick, Theatre Royal, Drury Lane (*c.* 1770)

Much Ado About Nothing had largely fallen out of the repertoire until David Garrick (1717–1779) revived its fortunes. He played the role of Benedick, destined to become a crowd-pleasing favourite, 113 times over twenty-eight years. Though Garrick was famously painted by Joshua Reynolds as torn between the figures of Comedy and Tragedy (1761), he acted in relatively few Shakespearean comedies, his other roles being Posthumus in *Cymbeline* (a tragedy according to its position in the First Folio) and Leontes in *The Winter's Tale* (later altered and retitled *Florizel and Perdita*). Neither of these parts offer the comedic potential he was able to exploit as Benedick in a bickering, bantering pairing with Beatrice.

Benedick was the last role he played before his marriage to Eva-Maria Veigel in 1749, and his first after resuming the stage with a nod to his new status as husband. His lines 'When I said I would die a bachelor, I did not think I should live till I were married' (2.3.220–1) elicited knowing laughter. *Much Ado* was the vehicle for his return to the London stage in 1765 (by royal command) after a long break during which he and his wife did the Grand Tour. For this he wrote a special prologue,

> With doubt – joy – apprehension – almost dumb,
> To face this awful court once more I come;
> Lest Benedick should suffer, by my fear,
> Before he enters, I myself am here.
> I'm told, (what flattery to my heart!) that you
> Have wish'd to see me, nay, have press'd it, too:
> Alas! 'twill prove another Much Ado.[1]

In this lively watercolour by Jean-Louis Fesch (Johann Ludwig Fäsch), Garrick wears a rich red frock coat with black cuffs and lapels, and gold decoration on the coat, waistcoat, and breeches. He is bewigged and flourishes a three-cornered hat. This is eighteenth-century modern-dress

Shakespeare. The epaulettes and sword remind us that Benedick is a soldier newly returned from war.

Garrick was renowned for the vitality of his performances and this is caught in the dynamic movement the artist conveys. Fesch (*c.* 1739–1778) was a Swiss-born engraver, who had worked on Robert Sayer and John Smith's *Dramatic Characters, or Different Portraits of the English Stage* (1770), but his preliminary sketches were almost certainly made from life, in the theatre.[2] In this sense his pioneering work – capturing the moment more spiritedly than the typically static and formal images that record Georgian theatre – anticipates the immediacy of stage photography two centuries later. A number of his works depicting members of the Comédie Française, Comédie Italienne, Opéra Comique, and Académie Royale de Musique, as well as London theatres, reside in the Harvard Theatre Collection.

1. Thomas Davies, *Memoirs of the Life of David Garrick*, vol. 2, p. 97.

2. [John P. Cavanagh], *The Drama Delineated*, p. 3.

Mr GARRICK in BENEDICT.
in Much ado about nothing.

66 Fair Princess, welcome to the court of
Navarre...99
Love's Labour's Lost (2.1)

13

Tyrone Guthrie's Old Vic production of *Love's Labour's Lost* (1936)

J.W. Debenham is not the best known of theatre photographers, but his work in the 1930s and 1940s at the Old Vic and Sadler's Wells captured some of the great performances of the time. It is thanks to him that we have images of Laurence Olivier, John Gielgud and Edith Evans in some of their great Shakespearean roles. The 1936 Old Vic *Love's Labour's Lost* was not regarded as particularly star-studded at the time but, like many Old Vic productions, it contained stars of the future. The middle-aged courtier Boyet was played by the twenty-two-year-old Alec Guinness (1914–2000); the King of Navarre and the Princess of France were Michael Redgrave (1908–1985) and his wife, Rachel Kempson (1910–2003), at the start of their careers. It was Redgrave's London stage debut.

Redgrave and Kempson joined a theatre famous for the Shakespeare productions which its manager, Lilian Baylis (1874–1937), had been presenting since 1914. The Old Vic operated on a shoestring, paying the minimum in salaries, using the most basic of settings, and constantly recycling costumes, but it acquired a loyal audience. Crowd-pleasing plays like *As You Like It* and *Romeo and Juliet* were regulars in the repertoire, but the theatre risked the less popular pieces as well. *Love's Labour's Lost* tended to be regarded as 'difficult', its wordplay and lack of action being cited by reviewers as barriers for a twentieth-century audience, though it had received three previous Old Vic productions and been staged at London's Westminster Theatre in 1932, and at Regent's Park Open Air Theatre in 1935 and 1936. The director of the Westminster Theatre version was Tyrone Guthrie (1900–1971), who became director of the Old Vic at the start of the 1936 season.

Guthrie had already directed a season at the Old Vic, in 1933–4, when his ideas, including the recruitment of West End stars, had led to disagreements with Lilian Baylis. However, she was prepared to reappoint him in 1936 and he introduced changes, bringing in famous names, extending the runs of popular plays, and improving the look of productions (while still keeping an eye on the budget). For *Love's Labour's Lost*, designer Molly McArthur created a permanent setting with small pavilions on either side of the stage, a central fountain, and steps leading to a gateway with trellised fencing on each side. In his autobiography *In My Mind's Eye*, Redgrave admitted that he was not happy with the design:

> the set had a distinctly utilitarian appearance. The skycloth had seen far better days, and a gauze had to be hung in front of it to hide its wrinkles and gashes, giving the whole play an autumnal, hazy look quite at odds with its springtime theme. And I hated my costume. It was absurdly frilly and over-pretty, marabout [a form of raw silk] edged in lace, like an illustration to a child's history book.[1]

Rachel Kempson was happier with her outfit, which she called 'comfortingly disguising' as it hid the fact that she was pregnant with her daughter, Vanessa.[2]

Reviewers did not share Redgrave's dislikes and Debenham's photographs make the set and costumes look respectable enough, and catch some of Guthrie's stagecraft, which emphasised the artificiality of the story by using symmetrical groupings and formalised movement, some to a musical accompaniment. 'Most of the players have the zest and artistic suppleness of youth and the play moves with a swift and flashing grace', wrote Stephen Williams in the *Evening Standard*.[3]

---

1. Michael Redgrave, *In My Mind's Eye*, p. 97.

2. Rachel Kempson, *A Family and its Fortunes*, p. 116.

3. Stephen Williams, *Evening Standard*, 15 September 1936. This was one of the reviews kept by Rachel Kempson in a scrapbook, now part of the Michael Redgrave Archive in the V&A.

François Boitard, illustration of *A Midsummer Night's Dream* (1709)

It may be that this illustration from Rowe's 1709 Shakespeare edition reflects the adaptation of *A Midsummer Night's Dream* as *The Fairy Queen* that was first staged at the Dorset Garden Theatre in 1692, with songs and music by Henry Purcell (1659–1695). The illustration conjures up the description of a moonlit wood in Act Three of *The Fairy Queen*: 'the Scene changes to a Great Wood; a long row of Trees on each side: a river in the middle: Two rows of lesser Trees of a different kind just on the side of the River.'[1]

Following the Restoration, *A Midsummer Night's Dream* originally belonged to the group of plays chosen by Killigrew for the King's Company, and Pepys saw it staged at the King's Theatre in Vere Street in 1662. Killigrew is credited with staging productions close to Shakespeare's original text, but Pepys remained unimpressed: 'to the King's Theatre, where we saw *Midsummers nights dreame*, which I have never seen before, nor shall ever again, for it is the most insipid ridiculous play that ever I saw in my life. I saw, I confess, some good dancing and some handsome women, which was all my pleasure.'[2] Pepys may be forgiven his reaction, since it is evident that Shakespeare's unaltered plays were not guaranteed to find favour with Restoration audiences, and were routinely altered to make them more appealing to contemporary taste. A shortened version of *A Midsummer Night's Dream* enjoyed popularity on the Restoration stage, and it may have been a production of this that Pepys witnessed. Entitled *The Merry Conceited Humours of Bottom the Weaver* (1661), it gives prominence to the comic antics of the low-life characters, and is advertised on the title page as having been 'often publicly acted by some of his Majesty's Comedians' as well as 'privately presented by several Apprentices for their harmless recreation with Great Applause'.[3]

The demand for scenery, music and dancing led to the growth of English opera, a hybrid of spoken drama interspersed with song. Purcell's

Dido and Aeneas was combined with *Measure for Measure* in an adaptation by Charles Gildon (*c.* 1665–1724) called *Beauty the Best Advocate*, in which Angelo celebrates his birthday with a masque in four parts telling the story of Dido and Aeneas. *The Fairy Queen* is described on the title page as 'an Opera represented at the Queen's Theatre', as the Dorset Garden Theatre had come to be known. The prompter John Downes records:

> *The Fairy Queen*, made into an Opera, from a Comedy of Mr Shakespear's… Superior… especially in Cloaths, for all the Singers and Dancers, Scenes, Machines and Decorations, all most profusely set off; and excellently perform'd, chiefly the Instrumental and Vocal part.[4]

The Fairy Queen was essentially Shakespeare's *A Midsummer Night's Dream* with masques, featuring the singers and dancers, performed between each of the play's acts. Act Two is followed by 'a Masque, involving Night, Mystery, Secresie and Sleep and their attendances. A dance of the Followers of the Night concludes all.' The masques become more and more elaborate, with the fourth masque featuring 'mighty Cascades' and 'a very large Fountain, where the Water rises above Twelve foot'. The whole culminates in a wedding masque inspired by the growing craze for chinoiserie: 'Six Pedestals of China-work rise from under the Stage; they support six large Vases of Porcelain, in which are six China-Orange Trees.'[5] The climax of the work is a dance performed by twenty-four dancers in Chinese costume. Downes recalled that 'The Court and Town were wonderfully satisfy'd with it; but the Expenses in setting it out being so great, the Company got very little by it.'[6]

1. George C.D. Odell, *Shakespeare from Betterton to Irving*, vol. 1, pp. 192–3.

2. *Diary of Samuel Pepys*, vol. 3, p. 208.

3. *The Merry Conceited Humours of Bottom the Weaver* (1661) (Cornmarket Press Facsimile, 1970).

4. John Downes, *Roscius Anglicanus*, p. 89.

5. Odell, *Shakespeare from Betterton to Irving*, vol. 1, pp. 193–4.

6. Downes, *Roscius Anglicanus*, p. 89.

Sally Jacobs, set model for Peter Brook's production of *A Midsummer Night's Dream* (1970)

Peter Brook's 1970 production of *A Midsummer Night's Dream* had a profound effect on a whole generation of theatre artists and audience members. It is still one of the most influential and frequently cited Shakespearean productions of the twentieth century, and Sally Jacobs' white-box set was key to its success.

Brook claims that he was surprised to find himself agreeing to the Royal Shakespeare Company's invitation to direct one of Shakespeare's 'prettier' plays. His last work for the RSC had been the hard-hitting and experimental *US*, examining the effect of the Vietnam War. Brook's original ambition was to make the magic in the play believable by mixing actors with Chinese acrobats, having been inspired by the performers he saw in the Peking Circus on their first visit to Europe. The acrobats were all dressed identically in white shirts and trousers which concealed their muscular bodies and 'vanished in anonymity, leaving in their place an impression of pure speed, of pure lightness, of pure spirit'.[1] When this proved unworkable, Brook asked Trevor Nunn to choose a cast for him from the RSC's company (including Frances de la Tour, Alan Howard and Ben Kingsley) and they began a period of intensive, unconventional rehearsal. Each day started with gymnastics, moving on to practising circus tricks, then singing and dancing, only reading the text at the end of the day when their bodies were exhausted. John Kane (Philostrate/Puck) and Alan Howard (Theseus/Oberon) discovered a facility for plate-spinning that allowed them to toss the magic flower (in the form of a spinning plate) from one to another on the tips of their 'wands'.

Brook and Jacobs developed the standard white-box set (widely used at Stratford at the time) into a fantastical gymnasium/circus space. Steel ladders from the ground ran up to a gallery where the musicians were stationed and where the actors waited when they were 'offstage', gazing down on the action, or providing sound effects and rough music. Trapezes were suspended from the ceiling and wire springs dangled down to form the Athenian wood in which the lovers and Mechanicals are ensnared. Puck walked on stilts, actors dangled from trapezes, and Titania's bed became a giant feather suspended on wires (as shown here). The actors wore loose clothes (kaftans and bell-bottoms) in white, or bright, jewel-like colours that allowed them to contrast with, or blend into, the set.

The play literally began with a bang – a loud percussive crash – followed by the cast rushing on to the stage to take their positions. The production was intensely aural, scored by composer Richard Peaslee using autoharps, bongos and tubular bells to create unearthly, vibrant soundscapes.

Sally Jacobs recreated this model for the V&A to celebrate the thirtieth anniversary of the production, reusing some of the original model parts. The scene she created shows Puck (in luminous yellow) on stilts, Demetrius and Helena entangled in a wire thicket, and Oberon (in purple) on trapeze, while Titania rests on her feather bed attended by floating fairies.

1. Peter Brook, *Threads of Time*, p. 149.

Title page of the rehearsal score of Georges Jacobi's ballet *Titania* (1895)

Many choreographers have been attracted to Shakespeare's *A Midsummer Night's Dream*. The most widely performed are the full-evening ballets by George Balanchine (originally for New York City Ballet in 1962) and John Neumeier (originally for Hamburg Ballet in 1977). There are many more, including Frederick Ashton's one-act *The Dream*. Some, including Alexander Roy's 1980 production, are small-scale but able to tour worldwide. Others – David Nixon's entertaining 2003 production for Northern Ballet, for example, which replaced courtiers at Theseus's palace with a troupe of dancers on an overnight train – show considerable reinterpretation. The theme was also popular in the late nineteenth and early twentieth centuries, with productions by Marius Petipa (1877) and Mikhail Fokine (1902) for the Imperial Russian Ballet in St Petersburg, and two productions called *Titania* at the Alhambra (1895) and Empire (1913) theatres, both in Leicester Square, London.

Between 1865 and 1914, ballet in London was the principal feature of these two large variety theatres, which generally presented two productions of forty-five minutes' duration, along with a range of music-hall turns. The V&A's Theatre and Performance Collections hold the musical scores for the majority of the ballets created for the Alhambra by their house composer, Georges Jacobi (1840–1906). The collection includes conductor's scores and (as here) piano répétiteurs (or rehearsal scores) for the majority of the 105 ballets Jacobi wrote. They were acquired by the Ballet Guild in 1944 from the family, who were concerned about safeguarding their future. That collection was transferred into the London Archives of the Dance, which became one of the major collections contributing to the V&A's holdings. For many productions there are working synopses, as well as the annotations on the répétiteurs detailing mime action and other observations, making this one of the richest collections relating to dance within popular theatres during the period.

In 1895, the London-based Italian choreographer Carlo Coppi, working with the German-born Jacobi (who had trained in Brussels and Paris), chose Shakespeare's play for their new ballet. This completely flouted the regulations of the 1843 Theatre Regulation Act by which performances presented in music halls must not have a narrative. Theatre managers were constantly trying to push the boundaries of what was permissible and the authorities clearly often turned a blind eye to this aspect of production. Certainly the Alhambra made no secret of *Titania* being a 'Grand Spectacular Ballet in 4 Tableaux' arranged by Coppi from 'Shakespeare's Fairy Comedy'.

Coppi was probably looking for a subject which could feature the Grigolatis Flying Ballet, who had starred in the Alhambra's ballet *Ali Baba* in 1894 and would became a staple of the Drury Lane pantomimes (also choreographed by Coppi) between 1895 and 1904. The aerial dancers played the fairies, with Preciosa Grigolatis as the Fairy Queen and Emma Haupt as Puck, but Oberon was the earthbound leading British travesty dancer Julia Seale. The Mechanicals, being character parts, were played by men, as were Theseus, Egeus and Demetrius, but Louise Agoust of the famous pantomime troupe was cast as Lysander. Other members of the Agoust family played Theseus, Demetrius and Bottom. The traditional ballerina role was Hermia, danced by the Italian Cecilia Cerri, who was featured during the marriage of Theseus and Hippolyta as 'the central figure in a scarf dance with six associates, to a delicate accompaniment of harps, flutes, and subdued horn'. The ballerina wore a tunic rather than the usual tutu. *The Magazine of Art* approved: 'we recognise gratefully the concession to advancing taste in attiring the "Hermia" of the première danseuse so as to suggest the character, and not the conventional practising-skirts.'[1]

Although *Titania* was Jacobi's ninety-eighth ballet, he found the subject matter challenging. In an interview in the *Sketch* he said he had composed it within two months but he had 'seldom had so many troubles with a score. We have kept strictly to Shakespeare's story, which is, as you know, suggestive of slow, dreamy measures, and yet a ballet must be lively.'[2] Jacobi's bright, melodious music was well received and *Titania* had a twenty-week run from 30 July 1895.

The annotated descriptions of the action in the piano répétiteur for *Titania* appear to be in Coppi's hand, and the V&A collection includes his original three-scene synopsis amended by Jacobi, as well as band parts for the string players.

1. 'The Chronicle of Art', *The Magazine of Art*, vol. 18 (September 1895), p. 434.

2. [Arthur Symons,] 'The New Ballet at the Alhambra. A Chat with Mons. G. Jacobi', *Sketch*, 7 August 1895.

Ballet

Piano:

"Titania"
"A Midsummer Night's Dream"

By
Carlo Coppi

!— 92

Music by
G. Jacobi

Overture

Maestoso

Anthony Dowell and Antoinette Sibley (as Oberon and Titania) in Frederick Ashton's *The Dream* (1964)

On 2 April 1964, as a feature of the British celebrations of the quatercentenary of the birth of Shakespeare, The Royal Ballet paid its own tribute to the Bard. Robert Helpmann's *Hamlet* was revived, and Kenneth MacMillan created *Images of Love*, inspired by nine brief passages from Shakespeare, spoken in performance by Derek Godfrey (two from *Twelfth Night*, four from *The Two Gentlemen of Verona*, and one each from *The Taming of the Shrew*, *Julius Caesar* and Sonnet 144). The presence of Rudolf Nureyev in these two works meant they attracted most attention at the premiere, but it was the third work, Frederick Ashton's *The Dream*, which secured a place in the international repertoire of ballet companies.

Using Felix Mendelssohn's scores on the theme of *A Midsummer Night's Dream* (1826 and 1842), arranged by John Lanchbery, *The Dream* took a deliberately Victorian approach, both in the sets and costumes (by Henry Bardon and David Walker) and in the choreography that fleetingly incorporated poses from Romantic ballet lithographs, including those of *Pas de quatre* (1845) – appropriately, given Mendelssohn's great admiration for the ballerina Marie Taglioni. Ashton's ballet effectively encapsulated Shakespeare's play from the perspective of the fairy world, cutting the roles of Theseus and Hippolyta entirely, and only briefly including the 'rude Mechanicals' to introduce Bottom into the action. *The Dream* was a company work, Ashton's first as Artistic Director of The Royal Ballet, but at its heart was the launch of the remarkable dance partnership between the established ballerina Antoinette Sibley and the twenty-one-year-old emerging star Anthony Dowell.

When initially called for rehearsal, the two dancers assumed they had been cast as a pair of quarrelling lovers, but gradually they realised they were playing Oberon and Titania, the King and Queen of Fairyland. Although subsequently danced by many others, no one has since matched the creators of the roles – whether in the poignancy of Sibley's sensuous yielding or in Dowell's fleet-foot skimming across the stage with beaten steps. Their perfect proportions made them the ideal stage couple.

The Dream is one of Ashton's abiding masterworks, presenting his narrative with clarity through movement and dance. The reconciliation pas de deux shown in the photograph is the highlight of the ballet: not a dance for a ballerina supported by her partner, but rather a danced conversation in which the two are equals. Much of the movement has Titania and Oberon dancing side by side, each mirroring the other; it has precision, abandonment, and is rich in detail, as the dancers swoop and float – fairy figures indeed. Some of the ideas for the movement material had apparently come to Ashton in a dream (appropriately enough), and the dancers were left to work out how such steps could be realised.

The Theatre and Performance Collection at the V&A holds the Houston Rogers Archive, one of the most important photographic records of the London stage, particularly for the 1950s and 1960s. Active as a photographer between 1934 and 1970, 'Bill' Houston Rogers (1901–1970)had initially worked as a pit player for musical productions. His musical perspective served as an asset when photographing ballet, which proved a particular interest. His earliest dance photographs were of Ballet Rambert and the Markova-Dolin ballet, and he began his association with the Royal Opera House after the Second World War. Houston Rogers would attend photo calls at which poses would be set up for photographers, as well as dress rehearsals to record the productions on stage.

This iconic photograph appears to be one of a series of specially posed photographs, probably taken just before the dress rehearsal. The pose shows a moment from the reconciliation pas de deux between Titania and Oberon – though Dowell is here wearing the long flowing cape from the more mimetic first part of the ballet, rather than the short one into which he changed to free his limbs as he skimmed over the stage in his solo to the scherzo.

Lillah McCarthy's costume as Helena in the Savoy Theatre production of *A Midsummer Night's Dream* (1914)

At the beginning of the twentieth century, British theatregoers could expect to see Shakespeare presented in realistic settings and appropriate period costume. The actor-managers who worked in London and the larger cities wanted productions to be artistic and historically accurate, with effects as elaborate as the budget would allow. At Her Majesty's Theatre in 1900, Herbert Beerbohm Tree staged a romanticised version of *A Midsummer Night's Dream*, with painterly vistas of temples and a moonlit sea. The mortals wore classical Greek dress, and the fairies had tiny electric lights in their headdresses and wings. This popular production was still in Tree's repertoire in 1911. It was the epitome of pictorial Shakespeare.

Three years later, Harley Granville-Barker (1877–1946) staged a production of *A Midsummer Night's Dream* at the Savoy Theatre which seemed a world away from Tree's painted scenery. Barker was a playwright and an established director of contemporary drama who brought a modern sensibility to Shakespeare. Although he only directed three of the plays (the others were *The Winter's Tale* and *Twelfth Night*, both 1912), Barker's productions were hugely influential.[1] He recreated the spirit of the Elizabethan stage with swiftly moving action unencumbered by intervals for scene changing. Location was indicated by stylised scenery and curtains. Costumes suggested period dress but did not imitate it.

Barker's *Dream* has become famous for its fairies: otherworldly beings with gilded faces, whose oriental costumes shimmered in shades of gold and copper. Puck stood out as a figure from English folklore in scarlet doublet and breeches. The lovers wore Greek dress as seen through English eyes. Designer Norman Wilkinson (1882–1934) created two outfits for Helena, played by Barker's then wife, Lillah McCarthy (1875–1960). The first was a simple white dress of crêpe de Chine with a stencilled border. The costume shown here, also crêpe de Chine, was for the Act Five wedding celebrations. It consists of a dress with a shorter fringed tunic over the top; the shape is based on a classical chiton but the stencilled pink flowers owe much to the contemporary Arts and Crafts movement. Mauve shoes and red beads completed the ensemble. The Savoy Theatre account book, also in the V&A, gives the price for both dresses, two cloaks, plus accessories, as £23. 6s. 9½d., the equivalent of an impressive £1,897 today.

Costumes are vulnerable to damage and delicate fabrics can easily rip. Barker's production ran for three months, so Helena's dresses would have experienced much wear and tear. The fact that this costume was worn for only one scene, in which the character spent most of her time reclining on a couch, has helped its survival. The dress worn for the active woodland scenes has been lost.

1. Granville-Barker went on to co-direct *King Lear* at the Old Vic in 1940, but insisted that he should not be credited.

Vivien Leigh's crown as Titania at the Old Vic (1937)

Director Tyrone Guthrie (1900–1971) wrote a programme note to explain his staging of *A Midsummer Night's Dream*: 'The style of this production is early Victorian. This has not been arranged merely to be amusing. It is one more attempt to make an union between the words of Shakespeare, the music of Mendelssohn and the architecture of the Old Vic.' The production opened on Boxing Day 1937 and its nineteenth-century prettiness delighted reviewers, who found it the perfect Christmas entertainment. There was a corps de ballet of what Guthrie called 'operatic fairies in white muslin flying through groves of emerald canvas'. The flying came courtesy of Kirby's Flying Ballet, more usually associated with *Peter Pan*. The groves and white muslin were designed by Oliver Messel (1904–1978).

Much of the production's magic was credited to Messel's sets and costumes. He devised gauze drop curtains painted with huge flowers, which seemed to shrink the fairies to diminutive size. Oberon, played by dancer Robert Helpmann in his first Shakespearean role, resembled a stag beetle. His Titania, who was praised both for her beauty and her verse speaking, was the twenty-four-year-old Vivien Leigh (1913–1967). Leigh was then two years away from international fame as Scarlett O'Hara. She had joined the Old Vic Company earlier in 1937 to play Ophelia at Kronborg Castle in Denmark, opposite the Hamlet of her future husband, Laurence Olivier. *Gone with the Wind* made her name, but Leigh became an accomplished Shakespearean actress, her roles including Lady Macbeth, Viola, and Lavinia in *Titus Andronicus*.

Oliver Messel was a personal friend of Leigh's and it is thanks to their friendship that the two headdresses worn by Titania have survived. Messel kept both, and they are now held by the V&A. One, a small beaded creation incorporating flowers of silver paper, rhinestones and imitation pearls, features in photographs of Titania's scenes in the wood near Athens. The other is this crown, worn when the fairies bless the triple marriage in the final scene. Messel was an ingenious designer, ever conscious of the Old Vic's small budget. The crown was formed of a wire circlet, to which are attached flowers of velvet and ribbon, organdie leaves, and gold cord and cellophane bows, all dotted with silver beads and sequins to catch the light. Artificial pearls on wires alternate with taller spikes of cellophane to create the 'points'. Strings of silver beads hang from the sides, and a bow of silver gauze ribbon decorates the back. Messel stored both headdresses in a hand-painted hatbox, inside which is his note describing the crown as very crushed: 'all the cellophane stood upright like gossamer prisms'. Thanks to the V&A Conservation Department, it is now possible to appreciate the original effect.

Tile depicting Charles Macklin as Shylock (*c.* 1780)

The ports of Liverpool and Bristol became centres of tile production in eighteenth-century England, using blank tiles imported from Holland to produce a wide range of printed examples. The printers Guy Green and John Sadler spent seven painstaking years perfecting the process of transferring designs from woodblock, or copperplate, onto blank tiles with an oiled gel pad. Coloured glaze dusted onto the tiles stuck to the oil and the design was fixed by firing. The two printers signed an affidavit on 2 August 1756 affirming to have printed more than 1,200 tiles of different designs in six hours, 'more in number and better and neater than one hundred skilful pot-painters could have painted in a like space of time'.[1] Designs were chosen from various printed sources, favourites being illustrations from Aesop's Fables and portraits of the leading actors and actresses of the day. This image of Charles Macklin (*c.* 1699–1797) is taken from Bell's 1773 illustrated edition of Shakespeare's plays and shows the actor in his signature role, fixed in the public imagination by the jingle supposedly written by the poet Alexander Pope: 'This is the Jew that Shakespeare drew.'[2] Pope was invited to the party given by Lord Bolingbroke after the success of Macklin's first performance as Shylock at Drury Lane in 1741, and he asked Macklin why he had played Shylock wearing a red hat. On Macklin's replying that he had discovered that Jews in Italy were obliged to adopt this distinctive dress code, Pope asked, 'And pray, Mr Macklin... do players generally take such pains?' To which Macklin replied, 'I do not know, Sir, that they do, but as I had staked my reputation on the character, I was determined to spare no trouble in getting at the best information.'[3] Like many of his contemporaries in the profession – such as George Farquhar, Peg Woffington, and the playwright Sheridan – Macklin was Irish. Coming from a poor background in Donegal, he had risen the hard way, even killing a fellow actor in a fight over a wig, but was now catapulted by his success as Shylock into the highest literary and social circles.

Macklin was a redoubtable legal campaigner, winning damages in a lawsuit against members of the audience who had waged a hissing campaign against him. As both a playwright and an actor, he fought to protect authors' rights; he also started a revolutionary school for actors, in which he strove to eliminate 'all the cant and cadence', training the young actor to 'first speak the passage as he would in common life... then giving them more force, but preserving the same accent, to deliver them on the stage'.[4] He anticipated his younger contemporary Garrick in aiming at greater naturalism, but unlike Garrick, who enjoyed immediate success and played leading roles from the start, Macklin had to wait for his major break, meanwhile playing such supporting roles as Justice Shallow, First Witch, First Gravedigger, Osric, Polonius, Mercutio and Touchstone, before his appearance as Shylock in 1741 made him a star. At the end of his long career, after almost fifty years of playing Shylock, Macklin still remembered the sweetness of his triumph in that first performance: 'No money, no title, could purchase what I felt... By God, Sir, though I was not worth fifty pounds in the world at that time, let me tell you, I was Charles the Great for that night.'[5]

1. Hans van Lemmen, *Tiles*, p. 28.

2. J.O. Bartley (ed.), *Four Comedies by Charles Macklin*, p. 17.

3. Diana de Marly, *Costume on the Stage, 1600–1940*, p. 51.

4. Francis Aspry Congreve, *Authentic Memoirs of the late Mr Charles Macklin, Comedian*, p. 23.

5. Bartley (ed.), *Four Comedies by Charles Macklin*, p. 17.

M.r MACKLIN

in the Character of SHYLOCK

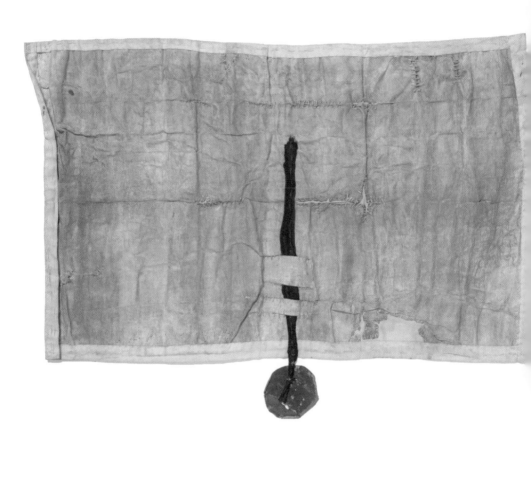

66 Go with me to a notary, seal me there your
single bond...**99**
The Merchant of Venice (1.3)

Henry Irving's property 'bond' as Shylock (1879)

This stage property bond was used in Henry Irving's 1879 production of
The Merchant of Venice and came to the V&A from the British Theatre
Museum Association. It had belonged to the collection of Sir Donald
Wolfit (1902–1968) and was donated by his widow, the actress Rosalind
Iden. Great importance was attached by Irving (1838–1905) to authenticity of costumes, settings and properties, and careful research was
undertaken to make the bond authentic to sixteenth-century Venice. It is
the legal document containing the terms of Shylock's loan of 3,000 ducats
to Antonio: if Antonio forfeits on repayment the bond entitles Shylock to
take one pound of his flesh.

The scenic designs for the Lyceum Theatre production by Hawes
Craven (1837–1910) were very much admired, and the V&A also owns
Craven's preliminary drawing of Shylock's house, which served as the
backdrop to a famously evocative piece of stage business introduced by
Irving in a short scene following Jessica's elopement. As Ellen Terry
described it, 'For absolute pathos, achieved by absolute simplicity of
means, I never saw anything in the theatre to compare with... Shylock's
return home over the bridge to his deserted house after Jessica's flight.'[1]
The curtain briefly fell after Jessica's exit but rose again immediately during the applause. 'When it went up again the stage was empty, desolate,
with no light but the pale moon, and all sounds of life at a great distance
– and then over the bridge came the wearied figure of the Jew.'[2] The curtain fell again as he was about to enter the house.

For his role as Shylock, Irving chose to wear a dark-brown Middle
Eastern costume, with a wide, brightly coloured sash, gold earrings and
a black and yellow cap. He drew his inspiration for the part from a Jewish
merchant he had seen that summer in Tunis when yachting in the
Mediterranean, who had made a great impression upon him: 'he was old,
but erect, even stately... As he walked beside his team of mules he carried

himself with the lofty air of a king.'[3] Irving chose to play Shylock less as a villain than as a victim, commenting, 'I look upon Shylock as the type of a persecuted race; almost the only gentleman in the play, and the most ill-used.'[4] Irving's liberal interpretation of Shylock's character is in tune with the assessment made by Hazlitt half a century earlier:

> He seems the depository of the vengeance of his race; and though the long habit of brooding over daily insults and injuries has crusted over his temper with inveterate misanthropy, and hardened him against the contempt of mankind… there is a strong, quick, and deep sense of justice mixed up with the gall and bitterness of his resentment.[5]

The balance of Irving's sympathies lay firmly with Shylock, as he unequivocally states: 'In *The Merchant of Venice* the Jew appears to less disadvantage than the Christian. *Both are animated by the spirit of intolerance*, the latter especially.'[6] Irving went on to play Shylock over a thousand times: he chose the role for his farewell appearance at the Lyceum Theatre in 1902, and at the time of his sudden death in Bradford three years later he was engaged to play Shylock the next evening.

1.   Alan Hughes, *Henry Irving, Shakespearean*, p. 232.
2.   *Ibid.*
3.   John Gross, *Shylock*, p. 128.
4.   *Ibid.*
5.   William Hazlitt, *Characters of Shakespeare's Plays* (1817), pp. 269–70.
6.   Alan Hughes, *Henry Irving, Shakespearean,* p. 240.

Ticket for David Garrick's Shakespeare Jubilee (1769)

It fell to George Garrick, general factotum of actor-manager David (1717–1779), to supervise the Stratford end of the 1769 Shakespeare Jubilee while his older brother masterminded preparations remotely from London. One of George's duties was to oversee the ticketing. The entrance price stated is one guinea (twenty-one shillings) and each and every ticket was signed and numbered by him. These went on sale at selected coffee houses and shops in London, and at The White Lion Hotel in Stratford.

The ticket shown here has been cropped on the left-hand side, detaching an image of Shakespeare pictured beneath the words, adapted from Hamlet's musing on his father, 'We ne'er shall look upon his like again' (1.2.188). The entertainments to which it admitted the jubilee-goer included Thomas Arne's oratorio *Judith*, the ball and fireworks, and the 'Ode' that David Garrick himself wrote in praise of Shakespeare, to be delivered as a rhetorical set piece in the temporary Rotunda, complete with musicians conducted by Dr Arne, interacting with Garrick's delivery. The *Oxford Journal* for Saturday, 9 September 1769 reported with considerable understatement that the weather on the second day proved 'rather unfavourable', but fulsomely praised the 'Ode' and its author/performer (whom it likened to the celebrated Roman actor Roscius):

> Mr. Garrick appeared in the Front of the Orchestra, wearing a fine
> Medallion of Shakespeare on his Breast, carved upon a Piece of the
> celebrated Mulberry Tree planted by our Great Bard, with a Wand of
> Office from the same wood. Soon after the Ode was performed, and
> performed in the most striking, as well as agreeable, Manner; the
> Recitative spoken by Mr. Garrick, and the Airs (which were in this
> Instance considered as a Part of the Recitative) echoed by the whole
> Band, vocal and instrumental. Mr. Garrick's Recitation was admirable,
> so admirable that it may be called *The Triumph of* SPEAKING *over*
> SINGING; for the excellent composition of Dr. Arne was in some
> Measure overcome by the Dramatic Powers of our English Roscius.

The success of the 'Ode' to some extent mitigated the misery of a day which had rained off the procession of Shakespearean characters planned to precede it. Although it attracted satirical mockery from those who viewed the whole festival as self-publicity for Garrick rather than a tribute to Shakespeare's genius, it appears to have entertained those who witnessed its first performance, despite the unfortunate line hoping that the Avon would be 'ever full'. In its swollen state the river was doing its best to join the audience in the amphitheatre.

After the Jubilee, Garrick left Stratford, leaving his brother to mop up – metaphorically, and perhaps literally. In its wake, Stratford, already a place of embryonic pilgrimage, would be indelibly marked on the map as a tourist shrine and cultural centre. Never again would a major Shakespearean anniversary go unmarked. A new Ode is planned for the 400th anniversary of Shakespeare's death in 2016.

See also Object 64: The Rotunda for David Garrick's Shakespeare Jubilee 1769, page 200.

SHAKESPEARS=JUBILEE,
the 6.th and 7.th of September,
at Stratford upon Avon.
This TICKET admits one on the 6.th to
The Oratorio.
The
DEDICATION ODE.
The
BALL.
And to the Great Booth at the Fireworks
One Guinea.
Geo: Garrick

N.º 335

66 Alas the day! what shall I do with my
doublet and hose? **99**
As You Like It (3.2)

23

Dorothy Jordan as Rosalind in Act Three, Scene Five of *As You Like It* (1795)

This stippled engraving, by Charles Knight (*c.* 1743–1826), is based on Henry Bunbury's depiction of Mrs Dorothy Jordan (1761–1816) as Rosalind, published in 1795. It is inscribed with a dedication from Bunbury 'To Mrs Jordan / In Gratitude for the Pleasure received from her Inimitable Performance as Rosalind'. A Royal Academician and a friend of Garrick and Reynolds, Bunbury (1750–1811) specialised in theatrical subjects and in caricature; his works were a popular subject for engraving by James Gillray and others.

In Dyce's opinion, Mrs Jordan 'was assuredly one of the most popular comic actresses that ever trod the British boards: and what added to the pleasure of her audience was the evident pleasure she herself took in the parts she played'. In his collection, Dyce had an engraving of Mrs Jordan as Nell in *The Devil to Pay*, a farce in which Nell, a shoemaker's wife, changes places with the rich Lady Loverule. In his *Reminiscences*, Dyce writes that 'Nothing in its kind could be more truthful or amusing than Mrs Jordan's representation of the bewilderment of Nell, when, waking in bed as Lady Loverule', and he quotes the lines from the play in which Nell is brought the new fashionable drink, chocolate, by a servant, and tries to conceal that she doesn't know what chocolate is, and thinks it might be something to wear. Dyce also particularly enjoyed her performance as Rosalind in *As You Like It* when 'with delightful archness, she sung into the ear of Orlando… the burden "Cuckoo, cuckoo," she at the same time made the powder fall from his wig by giving it a smart brush with the back of her hand.'[1] Her role as Viola in *Twelfth Night* was another favourite with Dyce, and the Theatre and Performance Department has a coloured engraving of her in the duel scene (Act Three, Scene Four).

Mrs Jordan epitomised the Comic Muse, as Mrs Siddons did the Tragic Muse, and she excelled in cross-dressing roles as Rosalind and Viola, and also as Imogen in *Cymbeline* and Helena in *All's Well That Ends Well*. She continued to play the same roles until her retirement from the stage in 1815. 'Latterly, of course,' commented Dyce, 'the effect of her performances was marred by the extreme unfitness of her figure for the juvenile parts, of which a large proportion of her repertoire consisted: yet there was such a charm about her… she continued to play youthful belles, and even hoydens of sixteen, to crowded and applauding houses.'[2] The theatre manager Tate Wilkinson takes credit for giving her the stage name of Jordan when she arrived from Dublin in Leeds in 1782, unmarried and pregnant, accompanied by her mother – whom Tate Wilkinson recognised as 'my first Desdemona in Dublin' in 1758.[3] The son of a clergyman, Wilkinson joked that he had played the role of godfather in giving her the name, saying, 'you have crossed the water, so I'll call you Jordan.'[4] She played many roles on the Yorkshire circuit, including Lady Teazle (in Sheridan's *The School for Scandal*), Jane Shore, and Imogen, before her child was born, staying three years in the north before moving down to London to become one of the most successful comic actresses of all time. She combined her acting career with motherhood: the father of her eldest daughter was her theatre manager in Dublin; three more children, of which two survived, were born to Richard Ford, son of one of the proprietors of the Drury Lane Theatre; and no less than ten children were born during her twenty-year relationship with Prince William, Duke of Clarence. He deserted her for a young heiress in 1811, but on becoming King in 1830, he commissioned a statue of her with two of their children from Francis Chantry. Originally intended for Westminster Abbey, the statue has been in the Royal Collection at Buckingham Palace since 1980.

The quality which her admirers all strive to capture in their descriptions of her was the sound of her voice, which, to Charles Lamb, 'sank, with her steady melting eye, into the heart'.[5] Leigh Hunt describes how 'Mrs Jordan seems to speak with all her soul' and for Hazlitt, her voice was 'a cordial to the heart, because it came from it, rich, full, like the luscious juice of the ripe grape; to hear whose laugh was to drink nectar… whose singing was like the twang of Cupid's bow.'[6,]

1. *The Reminiscences of Alexander Dyce*, ed. Richard J. Schrader, p. 102.

2. *Ibid.*, pp. 103–4.

3. Tate Wilkinson, *The Wandering Patentee*, vol. 2, p. 133.

4. Brian Fothergill, *Mrs Jordan*, p. 52.

5. Philip Highfill (et al.), *A Biographical Dictionary of Actors… 1660–1800*, vol. 8, p. 252.

6. *Ibid.*, pp. 252–3.

Nick Ormerod's costume design for Audrey in *As You Like It* (1991)

This design for Audrey's wedding dress is from Cheek by Jowl's celebrated 1991 all-male production of the play and is typical of the company's pared-down aesthetic. Founded by director Declan Donnellan and designer Nick Ormerod in 1981, Cheek by Jowl began as a small-scale touring company with an ambition to 're-examine classical texts, avoiding directorial and design concepts, and to focus on the actor's art'.[1] They quickly gained a reputation for their innovative, atmospheric productions that combined music, simple but effective design, and an immediacy between actors and audience. The intimacy between audience, actor and text was a central ambition of the company's work, and their name, taken from *A Midsummer Night's Dream* (3.2.338), was chosen to reflect that ambition.

In 1991, for their tenth-anniversary tour, Donnellan and Ormerod decided to produce an all-male version of *As You Like It* so that they could examine gender politics. Adrian Lester played Rosalind, Tom Hollander was Celia, and Richard Cant played Audrey. The show was a great success and toured Britain, Europe, New Zealand and Brazil. It was revived in 1994 for a second world tour before ending up in the West End.

Ormerod's design began in stark monochrome, reflecting the macho conventions of Frederick's court, and alternated between black-and-white box sets which represented the court and the forest for the winter scenes, while for spring, the white-box set was draped with rolls of green cloth and softly lit, with the actors costumed in bright shades. Many of the costumes were off-the-peg, shop-bought items like the black and white shirts and trousers the company assembled in at the beginning of the play. Audrey's wedding outfit, shown here, was a garish yellow dress that emphasised the comic nature of the character. In the costume sketch, the dress looks slightly vulgar; a little bit too short and tight for dignity (as befits a rustic comic character's idea of style). In performance, Richard

Cant's slender frame gave the outfit a touch of girlish anticipation. At one performance, there was 'a smatter of applause' for Audrey's wedding frock, with the stage manager drily noting, 'Zandra Rhodes, eat your heart out.'[2]

The V&A holds Cheek by Jowl's archive from 1981 to 1999, including prompt-books, production photographs, costume designs and administrative material. Because of the impact and importance of the production of *As You Like It*, the museum also acquired the set and costume designs and two costumes from the production, and filmed it for the National Video Archive of Performance during its run at the Albery Theatre, now the Noël Coward, in 1995.

1. Cheek by Jowl company website: <www.cheekbyjowl.com/history.php>, accessed 20 June 2013.

2. Show report for *As You Like It*, Cheek by Jowl Archive, THM/24/2/13.

AUDREY
(WEDDING)

RICHARD CANT

Hester Booth as a Harlequin Lady (c. 1725)

Although neither signed nor dated, the museum's portrait of Hester Booth (née Santlow) dancing as a Harlequin Woman, dating from the early to mid-1720s, was acquired at auction in 1989 as the work of John Ellys (1701–1757), who in 1736 became principal painter to Frederick, Prince of Wales. In 1710, Zacharias Uffenbach, a German visitor to London, saw the dancer-actress Hester Santlow (c. 1690–1773) playing the lead role in Charles Shadwell's comedy *The Fair Quaker of Deal*. He noted how 'universally admired' she was 'for her beauty, matchless figure, and the unusual elegance of her dancing and acting', and that she was 'visited by those of the highest fashion in England'. Between two acts of the play she also 'danced charmingly as Harlequin, which suits her excellently and much pleases the English. They make such a to-do about her that her portrait in this costume is painted on snuff-boxes and frequently sold'.[1] First recorded as dancing in the role of a female Harlequin in 1706, her success was so great that a year later she was invited to dance before Queen Anne at St James's Palace in *The Union*, an entertainment celebrating the uniting of the kingdoms of England and Scotland.

Having made her debut as an actress in 1709 as Prue in Congreve's *Love for Love*, she had success in a number of Shakespearean, and pseudo-Shakespearean, roles. In 1710 she appeared as Dorinda in Davenant and Dryden's adaptation of *The Tempest*, and Ophelia and Lady Percy in *Henry IV, Part One*. She retained the latter role at Drury Lane until her retirement from the stage in 1733, along with that of Cordelia in Nahum Tate's adaptation of *King Lear* (in which, notoriously, Lear does not die at the end of the play, and Cordelia survives to marry Edgar). Hester's fine legs were shown off to advantage in the breeches role of Violante in *Double Falsehood*, a play by Lewis Theobald which he claimed to have adapted from *Cardenio*, a lost original by Shakespeare and Fletcher. Her other Shakespearean role was Desdemona in *Othello*, in which she played opposite her future husband Barton Booth as Othello, who so excelled in the role that Theophilus Cibber observed: 'the heart-breaking Anguish of

81

his Jealousy would have drawn Tears from the most obdurate'.[2] William Chetwood, prompter at Drury Lane, recalls:

> I remember in the 5th Act of Othello, while he is listening to *Emilia's* speaking to *Desdemona*, after she is suppos'd to be strangled, he suited his Attitude and Countenance to the Circumstance of the Scene, that I have not the Art to describe, but the treble repeated Applause of the Audience, while he was silent, spoke such high Approbation, that Miss *Santlow* (afterwards Mrs *Booth*) us'd to say 'She thought the Audience were pleas'd poor Desdemona was strangled out of the Way.'[3]

When, after ten years of acting together, the two leading actors became romantically involved and eventually happily married, Booth's former partner Susan Mountfort is reported to have rushed madly on to the stage when Hester was playing Ophelia, and had to be forcibly removed from the theatre. Although Booth had proposed marriage to Susan, she is said to have preferred to retain a £300 annuity paid on condition that she remained single. Her relationship with Barton Booth reputedly soured after they bought a winning lottery ticket together in 1714 with a prize of £5,000, and Susan refused to share the money with him. Hester already had a daughter by a former lover, the highly placed James Craggs, future Minister of War and Secretary of State, who had fought a duel to defend her honour, but the relationship did not end in marriage, and Hester married Barton Booth in 1719. She retired from the stage after her husband's death in 1733, living for a further forty years in retirement, and erecting a memorial to her husband in Westminster Abbey before her own death in 1773. The allure of her person and her dancing is celebrated by her husband in the poem he wrote for her, 'On Mira Dancing':

> So round her Neck, her Eyes so fair!
> So rose her swelling Chest, so flow'd her Amber Hair!
> While her swift Feet outstripp'd the Wind…
> The Pulse still answers to the strains,
> And the Blood dances in our Veins.[4]

1. James Fowler, 'Hester Santlow: Harlequin Lady', p. 47.

2. Moira Goff, *The Incomparable Hester Santlow*, p. 67.

3. *Ibid.*, pp. 67–8.

4. Philip Highfill (et al.), *A Biographical Dictionary of Actors… 1660–1800*, vol. 2, p. 228.

"Doublet and hose ought to show itself courageous to petticoat..."
As You Like It (2.4)

'Scrap' depicting the Kendals as Rosalind and Orlando (*c.* 1890)

This glossy 'scrap' depicts Madge Kendal as Rosalind and William Henry Kendal as Orlando, in a characteristically convoluted girl-disguised-as-boy incident in *As You Like It* when Rosalind, dressed as Ganymede, encourages the hoodwinked Orlando to woo 'him', to vent his feelings about his hopeless love for Rosalind (4.1). The Kendals first played the roles together at London's Haymarket Theatre in October 1871, and Rosalind and Orlando remained popular characters in their repertoire during their long acting career as a married couple.

Madge Kendal (1848–1935) was a seasoned Shakespearean actress by 1871. A theatre manager's daughter, she made her first London stage appearance in 1854 at the Marylebone Theatre aged six when her father was co-lessee of the theatre.[1] After the family moved to Bristol the fifteen-year-old Madge played a Fairy in *A Midsummer Night's Dream* at the newly opened Bath Theatre, with the young Ellen Terry as Titania.[2] She made her adult London debut in the summer of 1865 at the Haymarket Theatre, playing Ophelia, Blanche in *King John*, and Desdemona, all within two months.[3] She married William Grimston (1843–1917) in 1869 and adopted his stage name Kendal, but the wedding was only sanctioned by her father William Robertson on the condition that they should always perform together.[4] Kendal was by then already a leading man with a gift for comedy, and had played Orlando at the Haymarket Theatre in 1867, with Mrs Scott-Siddons as Rosalind. He later proved his skills as a theatre manager, managing both the Court Theatre and the St James's Theatre with John Hare in the 1870s and 1880s.

The scrap is a sheet from a series issued by Siegmund Hildesheimer & Co. in around 1890, depicting popular British actors in well-known Shakespearean roles. Some of the actors, like David Garrick, Sarah Siddons, and Edmund Kean, made their names much earlier than the Kendals, but had earned their place as scraps due to legendary performances – Garrick as King Lear, Siddons as Lady Macbeth, and Kean as

Richard III. Making scrapbooks, or decorating screens, boxes, or greetings cards with scraps was a popular Victorian pastime. The earliest scraps appeared in the early nineteenth century as engravings that could be bought plain or hand-coloured. By the 1820s they were more elaborate and sometimes embossed, and by the middle of the century they were manufactured in colour by the process known as chromolithography, patented in 1837 by the printer Godefroye Engelmann, and the printing and embossing processes were automated. After being embossed, scraps were coated with a gelatine and gum layer to give them a gloss finish. Finally they were put through a stamping press where the surplus paper was cut away by a cutting die, leaving the individual images on one sheet connected by small strips of paper. The trade in scraps boomed from the 1870s until the end of the century, and Siegmund Hildesheimer & Co. appears in London directories from 1877 until 1929, also selling greetings cards and fancy stationery. In 1884, an advertisement in the *Stationery Trades Journal* shows the firm offering a range of forty-four different sheets of scraps, or 'New Penny Reliefs', of 'flowers, figures, fruits, birds, animals etc.' printed by the Berlin-based printer Wolff Hagelberg.

Although these scraps may appear to be a colourful item of fanciful ephemera, comparisons with photographs – where the subjects were born late enough to be photographed – show them to be an accurate record of costume, if not of colour. This image was reproduced from a photograph by the well-known portrait photographer Herbert Rose Barraud. The Kendals are seen here in the costumes designed by Lewis Wingfield for the production that opened at the St James's Theatre in January 1885, which prompted one contemporary critic to comment on Kendal's concern during the wrestling match with Charles, 'not to do anything likely to derange the symmetry of his wig', and the fact that Mrs Kendal appeared 'disadvantageously' in doublet and hose, owing to her trick 'of bending her knees inward when she seeks to express emotion becoming apparent in the absence of petticoats'.[5]

1. As Marie in Edward Stirling's nautical drama *The Struggle For Gold*, Marylebone Theatre, 20 February 1854.

2. Bath Theatre, March 1863.

3. Haymarket Theatre, *Hamlet*, 29 July 1865; *King John*, 10 August 1865; *Othello*, 21 August 1865.

4. Originally 'Kendall', but he later dropped the second 'l'.

5. *Illustrated Sporting and Dramatic News*, 7 February 1885.

ROSALIND.
(MRS KENDAL.)

ORLANDO.
(MR KENDAL.)

CHARACTERS FROM SHAKSPEARE. SHEET 4.

ROS. Men have died from time to time, and worms have eaten them, but not for love.

ORL. I would not have my right Rosalind of this mind; for I protest, her frown might kill me.

ROS. By this hand, it will not kill a fly. But come, now I will be your Rosalind in a more coming-on disposition; and ask me what you will, I will grant it.

ORL. Then love me, Rosalind.

ROS. Yes, faith will I, Fridays and Saturdays and all.

ORL. And wilt thou have me?

ROS. Ay, and twenty such.

AS YOU LIKE IT.
Act IV.
Scene 1.

Nº 431.

"DER WIEDERSPENSTIGE ZÄHMUNG"
KATE — HAYDEE/ REYN —
ACT II SC I

Elisabeth Dalton
'69

Elisabeth Dalton's costume design for Katherina in John Cranko's ballet of *The Taming of the Shrew* (1969)

The Taming of the Shrew is a good example of the ability of the choreographer John Cranko (1927–1973) to create characters and narratives through dance and movement so that his audiences could easily follow the action of a ballet. He recognised that with any literary text there was a need to adapt it to suit his purpose and with *The Shrew* he dropped the Induction and reduced the number of named characters. He also created a scene in which Hortensio and Gremio (roles memorably created by John Neumeier and Egon Madsen respectively) are tricked into marrying a pair of harlots whom Lucentio has disguised to look like Bianca – a subplot that many viewers believed came from Shakespeare's play. For ballet it is important that any adaptation of a play does not depend on its language and *The Shrew* lent itself to knockabout comedy. Genuinely funny ballets are very rare and *The Shrew* is one at which audiences still laugh out loud.

While including scenes for his corps de ballet, Cranko's *The Taming of the Shrew* was undoubtedly a vehicle for two great character dancers: the Brazilian ballerina (and Cranko's muse) Marcia Haydée as Kate, and Richard Cragun, a newer recruit to the Württemberg State Ballet (widely known as the Stuttgart Ballet), as Petruchio. Cragun's astonishing physical strength, breathtaking virtuosity, and the fun he brought to his role has never been surpassed. For Haydée, *The Shrew* was a new departure as it was a comic role and her great parts had been dramatic heroines, including Shakespeare's Juliet and Tatiana in *Onegin*. Cranko would give Haydée steps but leave her to slowly work out their interpretation. Devising the piece in the late 1960s, Cranko was sensitive to the rise of feminism and, in Kate, he and Haydée created a lively, feisty woman who, although she tosses her frowning, angry head and stomps along in a flat-footed walk, is quite capable of giving every bit as good as she gets. John Percival in his biography of Cranko recalled that the choreographer said that in his production Kate is tamed but not defeated; Katherina and

Petruchio become equal partners out of choice: 'the essential plot of the ballet was conveyed in their three big duets. In the first Kate is the stronger; by the second, Petruchio has the upper hand; and in the third, they find a balance.'[1]

It was typical of Cranko that he should commission designs for a major production from a relatively little-known designer, Elisabeth Dalton (1940–2004). Dalton had trained at the Wimbledon School of Art and the Slade, and began working in design for dance as an assistant to Nicholas Georgiadis. This experience meant that she was already aware that the set had to allow plenty of space for the dancers to move and that the costumes should not restrict their movements.

Dalton created a fixed, adaptable architectural setting and, unusually, Cranko came to an agreement with his designer whereby Dalton was allowed to create costume designs ahead of the choreography. Dalton recalled in an interview that John said, 'I'll choreograph round what you design, but you must work in chronological order.'[2] Together they built up the characters but, in spite of the liberty Cranko gave her, Dalton claimed that 'I don't think I put a single design on paper before consulting John and his agreeing it despite our fun race to get to the characters first.' She found inspiration for the costumes from artists of the Northern Renaissance, most notably for the bodices of the women's dresses from Lucas Cranach. The peachy-pink dress in the illustrated design was the basic shape for most of the women's costumes. This costume was designed for Act Two, Scene One of the ballet, in which the still-rebellious Kate and her new husband journey to Petruchio's home. Dalton has stuck paper over the dancer's hair on the design, clearly having had second thoughts about Kate's hairstyle for this scene. The design is annotated with the name of two dancers, since in ballet artists alternate in leading parts and from the start the Rhodesian dancer Judith Reyn was also learning this role.

Cranko's *The Taming of the Shrew* was premiered in Stuttgart on 16 March 1969, and was first seen in Britain at the company's first season at the Royal Opera House, Covent Garden, in the summer of 1974.

1. John Percival, *Theatre in my Blood*, pp. 196–7.
2. Mary Clarke and Clement Crisp, *Making a Ballet*, p. 101.

Chris Castor as the Widow in Barry Jackson's production of *The Taming of the Shrew* (1928)

In 1913, Barry Jackson's Birmingham Repertory Theatre opened with *Twelfth Night*. His stated aim was 'to enlarge and increase the aesthetic sense of the public… in short, to serve art instead of making that art serve a commercial purpose'.[1] A man of means (his family owned the Maypole Dairies: at its height, a chain of over a thousand grocer's shops) with a love of theatre and the arts, Jackson (1879–1961) had founded the Pilgrim Players in Birmingham in 1907, an influential amateur group that developed into the basis of Jackson's Birmingham Repertory Company. As its director, he experimented with approaches to presenting classic plays, with the aim of finding new interpretations which could link them with the present. His series of modern-dress productions of Shakespeare continue to be seen as a major landmark in the staging of Shakespeare.

The series began with *Cymbeline* in 1923, followed by *Hamlet*, *All's Well That Ends Well*, *Macbeth* and *The Taming of the Shrew*, finishing with *Othello* in 1929, all directed by H.K. Ayliff (1871–1949). Reviewing *Cymbeline*, the critic of the *Birmingham Evening Despatch* commented that in the characters' passages of 'fine emotion': 'we were moved more deeply because they looked like people of our own familiar world.'[2] This would greatly have pleased Jackson, who stated the purpose of his modern-dress productions in programme notes and newsletters. Alan Bland, the theatre's publicity manager, wrote an introduction to Jackson's production of *Macbeth*, saying:

> People who did not see *Hamlet* when it was produced in modern dress may still imagine that such a presentation of a great work is a silly 'stunt' amounting almost to blasphemy. It is fair to say that by far the great majority of those who did see it, came away feeling that, perhaps for the first time, they had fully appreciated that Hamlet was a human being and not a philosophical abstraction in a black cloak.[3]

It is thanks to Barry Jackson and his pioneering work that such programme notes would be superfluous today.

Jackson did not always feel that his efforts were fully appreciated by his home city. For a period, he relocated his company to London in 1924, before being wooed back to Birmingham the following year. The production of *The Taming of the Shrew* illustrated here was first presented for four weeks at the Royal Court Theatre in Sloane Square, opening in April 1928. It was deemed to be particularly successful, featuring amusing modern touches, such as an electric stove, speaking tubes, a cine-cameraman for the wedding scene and a Ford motor car. As demonstrated by this image from Barry Jackson's own photograph albums, the costumes, designed and created by Elspeth Fox-Pitt, also reflected the height of 1920s fashion.

On the whole, the critics were prepared to enjoy the production as a light-hearted entertainment and to respond to it in a similar vein. One critic commented that Paul Shelving's scenery 'was like nothing ever seen in Padua, and much of it reminded one of the classier portions of Southend'.[4] Chris Castor was the first wife of the actor Donald Wolfit (1902–1968), whom she married in the same year as this photograph was taken. The rest of the cast included two actors who became stars (and knights) of the stage: Laurence Olivier and Ralph Richardson. The Birmingham Repertory Company was responsible for launching the careers of many other successful actors, and for spotting talent in actors such as Peggy Ashcroft and Edith Evans.

In 1935, Sir Barry Jackson (he was himself knighted in 1925) passed on his theatre to a Board of Trustees, although he remained its Director. He went on to found the Malvern Festival, dedicated to Bernard Shaw, and between 1946 and 1948 he was Director of the Shakespeare Memorial Theatre in Stratford-upon-Avon, which he restored to being a theatre of distinction after a period of creative inertia. His contribution to the staging of Shakespeare during the first half of the twentieth century cannot be overestimated. He brought Shakespeare to new audiences and opened their minds to the relevance of his plays to the modern world.

1. Jonathan Bate and Russell Jackson (ed.), *Shakespeare: An Illustrated Stage History*, p. 140.

2. E.M.W., *Birmingham Evening Despatch*, 23 April 1923.

3. Programme for *Back to Methuselah*, Birmingham Repertory Theatre, October 1928.

4. Uncredited review in V&A Production File for *The Taming of the Shrew*, Royal Court Theatre, 1928.

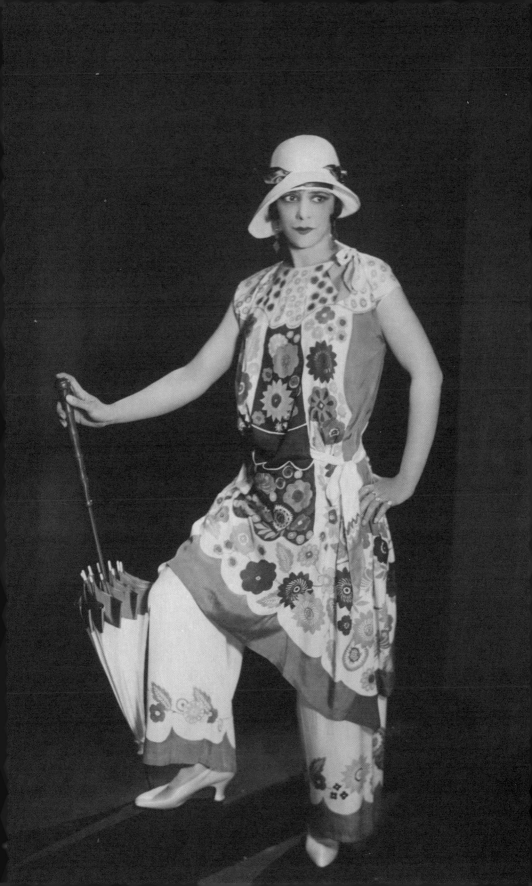

ALL'S WELL THAT ENDS WELL

BY WILLIAM SHAKESPEARE

ROGER ALLAM *MORGAN* PEGGY ASHCROFT *COUNTESS OF ROSSILLION* CHERYL CAMPBELL *DIANA* PETER CHELSOM *GENTLEMAN* ROBERT EDDISON *LAFEU*
JOHN FRANKLYN ROBBINS *KING OF FRANCE* PHILIP FRANKS *DUMAINE THE YOUNGER* MIKE GWILYM *BERTRAM* DIANA HARDCASTLE *MAID*
JULIA HILLS *MAID* CHRISTOPHER HURST *GENTLEMAN* GEOFFREY HUTCHINGS *LAVACHE* GRIFFITH JONES *THE KING'S GENTLEMAN* PETER LAND
DUMAINE THE ELDER NIGEL LE VAILLANT *GENTLEMAN* JOHN McANDREW *GENTLEMAN* LEONIE MELLINGER *MAID* JULIETTE MOLE *VIOLENTA*
STEPHEN MOORE *PAROLLES* BERT PARNABY *RYNALDO* JOHN ROGAN *DUKE OF FLORENCE* JULIA SWIFT *MARIANA* ELIZABETH RIDER *MAID*
GRAHAM TURNER *GENTLEMAN* HARRIET WALTER *HELENA* GILLIAN WEBB *WIDOW*
DIRECTED BY TREVOR NUNN DESIGNED BY JOHN GUNTER COSTUMES BY LINDY HEMMING LIGHTING BY ROBERT BRYAN MUSIC BY GUY WOOLFENDEN

RSC
Royal Shakespeare Theatre
STRATFORD-UPON-AVON
BOX OFFICE (0789) 295271
AMEX CARDS (0789) 297129

THE RSC IS
Arts Council
OF GREAT BRITAIN

Ginni Moo-Young poster for Trevor Nunn's RSC production of *All's Well That Ends Well* (1981)

A play needs an eye-catching poster. This poster for the Royal Shakespeare Company's 1981–2 production of *All's Well That Ends Well* is actually merchandising, not advertising, and was designed for sale in the RSC shops and for display in its theatres, rather than as a means of attracting passers-by in the street. Its designer, Ginni Moo-Young, created a striking image of a dancing couple, the pattern formed by the swirling skirt leading the eye upwards to the dancers' faces and the archway behind them. It creates an impression of *fin de siècle* romance, of officers and their ladies waltzing to Strauss. The lettering and the curving lines of the skirt borrow the style of art nouveau. What the image does *not* suggest is Shakespeare.

It does, however, capture the spirit of the production. Director Trevor Nunn set the play in the France of the *belle époque*. The poster was, he said, intended to reflect the period, preparing the audience for the play's updating, and capturing a theme: 'since among other things the play challenges the traditional social roles of men and women, the ritual and sexuality of the dance was to be an important visual image of the staging.'[1]

Nunn's *All's Well* belongs to a twentieth-century development in the presentation of Shakespeare: the locating of the play in a recognisable historical period which is not that of its imagined setting. In Britain the modern-dress experiments of the 1920s prepared the way for design that was contemporary neither with the play's creation nor with that of its audience. Surprisingly, perhaps, one of the earliest productions to re-imagine a play in another era was directed by William Poel (1852–1934), famous as a pioneer of Elizabethan staging. His 1931 production of *Coriolanus* for the Elizabethan Stage Circle did not attempt a consistent representation of a particular time and place but rather intended, as Poel wrote in a programme note, 'to show the ageless spirit of militarism', dressing the characters in the uniforms of the Napoleonic Wars (which baffled many of the reviewers). When David Thacker set the play in the same period in an RSC production of 1994, no one batted an eyelid. By the late twentieth century the historical re-imagining of Shakespeare's plays had become an accepted convention, enabling audiences to bring their own knowledge of a period to bear and draw parallels between the drama and its new setting. It has also become a useful way of suggesting class and status, particularly if the characters can be put into uniform.

All's Well That Ends Well sends its characters off to war in Italy. By updating it, Nunn's production hinted that the horrors of the First World War might not be far away, and so created a bittersweet atmosphere for the story of physician's daughter Helena and her love for the upper-class Bertram. Helena, played by Harriet Walter, became the poor relation brought up in an aristocratic household. The shock shown by Bertram at his forced marriage to his mother's ward suggested the snobbery of the pre-war officer class. The action took place on a set by John Gunter, which used a basic pillared construction that variously became the wrought-iron columns and arches of a country-house conservatory, a ball-room, a gymnasium, a railway station, a field hospital and a café. The arches are shown in the poster.

And, as the poster suggests, the production began and ended with a dance. Helena and Bertram began in silhouette – dancing 'a hesitation waltz', speculated Robert Cushman in the *Observer* – and they ended, reunited and dancing again, though whether this was the start of a long and happy marriage or a relationship fated to end in tears was left for the audience to decide.[2]

1. Trevor Nunn, quoted in Catherine Haill, *Theatre Posters*, p. 13.

2. Robert Cushman, *Observer*, 22 November 1981.

The Great Bed of Ware (c. 1590)

Some of the topical references in Shakespeare's plays are lost to us. 'The Lady of the Strachy married the yeoman of the wardrobe,' muses the steward Malvolio, as he fantasises about marrying his employer (*Twelfth Night*, 2.5), but the identities of the lady and her yeoman remain a subject for scholarly speculation. When, however, later in the same play, Sir Toby Belch tells Sir Andrew Aguecheek to write a letter containing 'as many lies as will lie in thy sheet of paper, although the sheet were big enough for the bed of Ware in England' (3.2), he alludes to an object which can still be seen today: the Great Bed of Ware, one of the treasures of the V&A.

The imposing four-poster bed of English oak dates from the early 1590s. Now refurbished with hangings in sixteenth-century style, it is a good example of Elizabethan craftmanship, its woodwork copiously carved with human figures, acanthus leaves and strapwork. Traces of paint remain on the figures, and in Shakespeare's day the bed would have been brightly coloured. What sets it apart from others of the period is its size. It is over three metres wide, more than twice as wide as the average Elizabethan bed, and could have accommodated eight people, though larger numbers have been claimed. It was alleged that in 1689 twenty-six butchers and their wives slept in it for a wager.[1]

Although its origins are uncertain, it is likely that the bed was made for an enterprising innkeeper in the Hertfordshire town of Ware as a means of attracting visitors to his establishment. Ware, on the River Lea, is twenty-two miles from London, then a day's journey by horseback or carriage, and was a convenient stopping-off point for travellers on the road north to Cambridge and beyond, or for those taking a boat to the Lea's junction with the Thames. The town had many inns, all looking for trade, and the bed's novelty value enticed customers through the door. The earliest recorded reference comes in a journal, written in verse by a young German prince, Ludwig of Anhalt-Köthen (1579-1650), who toured England in 1596. A translation runs:

> At Ware was a bed of dimensions so wide
> Four couples might cosily lie side by side
> And thus without touching each other abide.[2]

Twelfth Night (1601–2) was not the only contemporary play to name it. The action of *Northward Ho* (1605), by Thomas Dekker and John Webster, begins and ends at Ware, and a complex plot involving the staples of Jacobean city comedy – illicit affairs, would-be illicit affairs, and the exposure of tricksters – is resolved amicably with a single couplet (5.1):

> This night let's banquet freely: come, we'll dare
> Our wives to combat i' th' great bed in Ware.

In Ben Jonson's *Epicœne, or The Silent Woman* (1609) the bed is again referenced for bawdy effect (5.1.58), and it continued to be mentioned in plays and poems, providing an opportunity for saucy humour and a proverbial example of great size. In George Farquhar's comedy *The Recruiting Officer* (1706), a potential recruit is bamboozled by talk of 'a mighty large bed, bigger by half than the great bed at Ware' (1.1.28–9), and in his poem *Don Juan* (1823), Byron joked that wise men eschew polygamy and 'forbear / To make the nuptial couch a "Bed of Ware"' (canto 6, stanza 12). The bed itself had a key role in Covent Garden's 1839 Christmas pantomime *Harlequin and the Merrie Devil of Edmonton, or, the Great Bed of Ware*, featuring in a transformation scene in which Henry VIII and his court appear.

The real bed passed between several inns in Ware, and in 1870 was bought for display by the Rye House Hotel in nearby Hoddesdon. It was sold to a London antique dealer in 1931, and acquired by the V&A for its historical and literary associations. These continue: in 2001 the Museum opened its British Galleries with the Great Bed of Ware in prominent position and Poet Laureate Andrew Motion celebrated the occasion in verse, mentioning the bed in his opening line.[3]

---

1. *London Chronicle*, 4 July 1765.

2. Quoted in the pamphlet *The Great Bed of Ware, exhibited at Frank Partridge (& Sons Ltd.)* (London: Frank Partridge & Sons Ltd, 1931), p. 5.

3. Andrew Motion, *The British Galleries*: <www.vam.ac.uk/content/articles/p/andrew-motion/>

SIR TOBY BELCH   TWELFTH   NIGHT

Greetings
Roger Livesey

Gilbert Sommerlad caricature of Roger Livesey as Sir Toby Belch, Old Vic Company (1950)

Gilbert Sommerlad (1904–1976), a professional pianist and violinist, began his career in Brighton as an accompanist at local cinemas and theatres, and in 1936 moved to the recently built New Theatre at Oxford, where his brother Roy, also a musician, was already working. Gilbert Sommerlad was an orchestral violinist and rehearsal pianist at the New Theatre for forty years, and when not required in the orchestra pit he occupied himself by sketching the performers, becoming well known in the profession for his ability as a caricaturist. The New Theatre was a receiving house for touring productions and Sommerlad's drawings are a record of the actors, entertainers, musicians and conductors who visited the theatre in the mid-twentieth century. 441 sketches, many signed by their subjects, were mounted in six albums which his son donated to the V&A in 2001.

The majority of the sketches show performers appearing in modern plays on pre- or post-West End tours, but productions of Shakespeare occasionally visited the New. In October 1950, the Old Vic Company, on a three-week tour, brought *Twelfth Night* with Peggy Ashcroft as Viola, directed by Hugh Hunt (1911–1993). Hunt had become the company's Artistic Director in 1949, when its links to the Old Vic were in name only, the theatre itself having closed following bomb damage in 1941. It remained derelict until 1950, when the Arts Council offered funding to enable the building to be restored in time for the 1951 Festival of Britain on London's South Bank. The Old Vic reopened on 14 November 1950 with a gala performance, in the presence of the King and Queen, much heralded in the press as the first visit by a reigning monarch to the Old Vic. The play chosen for the occasion was the *Twelfth Night* seen by Sommerlad.

Hugh Hunt, a scholarly man who became Professor of Drama at Manchester University in 1961, wrote a series of prefaces to the plays that he directed at the Old Vic. These were read to his actors at rehearsal, and were later collected and published. Hunt described them as representing his personal approach to each play, explaining his ideas at that particular time. He imagined the setting for *Twelfth Night* as a small island off the Dalmatian coast which would fit the nominal location of Illyria, with the action unfolding in a small seaport. The houses of Olivia and Orsino would be set on either side of a piazza, with the majority of scenes taking place out of doors, including the disruptive drinking session of Sir Toby and his cronies in Act Two, Scene Three. In Hunt's interpretation, the revellers would be locked out of the house, which would afford opportunities for comic business with a ladder: 'But with all his boisterousness, Toby must always remain a gentleman. In his most drunken moments we must see his ludicrous attempts to maintain his dignity.'[1]

Roger Livesey (1906–1976), who became famous for his roles in the films of Powell and Pressburger in the 1940s, was an experienced Shakespearean actor and had played Sir Toby in a previous Old Vic production in 1933. Some of the London critics felt that Hunt allowed the play's romantic elements to take second place to the comedy, but still enjoyed the buffoonery of Livesey's surprisingly acrobatic old reprobate, who managed to fall down stairs and tumble off his ladder without losing the suavity and 'drunken serenity', which, according to Harold Hobson, supplied 'a glorious contribution to the evening's entertainment.'[2]

1. Hugh Hunt, *Old Vic Prefaces*, p. 67.
2. *Sunday Times*, 19 November 1950.

Ebenezer Landells after H.K. Browne, illustration of Mrs Jarley's caravan of waxworks, from Charles Dickens's *The Old Curiosity Shop* (1841)

The V&A has a four-part collection of booklets, published by Samuel French (*c.*1889), entitled *Mrs Jarley's Far-Famed Collection of Waxworks, With full Directions for their Arrangement, Positions, Movements, Costumes, and Properties*. The booklets are devised for amateur theatricals, in which the participants represent movable wax figures, with French's offering a hire service for costumes and properties. The text by G.B. Bartlett and W. Gurney Benham is an extended running commentary by Mrs Jarley, a character from Charles Dickens's *The Old Curiosity Shop* (1841). Mrs Jarley, the proprietor of a travelling waxworks, is accompanied by Little Nell, who helps her with the arrangement and 'winding up' of the figures, and two assistants, Peter and John, 'one of whom places little wedges to keep [each figure] upright, and the other pretends to adjust and oil the joints before winding up... The noise of winding is made with a watchman's rattle.'[1] Much amusement can be had 'by means of by-play with the figures, turning them the wrong way, giving them the wrong properties' and by 'the fall of the figures at critical moments'.[2] A wide range of characters, drawn from fiction, history and folklore, are organised into categories: 'The Chamber of Beauty', 'The Chamber of Horrors', 'The Historical Chamber', and 'The Shakespearean Chamber' – which includes Shylock ('sharpens his knife angrily on an old slipper'), 'Richard No. 3 – Suit of armour; holds sword; sits on a rocking horse', and Titania ('Lovely little girl; white gauze dress, spangled; holds wand').[3]

Shakespeare himself features as a character, sandwiched between Little Jack Horner and the Goddess Flora. The lines from *Hamlet*, 'Aye, there's the rub' (3.1.65), are accompanied by an invitation to buy a bottle of 'Parkinson's Embrocation'. When wound up, the poet's figure 'Writes furiously, rolling his eyes vigorously at the audience' in illustration of the reference in *A Midsummer Night's Dream* to 'The poet's eye, in a fine frenzy rolling' (5.1.12). He holds a quill pen and has a bottle labelled 'Embrocation' displayed in the breast pocket of his Elizabethan costume.[4]

Mrs Jarley's caravan advertising her waxworks can be seen in this illustration from *The Old Curiosity Shop* by Ebenezer Landells (1808–1860), with the fugitive Little Nell and her grandfather walking beside it. In Dickens's novel, kindly Mrs Jarley employs the girl to dust the figures and comment on the displays, until the wanderers are recognised by 'a man of the name of Jerry… wot keeps a company of dancing dogs', shown in the foreground here, and have to leave the waxworks to resume their travels.[5]

Dickens based the character of Mrs Jarley upon the famous Madame Tussaud, who led an itinerant life for more than thirty years before establishing a permanent exhibition on London's Baker Street in 1835. No expense was spared to achieve authenticity in the displays but not everyone was impressed by the result, with one visitor complaining of 'Miserable caricatures of Napoleon, Washington, Cromwell, Shakespeare, and Byron… Shakespeare is represented as a modern dandy, who "cultivates his hair".'[6] A major attraction, then as now, was the Chamber of Horrors: 'Madame Tussaud made the discovery that the effigies of a dead criminal would bring in thousands of shillings, while no one would expend a solitary sixpence to look upon the image of Innocence herself'.[7] The sentiment is one that Autolycus – Shakespeare's own itinerant pedlar in *The Winter's Tale* – would have recognised: 'The ballad is very pitiful, and as true' (4.4.275).

1. *Mrs Jarley's Far-Famed Collection of Waxworks*, Preface to Part 2, p. 2.

2. *Ibid.*, Preface to Part 4, p. 5.

3. *Ibid.*, Part 4, p. 31; Part 2, p.5.

4. *Ibid.*, Part 3, p. 14.

5. Charles Dickens, *The Old Curiosity Shop*, p. 287.

6. Richard D. Altick, *The Shows of London*, p. 336.

7. *Ibid.*

DANCING DOGS.

Judi Dench (Perdita) and David Bailie (Florizel) in Trevor Nunn's RSC production of *The Winter's Tale* (1969)

When photographer Douglas H. Jeffery (1917–2009) died, he left an archive of over two million negatives, representing his life's work as a recorder of stage productions. Shortly after his death, this collection was acquired by the V&A: Jeffery's obituary in the *Guardian* called it 'one of the most comprehensive libraries of theatre photography in Britain'.[1] Jeffery, who always worked with film and never adopted digital technology, was, by all accounts, a determined and demanding character. In the 1950s, when theatres did little to help anyone wishing to photograph their productions, he was instrumental in setting up the system of 'photocalls' to give photographers the opportunity to take pictures for the press. He recorded over 10,000 productions himself, of which more than 700 were Shakespeares. They include all the major stagings by the Royal Shakespeare Company and the National Theatre from the 1960s until the 1990s, and some of the finest Shakespearean performances of the late twentieth century. A recurrent name in Jeffery's archive is Judi Dench, who began her professional acting career at the Old Vic in 1957 and went on to become a leading light of the Royal Shakespeare Company. Jeffery recorded many of her RSC performances, including Viola, Portia, Beatrice, Lady Macbeth, Imogen, and both Hermione and Perdita in Trevor Nunn's 1969 production of *The Winter's Tale*.

The 1969 Stratford season was Nunn's first as sole Artistic Director of the company. It was a season of comedies and late works. Judi Dench, who was cast as Viola in *Twelfth Night*, was also offered the role of Hermione. When the play opened she would be thirty-four. Conscious of her age, she sent Nunn a postcard, jokingly enquiring, 'Is it mothers' parts already?'[2] Three weeks later Nunn contacted her again, suggesting that she play both Hermione and Perdita. This doubling of mother and daughter roles had been tried once before, when American actress Mary Anderson played them at the Lyceum Theatre in 1887. It would, thought Nunn, give a greater coherence to the play and point up the ironies between the tragic first section and the central pastoral scenes.

Dench's portrayal of both women was highly praised. The production used a simple white-box set, designed by Christopher Morley to put the focus on the actors. In Sicilia the court dressed in white, pale grey or green, the suits and Empire line gowns suggesting both the nineteenth century and the high fashion of contemporary Chelsea boutiques. In Bohemia the production exploded into the present day in a riot of orange and yellow, with the sheep-shearing feast becoming a hippy festival accompanied by rock music, and the cast in mini-dresses, flared trousers, waistcoats, and beads. Perdita, first seen relaxing with Florizel beside a fallen tree, was 'pranked up' for the celebrations as a tousle-haired Botticelli Flora. According to Gerald Jacobs, Judi Dench's first biographer, 'She had aimed to lend a "slightly earthy, slightly Yorkshire" quality to Perdita, and while she did this she still maintained the girl's *apartness* from Mopsa, Dorcas and the rest. It was her finest Shakespearean performance yet.'[3]

1.   Eamon McCabe, *Guardian*, 14 February 2009.

2.   John Miller, *Judi Dench*, p. 107.

3.   Gerald Jacobs, *Judi Dench*, pp. 77–8.

Sarah Siddons's self-portrait in sculpture (*c.* 1790)

Sarah Siddons (1755–1831) was born into a touring company of actors led by her father Roger Kemble, and she and her brother, John Philip Kemble, became the leading stars of their generation. Although Sarah's debut on the London stage in 1775 under the tutelage of David Garrick was not a success, when she was invited back to London after her triumph at the Theatre Royal in Bath, she became the talk of the town, much favoured by the Royal Family. As she herself recounts:

> The Royal family very frequently honoured me with their presence. The King was often moved to tears which he as often vainly endeavoured to conceal behind his eye-glass, and her Majesty the Queen, at one time told me in her gracious broken English that her only refuge from me was actually turning her back upon the stage.[1]

She was admired in her private life for her virtue as a wife and mother, and on stage she was acclaimed as the embodiment of the tragic muse, as immortalised by Reynolds in his portrait of 1784:

> When I attended him for the first sitting, after many more gratifying encomiums than I dare repeat, he took me by the hand, saying, 'Ascend your undisputed throne, and graciously bestow upon me some grand Idea of The Tragick Muse'. I walked up the steps & seated myself instantly in the attitude in which She now appears.[2]

Her image is fixed for posterity in portraits by all the leading artists of the day, including Thomas Gainsborough and George Romney. Thomas Lawrence, fourteen years her junior, had a lifelong fixation with her beauty, dating from his first encounter with her in Bath when he was a child. She herself adopted sculpture as a hobby, in order to accurately preserve her likeness in a mode in keeping with the simplicity and grandeur of classical sculpture. This portrait bust dates from around 1790 and resembles a classical bust, except for the fashionable headdress with chin strap. Her interest in classical sculpture coincided with the fashion for neoclassicism in the 1790s and, feeling that 'tragedy was debased by the flutter of light materials', she adopted a trend-setting high-waisted style of dress in restricted tones.[3] Although best known for tragic rather than comic roles, she was commended for her portrayal of Rosalind in *As You Like It*, and when it was remarked to her friend Mrs Piozzi that Sarah 'gave one a notion of a wicked unhappy Queen', Mrs Piozzi said that:

> her friend Mrs Siddons could be infinitely comic when she pleased, and was among her intimates... She then added a very amusing description of her having a family party, ordering the parlour-door to be made fast, and proceeding to perform most of the part of Sir Anthony Absolute [in Sheridan's *The Rivals*], with astonishing spirit and pleasantry.[4]

Shakespeare provided her with the roles in which she was most acclaimed, including Katharine in *Henry VIII*, Volumnia in *Coriolanus*, and Hermione, the much-abused heroine of *The Winter's Tale*, where – fittingly – her 'statue' comes to life in the final scene. The role in which she most excelled, however, was Lady Macbeth, ever since being struck by panic on reading the assassination scene for the first time aged twenty: 'I snatched up my candle, and hurried out of the room in a paroxysm of terror. My dress was of silk, and the rustling of it, as I ascended the stairs to go to bed, seemed to my panic-struck fancy like the movement of a spectre pursuing me.'[5] Her portrayal of Lady Macbeth sprang from a profound engagement with the character, whom she saw as 'most captivating to the other sex, – fair, feminine, nay, perhaps, even fragile – ... captivating in feminine loveliness... a charm of such potency as to fascinate the mind'.[6] Lady Macbeth was the last role she performed before retiring from the stage in 1812, and then returning to revive it several more times. Hazlitt's description of her performance in his *Characters of Shakespeare's Plays*, is itself unforgettable: 'In coming on in the sleep-walking scene, her eyes were open, but their sense was shut. She was like a person bewildered and unconscious of what she did... She glided on and off the stage like an apparition. To have seen her in that character was an event in every one's life, not to be forgotten.'[7]

1. Roger Manvell, *Sarah Siddons*, p. 77.

2. *Ibid.*, p. 98.

3. Aileen Ribeiro, 'Costuming the Part', p. 116.

4. Manvell, *Sarah Siddons*, p. 133.

5. *Ibid.*, p. 22.

6. *Ibid.*, p. 120.

7. William Hazlitt, *Characters of Shakespeare's Plays* (1817), p. 22.

66 There's no art to find the mind's construction
in the face...99
Macbeth (1.4)

35

Michael Rysbrack, terracotta bust of Shakespeare (*c. 1730*)

The son of the landscape painter Peter Rysbrack, Michael Rysbrack (1694–1770) trained as a sculptor and quickly established himself after his arrival in London from Antwerp in 1720 with commissions in Poets' Corner in Westminster Abbey. He completed the tomb of the poet Matthew Prior in 1723 and a marble relief portrait of Ben Jonson at about the same time. These were followed in the next decade by memorials with portrait busts of John Gay (1736), John Milton (1737), and Shakespeare's editor, the dramatist Nicholas Rowe, in 1742. A campaign was meanwhile growing for a memorial to Shakespeare in Westminster Abbey: funds were raised by benefit performances of *Hamlet* and *Julius Caesar* with parallels drawn between the ghosts in these plays and Shakespeare's ghost in search of a final resting place:

> For, like Caesar, thou art mighty yet!
> Thy spirit walks abroad; and at our hands
> The honorary tomb, thy right, demands.[1]

The Trustees of the Shakespeare Memorial project were Lord Burlington, Alexander Pope and Dr Richard Mead. Lord Burlington's close associate William Kent was chosen to design the Shakespeare monument, having already designed the monuments of Isaac Newton and the explorer Lord Stanhope in the nave of the Abbey, both executed by Rysbrack. The memorials already completed made Rysbrack a likely choice of sculptor for the Shakespeare statue, but instead the commission went to Peter Gaspar Scheemakers (1691–1781), a friend of the trustee Richard Mead.

Rysbrack did, however, create a bust of Shakespeare, the first since the memorial bust of the poet was installed in Holy Trinity Church, Stratford, by 1623. Unlike Roubiliac's later statue of Shakespeare, Rysbrack's bust owes more to the Stratford memorial than to the more romanticised Chandos portrait, popular in the eighteenth century. The work illustrated here is a terracotta bust cast from a mould after the stone bust carved by

Rysbrack for the Temple of British Worthies in the gardens at Stowe. Lord Cobham had begun building his temple in 1726 to house 'a sacred Band Of Princes, Patriots, Bards and Sages'.[2] Rysbrack contributed eight busts, including those of Queen Elizabeth, William III and Shakespeare. The collection was moved in 1735 to a temple designed by William Kent, enlarged to include a further seven busts by Peter Scheemakers.

Portrait busts of national figures had become a must-have for the aristocracy and monarchy, and Rysbrack received a commission from Queen Anne ('Her Majesty has ordered Mr Risbrack [sic] to make the bustos in marble of all the Kings of England from William the Conqueror in order to be placed in her new buildings in the gardens at Richmond'), and he also carved statues of the Black Prince and King Alfred for the octagon in the garden of the Princess of Wales in Pall Mall.[3] The sculptor is perhaps most famous for his statue of Hercules at Stourhead, which took him five years to complete and which was 'compiled from various parts and limbs of seven or eight of the strongest and best made men in London, chiefly the bruisers and boxers of the then flourishing ampitheatre for boxing; the sculptor selecting the parts which were most truly formed in each'.[4] Although Rysbrack's prestige suffered from the loss of the commission for the Shakespeare memorial in Westminster Abbey, his work continued to be greatly admired by his contemporaries: Horace Walpole pronounced him 'the greatest master the islands have seen', with the chronicler of the art world George Vertue declaring his work 'beautifully and masterly done, admired by all artists and lovers of art'.[5]

1. Ingrid Roscoe, 'The Monument to the Memory of Shakespeare', p. 73. Compare: 'O Julius Caesar, thou art mighty yet! / Thy spirit walks abroad and turns our swords / In our own proper entrails' (*Julius Caesar*, 5.3.94–6).

2. Malcolm Baker, *Figured in Marble*, p. 135.

3. Rupert Gunnis, *Dictionary of British Sculptors 1660–1851*, vol. 5, p. 334.

4. *Ibid.*

5. *Ibid.*, p. 335.

Oliver Rix and Alex Hassell in the National Video Archive of Performance recording of Gregory Doran's RSC production of *Cardenio* (2011)

First attributed jointly to Shakespeare and John Fletcher in 1653, when it was entered in the Stationers' Register, *Cardenio* holds a special place in the Shakespearean Apocrypha. Regardless of whether its entry is reliable, the piece had certainly been performed at Court forty years earlier. The play produced at the Swan Theatre, Stratford-upon-Avon, as part of the Royal Shakespeare Company's fiftieth-birthday season (2011), has a complicated pedigree, derived principally from *Double Falsehood* (1727) by Lewis Theobald, with gaps made good by material culled from the original source of the story, Cervantes' *Don Quixote* in the 1612 translation by Thomas Shelton. This is further augmented by snatches from other Fletcher plays based on stories by Cervantes.

Theobald (1688–1744) claimed his play was based on a manuscript in the possession of the prompter to the company of the playwright William Davenant, who did little to discourage rumours that he might be Shakespeare's illegitimate son. Whether Theobald actually had a copy of *Cardenio* is unknowable, but the association of Shakespeare's name doubtless did his play no harm. It ran for ten performances at Drury Lane in 1727, which in those days constituted a successful run.

Gregory Doran, who co-authored this version with dramatist and director Antonio Álamo, also directed the production, marketed as 'Shakespeare's "lost play" re-imagined', reinforcing its Hispanic setting with the look and feel of a Spanish Golden Age play, with actors in period costumes and guitar music. This 'revival', not so much breathing life into an old text as establishing a text to revive, displayed many of the themes common to Fletcher's tragicomedies and the mood and style of Shakespeare's last plays: honour threatened, thwarted lovers, a pastoral interlude, and a girl disguised as a boy. It was critically well received, but its 'Shakespearean' credentials met with general scepticism. The production reopened the Swan Theatre following its closure during the redevelopment of the Royal Shakespeare Theatre (2007–2010).

This still from the museum's archival recording depicts Cardenio (Oliver Rix, left) and Fernando (Alex Hassell, right) in Act One, Scene Five, an episode largely fabricated by Doran from other sources to flesh out the plot.[1] The National Video Archive of Performance at the V&A makes high-quality archival recordings of live performance in the UK for research purposes. The archive was launched in 1992 and made a strong start with two Shakespearean productions: *Richard III* (Royal National Theatre, with Ian McKellen in the title role) and the RSC's 1992–3 *Hamlet* (starring Kenneth Branagh as the prince). By 2013 it had recorded over thirty productions of Shakespeare plays or Shakespearean analogues, all of which may be viewed by appointment. One of the selection criteria for filming productions for the archive is 'rarity', for which *Cardenio* certainly fits the bill.

1. Gregory Doran, *Shakespeare's Lost Play*, pp. 189–93.

Histories

Charles Buchel, portrait of Herbert Beerbohm Tree as King John (1900)

King John is a rarity on the modern stage but was a popular play in the nineteenth century. Although not the first Shakespearean production to use historically accurate costumes, Charles Kemble's lavish 1823 version was the first to attempt a large-scale recreation of the past, with every costume reproduced from a surviving historical source, all thoroughly researched down to the smallest detail. This 'archaeological' attempt to bring history to life was so successful that it inspired other elaborate Shakespeare productions, and *King John*, with its opportunities for pageantry, became a favourite with actors and audiences. The play was presented with similar splendour by William Charles Macready in 1842, and Macready's production then formed the template for subsequent stagings in London and the United States. The 1899 production by Herbert Beerbohm Tree (1852–1917) at Her Majesty's Theatre, London, was the last in this line of spectacular versions of the play.

Tree's production was hugely popular, playing for 114 performances to a total estimated audience of 170,000 people. It benefited from a totally new form of publicity, having the distinction of being the first filmed production of a Shakespeare play: while still in rehearsal, three short episodes were recreated for the camera in a nearby film studio. The result, which only lasted three or four minutes, was first shown to the public at the Palace Theatre, then a variety venue, on 20 September 1899, the same day as the play opened down the road at Her Majesty's.[1]

King John was the second of Shakespeare's plays to be presented by actor-manager Tree at his new theatre. Determined to give it 'a setting which should place before the public a living picture of the times as designed by Shakespeare', he expanded the action by including tableaux of the Battle of Angiers and the signing of the Magna Carta, events which are not depicted in the play.[2] Photographs of the tableaux show the stage crowded with extras, with painted figures on the backdrops swelling the numbers. A journalist from the *Daily Chronicle* who asked Tree's stage manager how many costumes were used in the production received the reply, 'Only 424'. Costume designer Percy Anderson told the same journalist that he had not based his designs on those of previous productions but had gone back to historical sources, adding, 'Necessarily, I had to rely on myself for the colors, to get an harmonious effect.' He described John's royal robe, which 'consists of a gown of gold silk, heavily embroidered with yellow topaz, over which is a cloak of cloth of gold, lined with Vair [a grey fur], and bordered with a deep band of gold and jewels. The crown is copied from an effigy at Worcester. The boots are of cloth of gold, stitched with jewels.' The interviewer also visited costume makers L. & H. Nathan, where the proprietor spoke proudly of the cloth-of-gold in Tree's robe: 'We do not pretend ever to have turned out anything better in quality of material.'[3]

The costume described is the one depicted in this portrait by Charles Buchel (1872–1850). Buchel worked with Tree for sixteen years, providing illustrations for the souvenir brochures that accompanied his productions, designing posters, creating murals to decorate Tree's apartment at Her Majesty's, and painting portraits of the actor-manager himself. King John was his third portrait of Tree in character and, at over two metres high, was the largest and grandest. It was painted at the artist's studio, where Tree arrived with full costume, make-up and dresser. The scene recreated is the play's Act Four, Scene Two. After victories in France, John is given a second coronation, but disaster is not far away: he learns of a French invasion and his mother's death, and is then deserted by his nobles, who believe him responsible for the death of his nephew Arthur, the rightful heir to the throne. A souvenir booklet, produced to celebrate the production's sixtieth performance, includes a photograph of Tree with orb and sceptre in the same scene. The picture gives an exact record of the actor in costume, but Tree, holding a pose for the photographer, seems stiff and lifeless. It is Buchel's portrait of the guilt-racked monarch that truly preserves the performance.

1. The film was lost for many years and, because filming took place at an outdoor studio beside the Thames, there was speculation that it showed the Magna Carta tableau, set by the river at Runnymede. This assumption was repeated as fact in a number of books, but in 1990 one scene of the film, showing John's death, was discovered, and subsequent research revealed that the lost scenes showed John plotting the murder of his nephew Arthur, and Constance denouncing her son's captors. See Judith Buchanan, *Shakespeare on Silent Film*, pp. 57–73.

2. Herbert Beerbohm Tree, introduction to the souvenir booklet commemorating the 60th consecutive performance of *King John*, Her Majesty's Theatre, 13 November 1899.

3. '"King John" at Her Majesty's Theatre', *Daily Chronicle*, 21 September 1899.

Audrey Cruddas's costume design for King John (1957)

Having supplied an opportunity for historical reconstruction and pageantry in the nineteenth century, *King John* fell out of favour in the twentieth. It was a history play unconnected to Shakespeare's other history cycles, featuring a large cast of monarchs and lords largely unknown to modern audiences. The patriotic declamations of the final scene, which Beerbohm Tree's 1899 production had accompanied by offstage angelic choruses, seemed jingoistic, and the vacillating John was not a role to attract leading players. As modern revivals have not been plentiful, it is a surprise to discover that one designer, Audrey Cruddas, was responsible for the settings and costumes for three separate productions of the play, designing for Michael Benthall at the Shakespeare Memorial Theatre in 1948, for Douglas Seale, again at Stratford, in 1957, and for Peter Potter at the Old Vic in 1961.

Audrey Cruddas (1911–1979) was born in South Africa and came to England in 1923.[1] She studied at the Royal Academy Schools and began a career as a painter, but illness forced her to rest for a year during the Second World War and it was while convalescing that she began to experiment with stage design, making watercolour drawings of costumes for imaginary productions of *Macbeth* and *A Midsummer Night's Dream*.[2] When her health had recovered she looked for work in the theatre, and her designs were seen by Robert Helpmann. Helpmann was a good spotter of design talent, and as a result Cruddas was employed to create costumes for Webster's *The White Devil*, directed by Michael Benthall at London's Duchess Theatre in 1947, with Helpmann as Flamineo. This was the beginning of a successful theatre career for Cruddas, which encompassed Shakespeare at Stratford and the Old Vic, West End plays and operas.

King John may not have been a favourite piece in the mid-twentieth century but it was given some effective productions. Benthall's version, with Helpmann as a 'suave, calculating devil' in the leading role, was summed up in *Theatre World* as 'enthralling as spectacle, eloquent in pageantry, a triumph for Audrey Cruddas', so it is not surprising that Cruddas was asked to design the new Stratford *King John* in 1957.[3] After his successes with the *Henry VI* plays at Birmingham and the Old Vic (1951–1953), director Douglas Seale (1913–1999) had gained a reputation for his ability to handle sprawling narratives. To give unity to the action, Cruddas designed a permanent setting, featuring a multifunctional central battlemented structure that could represent interiors and exteriors and allow the action to flow uninterrupted. Lighting was key to the stage picture. Harold Hobson summed up the effect: 'when the warring kings of France and England for a moment cease their quarrels beneath the frowning walls of Angiers, the light is sulphurous… Mr. Seale and his designer, Audrey Cruddas, have conceived the heavens as though the sun had been extinguished, and the world were lit only by the reflection of flames from the nether pit.'[4]

Seale's John was Robert Harris (1900–1995), an actor with a long list of Shakespearean roles to his credit. He had played Hamlet at the Old Vic in 1932, Edgar in Gielgud's 1940 *King Lear*, and Prospero, Macbeth and Richard II at Stratford in the late 1940s. His John was 'a man of moral stature' struggling with his conscience with a fervour that, wrote Kenneth Tynan, 'gives the play an emotional centre, which in my experience it has always lacked'.[5] John's mother, Queen Elinor, was played by Molly Tapper ('forceful, but never over-played', according to Rosemary Anne Sisson).[6] Cruddas dressed the company in thirteenth-century style. Her design for John and Elinor has not been annotated, but it was published in the Memorial Theatre's 1957 souvenir booklet along with a handwritten note which gave details of colour and fabric. John's silver cloak is to be lined in scarlet 'veering towards orange', and Elinor's heavy red silk cloak, described as 'not shiney' [sic], is worn over a velvet dress and a chain mail tunic 'with more glitter than the men's'. The colourful costumes were designed to stand out as the actors moved in pools of light against the sombre background.

1. Audrey Cruddas's date of birth has been variously reported as 1912 and 1914, but her biographer, Aurèle Letricot, believes that she was born in 1911.

2. A design for female fairies in *A Midsummer Night's Dream* held by the V&A (S.338–1999) may be one of these early designs.

3. T.C. Kemp and J.C. Trewin, *The Stratford Festival*, p. 226; H.G. Matthews, *Theatre World* 44 (July 1948), p. 29.

4. Harold Hobson, *Sunday Times*, 21 April 1957.

5. Kenneth Tynan, *Observer*, 21 April 1957.

6. Rosemary Anne Sisson, *Stratford-upon-Avon Herald*, 19 April 1957.

Paul Scofield as Richard II (1952)

Paul Scofield (1922–2008) was one of the twentieth century's most respected actors, noted for his distinctive vocal style, for the intensity and focus of his acting, and for his versatility. He appeared in both classic plays and in contemporary works by some of the century's leading playwrights, and was particularly noted for his interpretations of the great Shakespearean roles. After training at the London Mask Drama School, Scofield spent the early years of the Second World War touring with ENSA (Entertainments National Service Association), the organisation set up in 1939 to provide entertainment for the British armed forces during the war. In 1944 he joined the Birmingham Repertory Company and when its founder, Sir Barry Jackson, left to become director at Stratford, Scofield was asked to join the company there. He quickly established his reputation, and many regarded him as a star even before his first major appearance on the London stage, in Vanbrugh's *The Relapse* in 1948.

At the time of this production of *Richard II*, the Lyric Theatre, Hammersmith, in West London, was managed by the Company of Four, a consortium comprising backers John Christie (creator of Glyndebourne Opera), the theatrical management company H.M. Tennent, and the Arts Theatre, Cambridge. The company's name was derived from the plan to rehearse a show for four weeks, and then play at Hammersmith for the following four weeks. Despite its distance from the West End, the theatre had enjoyed a very successful period in the 1920s under Sir Nigel Playfair's direction, especially remembered for its production of *The Beggar's Opera*, which ran for a total of 1,463 performances. The theatre's location clearly presented no obstacle to attracting audiences.

The Company of Four began operating at the Lyric Hammersmith in 1946, and the 1952–3 Gielgud Season (which also included a production of Congreve's *The Way of the World*) was a highlight of the company's ten-year residency at the Lyric. This production of *Richard II* opened to mixed reviews but most praised Scofield's verse speaking, and one critic called his performance 'almost intolerably moving'.[1] Gielgud later wrote that he should never have tried to direct an actor in a role so familiar to him, and one in which he had himself earned universal acclaim, having played Richard at the Old Vic in the 1929–30 season, and then at the Queen's Theatre in 1937.[2] Despite being somewhat overshadowed on this occasion by the critics' recollections of Gielgud's interpretation of the role, Scofield went on to be regarded as a superlative actor of Shakespeare. His playing of King Lear, directed at Stratford by Peter Brook in 1962, was voted the greatest ever Shakespearean performance when Royal Shakespeare Company members were polled in 2004.[3]

Scofield was photographed here by Angus McBean (1904–1990), in his own right a significant figure in any work on representations of Shakespeare. McBean photographed all Shakespeare's plays during his career, some of them several times, and is regarded as possibly the greatest of all theatrical photographers. Scofield was one of McBean's favourite sitters, and was photographed by him repeatedly over a period of twenty-five years. In 1946, McBean was commissioned by the Shakespeare Memorial Theatre to become its in-house photographer. Scofield had fond recollections of his work there:

> He generated a sense of excitement in the theatre and company when he arrived to photograph a production... His concentration was so total to the point of being electric and was perhaps the reason why his posed photographs had the quality of lively performance.[4]

1. Unsigned review, *Sketch*, 14 January 1953.

2. John Gielgud with John Miller, *Shakespeare: Hit or Miss?*, p. 41.

3. *Daily Telegraph*, 22 August 2004.

4. Bob Workman, 'Still Clicking', *Plays and Players* (June 1984), p. 16.

Kevin Spacey as Richard II (2005)

Since 2003, Kevin Spacey has been Artistic Director of the Old Vic Theatre in London, acting in, directing, administrating and programming a series of productions that have continued to strengthen the theatre's reputation for quality and innovation. With this modern-dress production of *Richard II*, directed by Trevor Nunn, Spacey made his UK Shakespearean debut in the title role, to good notices. Spacey was the twelfth Richard II to appear on the stage of the Old Vic, a theatre with an illustrious past and which, in the early years of the twentieth century, established itself as London's premier theatre for Shakespeare, largely thanks to the vision and energy of its then lessee and manager, Lilian Baylis (1874–1937).

The Old Vic embarked on staging Shakespeare in 1914 with an ambitious plan to present all the plays included in the Shakespeare First Folio. The series was completed in 1923 with a production of *Troilus and Cressida*, coinciding with the tercentenary of the First Folio's publication. In the years running up to the Second World War, the Old Vic was associated with a series of landmark Shakespeare productions, attracting established stars and launching the careers of many others. In 1929, Baylis appointed Harcourt Williams (1880–1957) as her new director, who invited John Gielgud to join the company as its leading actor. Gielgud's period at the Old Vic developed him as a classical actor and also brought commercial success to the theatre. His 1930 *Hamlet* was the Old Vic's first production to transfer to the West End.

By 1931 Lilian Baylis had also succeeded in rescuing and reopening the derelict Sadler's Wells Theatre in Islington, which was to be run in partnership with the Old Vic. The two theatres had first been run as a pair of related venues in the 1870s, sharing productions and also their costs as a means of capitalising on local audiences in two different London neighbourhoods. Although *Twelfth Night* was Sadler's Wells's opening production, and the opera, drama and ballet companies formed by Baylis continued to switch between the two theatres during the early years, by 1935 the ballet and opera companies were firmly established at Sadler's Wells and the drama company at the Old Vic.

Lilian Baylis died in November 1937, and after a period of closure during the Second World War when the building was damaged by bombing, the Old Vic reopened in 1950. Between 1953 and 1958, under the direction of Michael Benthall (1919–1974), the complete First Folio works were staged for a second time, beginning with *Hamlet*, starring Richard Burton.

In 1963, the Old Vic entered a major new phase of its history when it became the home of the National Theatre Company. The opening production was *Hamlet* with Peter O'Toole. The company remained at the Old Vic until its new theatre building opened on the South Bank in 1976, and during its residency, and that of the Prospect Theatre Company which succeeded it, the stage of the Old Vic saw a succession of superlative Shakespeare productions.

In 1998, the recently refurbished theatre was put on the market and acquired by The Old Vic Theatre Trust. After a series of award-winning productions, an announcement in 2003 confirmed that the theatre would once again become a producing house, with Kevin Spacey appointed the first Artistic Director of the Old Vic Theatre Company.

This photograph was taken by the V&A's own photographer, Graham Brandon, who has been recording the performing arts for the Theatre and Performance Department since the 1980s. By 2013 the Performance Documentation Programme comprised photographs taken at over 1,200 photo calls, rehearsals, performances and interviews.

Ian McKellen's tabard as Richard II (1968)

This costume was made for Prospect Theatre Company's 1968 production of *Richard II*, featuring twenty-nine-year-old Ian McKellen in his first leading role as a king 'so cocooned in ceremony he seemed to be gliding on castors'.[1] McKellen claims that this effect was achieved by him copying the 'roller-skating gait' of renowned drag act Danny La Rue.[2] The production and its leading man were so successful during its five-week tour that a second tour was staged, beginning at the Edinburgh Festival and ending in a sell-out London run. The play toured Europe, including a memorable performance in Soviet Czechoslovakia when the audience wept for their lost country when Richard weeps for joy on his return to England. The production was filmed by the BBC in 1970.

Prospect was a small company with limited funds, and designer Tim Goodchild decided, unusually, to reserve most of the money for the costumes. Richard made his first entrance in this sweeping gold tabard embroidered with heraldic lions and glistening with jewels (in reality it was encrusted with bottle tops and gold paint). The train of the tabard was covered in cling film to preserve the fabric during its many performances. The tabard was a fashionable piece of clothing in Richard II's time and wearing one made entirely of gold cloth was an unambiguous statement about the wealth and power of the Crown. Richard is closely associated with the colour Goodchild chose for the tabard. The Westminster portrait shows him against a background of gold while the Wilton Diptych sees him dressed in gold, also against a gold background. McKellen, looking for a way to convey Richard's belief that his role was divinely appointed to a modern secular audience, described his character's journey as the 'fall from the golden stardom of Godship to the obscurity of humanity'.[3] He took inspiration from the Dalai Lama: 'Did the god-emperor in exile suffer something like Richard's dejection and determination in his imprisonment? And one magical day in rehearsal, we discovered a gesture, a regal, priestly upraising of the arms, symbolic but deeply felt.'[4] Once he had this gesture, he was able to build the rest of the character. McKellen's interpretation rejected the idea of Richard as an effete and ineffectual ruler and portrayed him instead as someone who was seduced by his own hype and only realised the danger he was in when it was too late.

Many years later, McKellen would go on to play a quite different Richard, the crookback Richard III in modern dress at the National Theatre in 1990. That production was one of the first performances ever recorded for the V&A's National Video Archive of Performance. The museum also holds the archive of the Prospect Theatre Company and a collection of scripts and recordings from Ian McKellen.

1. Michael Billington, comparing McKellen and Eddie Redmayne in a review of the 2011 Donmar Warehouse production, *Guardian*, 7 December 2011.

2. <www.mckellen.com/stage/r2/words.htm>, accessed 25 March 2013.

3. Ian McKellen, 'The Czech Significance', in *A Night at the Theatre*, ed. Ronald Harwood, p. 105.

4. *Ibid.*

> **❝**I am not only witty in myself, but the cause
> that wit is in other men...**❞**
> *Henry IV, Part Two* (1.2)

42

Coloured illustration from *The Wits* (1662) showing Falstaff and the Hostess (1809)

The earliest published images of characters from Shakespeare's plays appeared in *The Wits, or, Sport upon Sport*, the first part of which was printed in 1662 and reissued in 1672. This 1809 reproduction of the original black-and-white frontispiece shows characters from *Henry IV* that feature in the work, which is subtitled: *Select Pieces of Drollery, Digested into Scenes by way of Dialogue. Together with Variety of Humors of several Nations, fitted for the pleasure and content of all Persons, either in Court, City, Countrey, or Camp. The like never before Published.* Falstaff stands at the front of the stage on the left-hand side with a bumper of wine in his hand, apparently being taken to task by the Hostess, Mistress Quickly. In the Preface to the second part of the volume, published in 1673 by Francis Kirkman, the publisher asserts that the extracts are derived from 'such Penmen as were known to be the ablest Artists that ever this Nation produced, by Name, Shake-spear, Fletcher, Johnson, Shirley and others'. He went on to explain:

> When the publique theatres were shut up, and the Actors were
> forbidden to present us with any of their Tragedies, because we had
> enough of that in earnest; and Comedies, because the Vices of the
> Age were too lively and smartly represented; then all that we could
> divert our selves with were these humours and pieces of Plays,
> which... were only allowed us, and that by stealth too, and under
> pretence of Rope-dancing, or the like; and these being all that was
> permitted us, great was the confluence of the Auditors... I have seen
> the *Red Bull* Play House, which was a large one, so full, that as many
> went back for as want of room as had entered; and as meanly as you
> may now think of these Drols [Drolls], they were then Acted by the
> best Comedians then and now in being; and I may say, by some that
> then exceeded all now Living, by Name, the incomparable Robert
> Cox, who was not only the principal Actor, but also the Contriver
> and Author of most of these Farces.[1]

The caption to the illustration describes the Red Bull Playhouse in Clerkenwell, which was well known during the Civil War as a venue for performing 'Drolls', or short entertainments and theatrical extracts, accompanied by singing and dancing. Robert Cox, mentioned above as the principal actor in the drolls, is depicted on the right of the stage as the 'Simpleton'. A French dancer with violin occupies the centre of the stage and at the rear on the left is a character from Thomas Middleton and William Rowley's *The Changeling*. Falstaff is depicted as wearing a pre-Civil War silk costume and lace collar familiar from Van Dyck's portraits of the 1630s.

Shakespeare's character of Falstaff remained hugely popular with audiences beyond the closure of the theatres. In the introduction to his 1709 edition of Shakespeare, Nicholas Rowe records the tradition that Queen Elizabeth 'was so well pleas'd with that admirable Character of *Falstaff*, in the two Parts of *Henry* the Fourth', that she commanded Shakespeare 'to continue it for one Play more, and to shew him in Love. This is said to be the Occasion of his Writing *The Merry Wives of* Windsor.'[2] Although Pepys saw *The Merry Wives of Windsor* three times at the King's Theatre between 1660 and 1667, his pleasure in the play did not increase. In 1660 he observed: 'The humours of the Country gentleman and the French Doctor very well done; but the rest but very poorly, and Sir J. Falstaffe as bad as any.'[3] In 1661, he saw the play again 'ill done', and in 1667 he found that the play 'did not please me at all – in no part of it'.[4] Despite Pepys's views, the character of Falstaff has remained one of the most popular of Shakespeare's creations. The scene of Falstaff examining the troops from *Henry IV, Part Two* is the first Shakespearean subject to be depicted by an English artist. An oil painting on the theme was completed by William Hogarth in 1730 (now belonging to the Guinness family), a preliminary sketch for which, owned by Her Majesty the Queen, is in the Royal Library at Windsor Castle.

1. R.A. Foakes, *Illustrations of the English Stage*, p. 159.

2. Nicholas Rowe, *The Works of Mr. William Shakespear* (9 vols), (1709), vol. 1, pp. viii–ix.

3. *Diary of Samuel Pepys*, vol. 1, p. 310.

4. *Ibid.*, vol. 2, p. 185; vol. 8, p. 386.

From Kirkman's Drolls.

Published 1672.

Inside of the RED BULL Playhouse.

The Red Bull Playhouse stood on a plot of ground lately called "Red Bull Yard" near the upper end of St John's Street Clerkenwell; and is traditionally said to have been the Theatre at which Shakespeare first held gentlemen's horses. In the civil wars it became highly celebrated for the representation of Drolls, to a collection of which pieces published by Fraunces Kirkman in 1672, this view of it forms a frontispiece. The figures brought together on the stage, are intended as portraits of the leading actors in each Droll. The one playing Simpleton, is Robert Cox, then a great favorite, of whom the publisher thus speaks in his preface. "I have seen the Red Bull Playhouse which was a large one, so full, that as many went back for want of room as had entred: Robert Cox, a principal actor and contriver of these pieces, how have I heard him cryed up for his John Swabber, and Simpleton, the Smith: In which latter, he being to appear with a large piece of Bread & Butter, on the stage I have frequently known some of the female spectators to long for it". The above print may be regarded not only as highly curious for the place it represents, but as a unique specimen of the interior economy of our antient English Theatres.

Published June 13th 1809, by Wm Herbert Lambeth, and Robert Wilkinson, No 58 Cornhill, London.

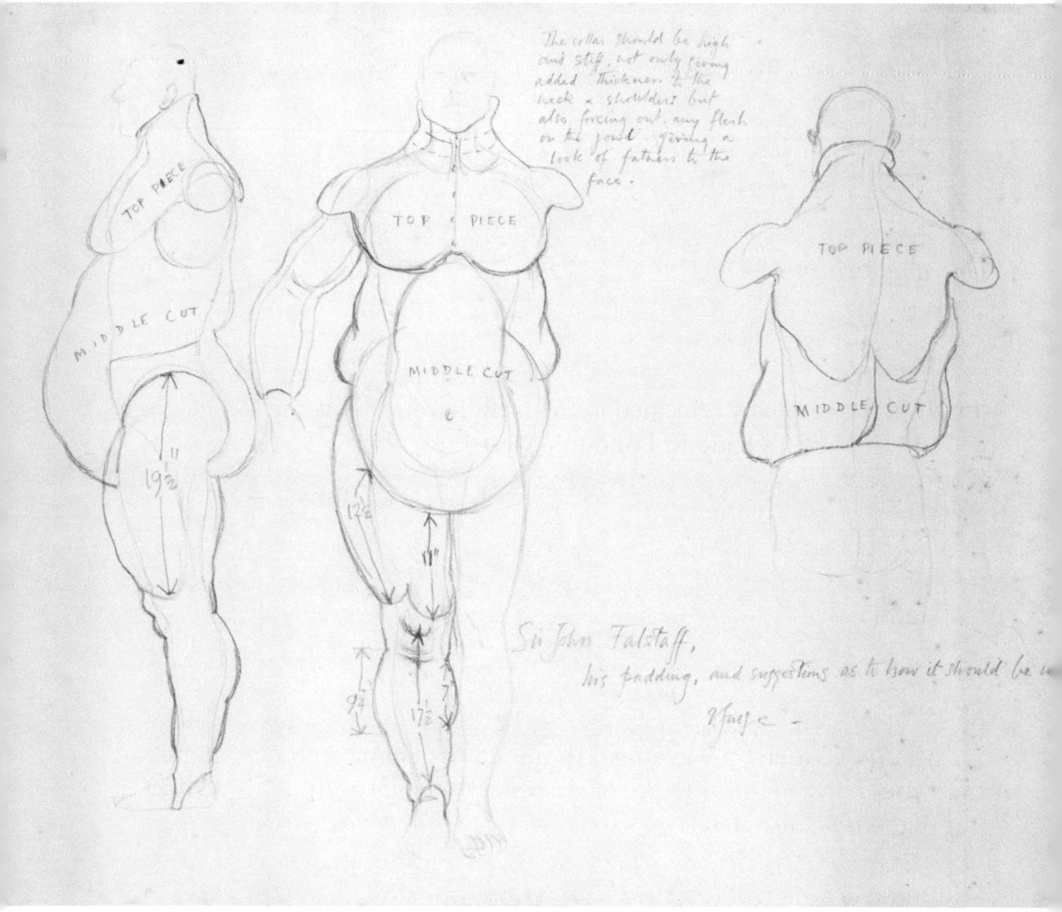

The collar should be high
and stiff, not only giving
added thickness to the
neck & shoulders but
also forcing out any flesh
on the jowl, giving a
look of fatness to the
face.

TOP PIECE

MIDDLE CUT

TOP PIECE

MIDDLE CUT

TOP PIECE

MIDDLE CUT

19½

12½

11"

9¾

17½

7

Sir John Falstaff,
his padding, and suggestions as to how it should be worn
V Jones —

66 That swoll'n parcel of dropsies, that huge bombard of sack, that stuff'd cloak-bag of guts...**99**
Henry IV, Part One (2.4)

43

Roger Furse's costume design for Ralph Richardson's 'fat-suit' as Falstaff (1945)

This drawing reveals the behind-the-scenes making of one of the most celebrated Falstaffs of the twentieth century: Ralph Richardson (1902–1983), who played the role for the Old Vic production of *Henry IV, Parts One and Two* in 1945. The Old Vic, one of Britain's most influential Shakespeare theatres, was the de facto national theatre in the 1940s under the leadership of star actors Richardson and Laurence Olivier (1907–1989). The theatre was badly bomb-damaged during World War Two and the company relocated to the New Theatre (now the Noël Coward) on St Martin's Lane in London's West End, often rehearsing in the National Gallery, which had been emptied of pictures to protect them from air raids.

Richardson was initially reluctant to take on the role of Falstaff, universally known as a rampant carouser, coward, braggart, and all-round bad influence on Prince Hal. He knew it was a part in which actors often failed and had to be convinced by Olivier to play the role. Once he had agreed, Richardson made a radical decision: rather than emphasising the crude comic aspects of the character, he focused on *Sir* John Falstaff, knight and gentleman. He aimed to imbue the character with a dignity that would bring pathos to the later scenes with Hal and Doll Tearsheet, but that would also make the comic scenes funnier. As Richardson said, 'Falstaff, well he's a little bit of a gent. If he's vulgar it's no good. If you're put into a laundry [sic], it's not funny unless it's an indignity.'[1]

It was the job of the costume designer and maker to produce a 'fat-suit' for Richardson that could maintain Falstaff's dignity. Roger Furse (1903–1972), who designed the costumes, was a frequent collaborator with Olivier. During World War Two he was released from the Navy to design the costumes for Olivier's most conspicuous contribution to the war effort, the film of *Henry V* (1944). He was a versatile and considerate designer who worked hard to ensure the comfort, as well as the appearance, of performers. His costume and set designs are a mine of information with details scribbled on their surfaces, and this drawing is no exception. The sketch is carefully labelled 'Sir John Falstaff, his padding, and some suggestions as to how it should be made', and also suggests that the collar should be stiffened to help force 'out any flesh on the jowls, giving a look of fatness to the face'. The suit was made by Alix Stone, a future star theatre designer, then in her first job as an assistant in the Old Vic workshops.

Furse and Stone created a convincing monstrously fat Falstaff who was both light on his feet and dignified. The padding was layered to give a more authentic and comfortable sense of bulk. Richardson wore a tow-elling suit covered in light mackintosh (rubber-coated fabric) to protect him from the outer layer of horsehair. Stone also constructed gnarled, veiny fat man's legs, using silk padding over which Richardson wore red stockings, adding to Falstaff's flamboyance and jollity. The addition of leg padding also allowed him to flaunt his stockings and dispense with the long boots that many a Falstaff had used to disguise his skinny legs. The costume and the performance received excellent reviews. Ivor Brown noted in the *Observer* that 'Mr Richardson grows to obesity downwards: the legs are dropsical trunks, the paunch is sketchy, the head is even pale and lean'.[2] Even James Agate, Richardson's harshest critic, conceded that 'He had everything the part needs – the exuberance, the mischief, the gusto, in a word. Falstaff is more than a "stuffed cloak-bag of guts". He is also "reverend vice" and "grey iniquity".'[3]

Richardson's interpretation had a huge influence on a younger generation of theatre-makers. Sir Peter Hall wrote that he considered his inability to get Richardson to do the role again one of the biggest failures of his career.[4] The critic Kenneth Tynan, who saw the performance as an undergraduate, described 'a Falstaff whose principal attribution was not his fatness, but his knighthood. He was Sir John first, and Falstaff second.'[5]

1. Garry O'Connor, *Ralph Richardson*, p. 123.

2. *Observer*, 30 September 1945.

3. *Sunday Times*, 30 September 1945.

4. *Peter Hall's Diaries*, p. 45.

5. John Miller, *Ralph Richardson*, p. 96.

Charles Kean as Henry V (1859)

Charles Kean (1811–1868) was the son of the celebrated actor Edmund Kean. Determined that his son should not follow him on to the stage, he sent Charles to Eton but, after only three years at the school, financial hardship forced the younger Kean back towards acting, a profession which could at least offer him a viable source of income. After an earlier career in London, the provinces, Scotland and the United States, in 1842 he married the popular actress Ellen Tree (1805–1880), and they toured the United States together.

In 1850, Kean became lessee of London's Princess's Theatre, where perhaps his most significant work was achieved. The Shakespeare revivals he staged there between 1850 and 1859 were founded on his desire to give accurate representations of the past. He wished not only to be seen as an actor-manager but also as a scholar and antiquarian; the approach he employed involved lavish sets and costumes, large casts and spectacular tableaux and processions (the latter sometimes interpolated from historical accounts, rather than representing scenes appearing in Shakespeare's texts).

The Shakespeare revivals began with *Twelfth Night* in 1850 and concluded with *Henry V* in 1859. Kean used as many historical sources as were then available to research his productions and, beginning with his 1853 production of *Macbeth*, the playbills and accompanying texts included copious background notes providing evidence for the productions' historical details.

The large playbill for this production of *Henry V* describes the spectacle awaiting the playgoer, including 'Old London Bridge from the Surrey Side of the River. Reception of King Henry the Fifth on entering London After the Battle of Agincourt'.[1] As illustrated by drawings also in the V&A, this scene involved a large number of extras dressed as prophets, maidens, and other attendants, with King Henry V himself on horseback. Although mentioned in passing by the play's fifth-act Chorus, the scene itself does not appear in Shakespeare's play. Kean defended its inclusion in his preface to the printed edition of *Henry V*, available to buy in the theatre:

> The introductions made throughout the play are presented less with a view to spectacular effect, than from a desire to render the stage a medium of historical knowledge, as well as an illustration of dramatic poetry. *Accuracy*, not *show*, has been my object; and where the two coalesce, it is because the one is inseparable from the other.[2]

Kean's scholarship was recognised in June 1857 when he was elected a Fellow of the Society of Antiquaries. His scenically lavish productions were clearly also appreciated by Victorian audiences. *Henry V* was performed eighty-four times. This trend for long runs marked a new departure in London theatre which had previously prospered through offering a varied and frequently changing diet of entertainment to a comparatively small, local population with limited opportunities to travel beyond their immediate localities. The railways, which had delivered millions of visitors to the Great Exhibition in 1851, also benefited other London attractions, including theatres; these larger audiences in turn made it possible to cover the costs of Kean's extravagant productions.

This photograph belongs to a series of images created for Charles Kean by Martin Laroche, thirteen of which are in the V&A's collection. For their period, they are exceptional records of nineteenth-century theatre. It is true that Charles Kean was very interested in electricity and how it might be used in the theatre. However, although giving the impression that this scene was photographed on stage, lighting technology was insufficiently advanced at this time to allow photographs to be created without natural light. The Princess's Theatre, at 73 Oxford Street, was only eight doors away from Laroche's studio at number 65, and we can therefore assume that actors, props and painted backcloths were moved between the two premises to create these photographs.

1. Playbill in V&A Collection, Princess's Theatre, 28 March 1859.

2. *Shakespeare's Play of King Henry the Fifth arranged for representation at the Princess's Theatre, with Historical and Explanatory Notes by Charles Kean, FSA* (London: Chapman and Co., 1859).

Richard Burton as Henry V (*c.* 1956)

Born Richard Walter Jenkins, the twelfth of thirteen children of a Welsh-speaking mining family, Richard Burton (1925–1984) said of himself: 'I am the son of a Welsh miner and one would expect me to be at my happiest playing peasants, people of the earth; but in actual fact I'm much happier playing princes and kings.'[1] Gaining his first acting role at Liverpool in 1943 in Emlyn Williams's play *The Druid's Rest*, Burton saw the vocation of acting in Wales as one developing naturally out of the role of the preacher, for whom the pulpit was 'the greatest stage of the world': 'You stood hovering like a great bird of prey over the people in the village; you said, "I will tell you what is wrong with you, and let me examine your soul".'[2] His first Shakespearean role was Angelo in Professor Nevill Coghill's production of *Measure for Measure* for the Oxford University Dramatic Society, and he went on to star in the London productions of Christopher Fry's *The Lady's Not for Burning* and *The Boy with a Cart* directed by John Gielgud. Having played Prince Hal and Henry V at Stratford in 1951, and *Hamlet* at the Old Vic in 1953, his performance as Henry V in 1955 at the Old Vic won him the Evening Standard Best Actor Award. This painting of him in the role, commissioned by the theatre management, was donated to the museum by his widow, Sally Burton. The artist, Frank Salisbury (1874–1962), was originally asked to portray the king seated on his throne but after seeing the production, he decided to focus on the moment when Henry recites the miraculously short list of casualties after the Battle of Agincourt (4.8.78–110), which concludes:

> When, without stratagem,
> But in plain shock and even play of battle,
> Was ever known so great and little loss
> On one part and on th' other? Take it, God,
> For it is none but thine.

After making his film debut in 1949, Burton went on to win dazzling acclaim as a Shakespearean actor, but when asked whether his next role was to be Macbeth or King Lear, he replied that his sole ambition was to be a millionaire. Although he never completely abandoned the stage, his main focus was increasingly on film work, to the dismay of those who hoped he might return to the fold as a classical actor. Burton's marriage to Elizabeth Taylor was famously tempestuous. When Franco Zeffirelli met them for the first time, they would not stop arguing: Burton wanted to discuss Shakespeare with Zeffirelli, while Taylor wanted Richard to rescue her pet bush baby, which had wrecked the hotel room, badly scratched the maid, and was now lurking out of reach in the bathroom. As Zeffirelli recalls:

> On and on they quarrelled, like Katherine and Petruchio in *The Taming of the Shrew*... I stopped, suddenly aware of what I was thinking: that they would be perfect in the roles if only they could be persuaded to do it. I could see that Richard would be no problem – he was desperate to get back into a classic part – it was Liz I would have to win over.[3]

Zeffirelli won her over by rescuing the exhausted bush baby from its perch in the bathroom; the film was made in Rome, where Elizabeth surprised everyone by delivering Katherina's speech of wifely submission with complete sincerity:

> Such duty as the subject owes the prince,
> Even such a woman oweth to her husband;
> And when she is froward, peevish, sullen, sour,
> And not obedient to his honest will,
> What is she but a foul, contending rebel
> And graceless traitor to her loving lord?
>
> (5.2.155–60)

Burton won high acclaim for some of his film roles: in 1959 he played Jimmy Porter in the film of John Osborne's *Look Back in Anger*, saying of the role: 'Up to that time... I'd only played princes, heroes, kings – dressed eternally in togas or whatever. It was fascinating to find a man who came presumably from my sort of class, who actually could talk the way that I would like to talk.'[4] Despite his status as a heart-throb, Burton did not see himself as a romantic actor: 'Romeo, for instance, I've never played; it's beyond my capacity... When I have to kiss a woman on the stage or on the screen, horrors start up. That is why I prefer to act with my wife rather than any other woman in the world.'[5]

1. Hal Burton (ed.), *Acting in the Sixties*, p. 18.

2. *Ibid.*, p. 28.

3. Franco Zeffirelli, *The Autobiography*, p. 201.

4. Burton, *Acting in the Sixties*, p. 24.

5. *Ibid.*, p. 20.

The Birmingham Repertory Theatre production of *Henry VI* (1953)

In 1906, Frank Benson presented the three parts of *Henry VI* at the old Shakespeare Memorial Theatre. The plays were rarely staged and Benson's productions could claim to be the first on record to be given consecutively. It was also the first time that *Part Three* had been performed at Stratford. Its appearance 'caused some brief excitement', wrote J.C. Trewin, 'though the piece was soon forgotten'.[1] Not, however, by Barry Jackson (1879–1961), then an amateur actor and theatre enthusiast, who was to found the Birmingham Repertory Theatre seven years later. 'To see all the histories in succession was the experience of a lifetime', he later wrote, and one that seemed 'unlikely to be repeated'.[2] In the first half of the twentieth century the plays – among Shakespeare's earliest – were not highly regarded. Commentators writing in earlier centuries had cast doubts on their authorship, reluctant to accept that the depictions of brutality in the Wars of the Roses, and, in *Part One*, the portrayal of Joan of Arc as a witch in league with demons, could be the work of the Immortal Bard. The twentieth century began to reclaim the plays for Shakespeare, but opportunities for them to prove themselves in performance were scarce. Jackson, writing in 1953, attributed the absence from the stage of these 'eminently actable' plays to their lack of obvious star roles.[3] He might also have added that they needed a theatre company prepared to take risks on unfamiliar work that might not draw the crowds. Jackson's Birmingham Repertory Theatre happened to be one.

The Birmingham 'Rep' had become famous for its modern-dress Shakespeare productions in the 1920s and Shakespeare remained essential to the theatre's repertoire, its later productions being generally well received but not attracting much critical attention outside the city. In 1948, the company was joined by director Douglas Seale (1913–1999), who had acted at Stratford and began his career at the Rep with a fast-paced production of *The Comedy of Errors* in *commedia dell'arte* style. Jackson asked Seale to look at *Henry VI, Part Two*, the piece that had made the greatest impression on him in 1906, and in 1951 Seale directed the play at Birmingham. It did not attract huge audiences and Jackson suggested that they may have been put off by the title – in Trewin's words, 'entering the second instalment of a serial, having missed the first and without chance of the third' – but reviewers were enthusiastic.[4] The following year Seale and Jackson began to make good the deficiency by staging *Part Three*, which played for sixteen performances at the Old Vic in July of that year, and in 1953 all three plays were staged at Birmingham and then taken to the Old Vic, where the full cycle played eight times, receiving an overwhelmingly favourable response from audience and critics. 'They were pronounced "impossible",' wrote Seale: 'But partly because of the challenge, perhaps, and partly because we were young and confident and a "company", they worked. In fact, they were a sensational success'.[5] 'Sir Barry Jackson has now shown that academic criticism is at fault,' declared Trewin in the *Sketch*.[6] The rehabilitation of these brilliant early plays had begun.

Designer Finlay James staged all three plays on a permanent set of three Gothic arches, which could serve for the exterior of a variety of buildings with the addition of doors or a portcullis and, with hangings or barred gates, become the interior of a palace or a prison cell. It gave unity to the action, framing the characters at key moments. In the photograph shown here, it represents the walls of York in *Henry VI, Part Three* (Act Two, Scene Two), with the severed head of the Duke of York visible on a pole as his son Edward confronts Queen Margaret. Seale encouraged his actors to remain still when they were not speaking and as a result 'achieved an undisturbed concentration upon the lines'.[7] 'The plays live in my mind as a series of savage tableaux,' wrote Kenneth Tynan, 'each held and lit for a moment as by a magnesium flare.'[8]

1. T.C. Kemp and J.C. Trewin, *The Stratford Festival*, p. 73.

2. Barry Jackson, 'On Producing *Henry VI*', p. 49.

3. *Ibid.*, p. 50.

4. J.C. Trewin, *The Birmingham Repertory Theatre*, p. 149.

5. Douglas Seale, in *Birmingham Repertory Theatre, 1913–1971*, ed. Roger Southern, p. 8.

6. *Sketch*, 29 July 1953.

7. T.C. Kemp, 'Acting Shakespeare: Modern Tendencies in Playing and Production', p. 125.

8. *Evening Standard*, 16 July 1953.

RSC

HENRY VI

Part 2

**Feliks Topolski, drawing of Alan Howard and Helen Mirren
in the RSC production of *Henry VI, Part Two* (1977)**

The work of Polish-born artist Feliks Topolski (1907–1989) is well represented in the collections of the V&A's Theatre and Performance Department. Topolski came to London in 1935, establishing a studio in the arches of Hungerford Bridge on the South Bank and taking British citizenship in 1947. An extraordinarily prolific artist who produced a vast body of work, he was an official war artist in the Second World War, a book illustrator, a painter of intimate portraits and huge murals, and the designer of several stage productions, notably *The Government Inspector*, starring Alec Guinness, at the Old Vic in 1948, and was famous as a recorder of contemporary life and events. *Chronicles*, a self-published broadsheet of sketches and commentary on any subject that caught his attention, appeared fortnightly from 1953 until 1982, and totals over 2,300 drawings. Topolski worked quickly, his subjects depicted in a shorthand of swirling lines and splashes of colour that capture the immediacy of the moment. Between 1975 and 1977 he drew many of the Royal Shakespeare Company's productions in both Stratford and London, sitting in the auditorium with his sketchbook and creating 'on-the-spot' pictures in felt-tip pen and crayon.

In 1977, the RSC staged all three parts of *Henry VI* at Stratford, directed by Terry Hands. The productions were another landmark in the plays' history. The Birmingham Repertory Company's productions of 1953 had reclaimed them for the theatre, but few companies had the resources, or the courage, to present a trilogy of lesser-known works that might not attract an audience. After his success in 1953, Douglas Seale directed them again at the Old Vic in 1957, but this time condensed into two parts, and the next staging was the RSC's celebrated *Wars of the Roses* cycle in 1963, with the three plays again reduced to two and performed with *Richard III* to complete Shakespeare's historical sequence. Terry Hands and the RSC's Artistic Director, Trevor Nunn, were prepared to take the risk of three rarities in one season: 'we have actually tried to show the plays simply as they are,' said Hands, 'without excessive rewriting and cutting, presenting them on their own as unfamiliar or little-known sagas with marvellous characters'.[1]

The trilogy proved far from easy. In her history of the RSC, Sally Beauman noted that their unfamiliarity made the plays difficult to cast, with actors reluctant to take roles they did not know.[2] All three plays were rehearsed together and treated as a single unit, and the company, which was also preparing a revival of *Henry V*, Hands's 1975 success, was exhausted by the time the productions opened on consecutive nights. As Beauman pointed out, this contributed to the tone of the first night reviews ('flawed in execution but redeemed by a passionate sense of purpose' was John Barber's verdict on *Part One*), but the productions had admirers – Michael Billington called *Part Two* 'little short of magnificent' – and having developed through performance, the plays transferred to London in the following year to great acclaim: 'the best Shakespeare production I have ever seen', wrote the *Financial Times* critic B.A. Young.[3]

Key to the production's success was Alan Howard's portrayal of Henry. In *Part One* he was an awkward adolescent, dwarfed by a huge crown and the high throne which prevented his feet from touching the ground. In *Part Two* he had grown up to become 'a king gifted with insight but no flair for action', who went to his death in *Part Three* as a willing sacrificial victim.[4] Topolski's sketch, one of two drawings of the production held by the V&A, shows Henry in the first scene of *Part Two*, when he is introduced to his bride, Helen Mirren's glamorous Margaret of Anjou. The sketchy figure to the right is recognisable as Graham Crowden's Humphrey, Duke of Gloucester.

1. Quoted in '*Henry VI*: "Which Oft Our Stage Has Shown"', in *RSC Newspaper* (Summer 1977), p. 2.

2. Sally Beauman, *The Royal Shakespeare Company*, p. 339.

3. *Ibid.*, p. 340; John Barber, *Daily Telegraph*, 14 July 1977; Michael Billington, *Guardian*, 17 July 1977; B.A. Young, *Financial Times*, 17 April 1978.

4. Billington, *Guardian*, 17 July 1977.

66 He dies, and makes no sign: O God, forgive him! 99
Henry VI, Part Two (3.3)

Caroline Watson, engraving after Joshua Reynolds, *The Death of Cardinal Beaufort* (1789)

The painting of the death of Cardinal Beaufort, from *Henry VI, Part Two* (Act Three, Scene Three) was commissioned from Sir Joshua Reynolds (1723–1792) by Alderman John Boydell for his Shakespeare Gallery in Pall Mall, and was among the first pictures to be exhibited in the gallery, which was open to the public from 1789 to 1805. Boydell had a highly successful trade in book illustration and engravings, and as well as being a popular visitor attraction, the paintings were intended to be a source of images for engraving in large or small format for the print market and illustrated editions of Shakespeare. Cardinal Beaufort is shown in his death throes, tormented by guilt for the murder he has sanctioned, and, as King Henry VI approaches his bed, declares:

> If thou be'st Death I'll give thee England's treasure,
> Enough to purchase such another island,
> So thou wilt let me live and feel no pain...
> O, torture me no more! I will confess.

(3.3.2–11)

Shakespeare's history plays were particularly popular with audiences during the time of the Napoleonic Wars, and no less than fourteen paintings of the *Henry VI* plays were exhibited in the Boydell Shakespeare Gallery, of which Reynolds's was the most popular. Nicholas Rowe in his edition of 1709 especially commends the death scene of Cardinal Beaufort, saying: 'There is a short Scene in the Second Part of Henry the Sixth... which I cannot but think admirable in its Kind. Cardinal *Beaufort*, who had murder'd the Duke of *Gloucester*, is shewn in the last Agonies on his Death-Bed, with the good King praying over him. There is so much Terror in one, so much Tenderness and moving Piety in the other, as must touch any one who is capable either of Fear or Pity.'[1]

The Reverend William Mason, who visited Reynolds's studio when the artist was working on the painting, was amused by the choice of model for the dying Cardinal: 'a porter, or coal heaver, between fifty and sixty years old, whom he had paid to grow a bushy black beard; he was unclothed to the waist, and sat with a fixed grin, showing his teeth, in illustration of Shakespeare's line *Mark* [sic] *how the pangs of death do make him grin.*'[2] In the early states of the print, following the original painting, a small devil squats on the pillow behind the Cardinal; this was later painted out from the picture and removed from later states of the print as too shocking, even though the image has its origin in Shakespeare's text: 'O, beat away the busy meddling fiend / That lays strong siege unto this wretch's soul' (3.3.21–2).[3]

Reynolds painted three canvases for the Boydell Shakespeare Gallery. On a visit to the artist's studio with a companion, Boydell was particularly taken by a painting of a baby, an infant Reynolds claimed he had found sitting on his doorstep. Boydell's companion is credited with the idea of transforming the painting into an image of Robin Goodfellow from *A Midsummer Night's Dream*: 'Well, Mr Alderman,' he is recorded as saying, 'it can very easily come into the Shakespeare, if Sir Joshua will kindly place him on a mushroom, give him Faun's ears and make a Puck of him.'[4] At the time of his death in 1792, Reynolds was still working on the third painting: a large canvas, measuring twelve feet by nine, of Macbeth and Hecate in the cavern of the three Witches. Boydell paid £1,000 for it to Reynolds's executors.

1. Nicholas Rowe, *The Works of Mr. William Shakespear* (9 vols), (1709), vol. 1, p. xxix.

2. Bernard Denvir, *The Eighteenth Century: Art, Design and Society, 1689–1789*, p. 146. (The line in fact reads: 'See how the pangs of death…')

3. *The Boydell Shakespeare Gallery*, ed. Walter Pape and Frederick Burwick, p. 260.

4. *Reynolds*, ed. Nicholas Penny, p. 322.

Henry Irving's boots as Richard III, Lyceum Theatre (1877)

The true character of Richard III, and indeed his physical appearance, remains a matter subject to heated, and often emotional, debate – though his recently discovered skeleton, excavated from a Leicester car park in 2012, confirms that he suffered from severe scoliosis, or curvature of the spine.[1] In his play, written *c.* 1593, Shakespeare characterised the monarch as a villainous tyrant, 'Deform'd, unfinish'd' and lame (1.1.20–23), making the hunched back and withered limbs of Tudor propaganda virtually synonymous with the role.

Surviving portraits and engravings depicting celebrated actors such as David Garrick (1717–1779) and Edmund Kean (1787–1833) as Richard III indicate that the late-eighteenth and early-nineteenth century may have witnessed a shift away from the original emphasis upon the protagonist's deformity. Subsequent images of Charles Kean (1811–1868), however, illustrate an effort to distort the actor's form, albeit through the subtle manipulation of the actor's sumptuous tunic to suggest a slightly raised left shoulder, rather than an obvious dramatic adoption of a hump or a manifest limp.

The mid-1850s, and Charles Kean's arrival at the Princess's Theatre in Oxford Street, heralded a new desire for historical accuracy in set and costume design. The lavish productions presented by Kean were founded upon painstaking research by expert designers, and, lest the audience should be left in any doubt regarding the authenticity of a piece, they were provided with lengthy explanations in their theatre programmes.

This increased emphasis on authenticity may have influenced Henry Irving's decision to set his production in the medieval era which corresponded with the historical events that had inspired the play, rather than the opulent Elizabethan settings favoured by his predecessors. It may also have contributed to his decision to return to Shakespeare's original text, in preference to the eighteenth-century adaptation by Colley Cibber (1671–1757), a version which cut many of the characters central to Shakespeare's narrative (Edward IV, Clarence, Queen Margaret and the

Woodvilles among them), and included a scene showing the murder of the innocent princes.

The Richard of Irving's version was not, according to Clement Scott,

> the truculent tyrant, who has so long stamped about the stage in scarlet doublet and flapping, russet boots, with black ringlet wig and bushy eyebrows, supposed to symbolise in their hue the darkness of his deeds of villainy. His deformity is no more obtrusive than is needful to justify the references of the text.[2]

While Irving (1838–1905) does appear to have retained the traditional 'russet boots', his costume reflects a much more restrained and subtle interpretation of the role. The boots themselves, made from a deep crimson suede, have been moulded to fit the actor's unusually narrow and long feet. Though clearly designed to reflect the wealth and status of the character, the glass jewels used to decorate the centre-front opening and ankle of the boots, with the additional gold metallic braid, add a comparatively conservative sparkle to an ensemble that was designed to be seen under the soft and shadowy beams of the gaslights. The fact that the heel of the right boot has been raised, forcing Irving to limp, has been carefully masked by adding a band of fabric (matching that used on the upper part of the shoe) to the heel. The only other modification Irving made to his form was the addition of a very small silk cushion, worn at the left shoulder, to create a barely noticeable hump.

The reviews for the production indicate that Irving's performance mirrored the style of his costume, choosing to play Richard as 'an arch and polished dissembler... the most subtle and the most merciless of assassins and conspirators'.[3] Even the mannerisms, in particular his stiff and awkward gait and somewhat clipped intonation, for which Irving was so frequently ridiculed, were felt by many critics to be perfectly suited to the part, and the production was a great success, running for nearly three months. It is perhaps not surprising therefore that Irving would later identify Richard III as among his four favourite roles.

1. See Philippa Langley and Michael Jones, *The King's Grave*, pp. 141–2, 171–3.

2. Clement Scott, *From 'The Bells' to 'King Arthur'*, p. 106.

3. Dutton Cook, *Nights at the Play*, vol. 2, p. 135.

Laurence Olivier's doublet as Richard III, Old Vic (1944)

Great performances pass into theatrical legend. Very occasionally they acquire a life beyond the theatre. Thanks to the 1955 film version, Laurence Olivier's stage performance as Richard III is familiar to people who weren't born when Olivier (1907–1989) was acting for the Old Vic Company. The clipped voice, based, Olivier said, on old actors' impressions of Henry Irving, is still imitated. When archaeologists located the grave of the historical Richard beneath a Leicester car park, the 2013 Channel 4 television programme that confirmed the king's identity included, without comment, a clip of Olivier limping malevolently towards the camera. Unfortunately for the real monarch, Olivier has become the popular idea of Richard III.

When the stage production, directed by John Burrell (1910–1972), opened in 1944, its star was predicting disaster. He felt that he could bring nothing to a part too closely associated with barnstorming actor-managers. Gradually, however, he began to develop a mental picture of the character. 'I wanted to look the most evil thing there was', he said in his book, *On Acting*.[1] Olivier liked to build his characters from the outside, finding the appropriate look for each. As Richard, he disguised himself behind an exaggerated beak-like putty nose and shoulder-length black hair tinged with red. A rubber glove became the withered left hand. But the performance did not rely on externals. The first entrance has been well documented: Richard opened a door noisily, limped through and carefully closed the door behind him, clicking the latch sharply to keep out intruders. Then he made his way slowly downstage to confide in the audience. His son, Tarquin, recalled the impact:

> He sidled down to the very edge of the stage, chuckling and leant towards us as if to a mirror, to explain his fascination with all that was dark and terrible and what fun it was going to be, his laughter hissing, his consonants like whip-lashes.[2]

The green-velvet doublet that Olivier wore for his first scenes was designed by Doris Zinkeisen (1898–1991) in a style which the historical Richard would have recognised. It echoes the shape of 1480s fashion, with hanging sleeves and fur trimming. But the play was taking place under wartime rationing restrictions and the 'make do and mend' philosophy of the time shows in the black fabric forming the infill at the neck and the tight-fitting sleeves, which is the material used for blackout curtains. The doublet is designed so that the decorative stitching at the back only hangs properly when the costume is padded out by a hump, and the neck infill is cut to give an irregular neckline that subtly emphasises the character's deformity.

1. Laurence Olivier, *On Acting*, p. 78.

2. Tarquin Olivier, *My Father Laurence Oliver*, p. 130.

Mr. Garrick in the Character of Richard the 3d.

"Is there a murderer here? No – yes, I am."
Richard III (5.3)

51

Charles Grignion, engraving after William Hogarth's portrait (1745) of David Garrick as Richard III (1746)

The eighteenth century witnessed an explosion of visual materials relating to Shakespeare's plays in performance, which were widely disseminated in illustrated editions and in prints and engravings. When William Hogarth started out on his career in the 1720s, there were only two print shops in London, with Continental prints the most in demand. By the end of the century, John Boydell (1720–1804) had opened a whole gallery of Shakespeare paintings produced in England, and had made his fortune exporting English prints to France. The earliest surviving painting of a scene from Shakespeare is by Hogarth, who painted *Falstaff Examining his Recruits* in 1730. In contrast to the low-life style of his painting of this scene from *Henry IV, Part Two*, Hogarth went on to paint a scene from *The Tempest* (*c.* 1735) in high-flown allegorical and historical style. Having begun his career as an engraver, Hogarth understood the commercial potential of making prints of theatrical subjects. This engraving by Charles Grignion (1721–1810) of his painting of David Garrick in the role of Richard III (1745) was phenomenally successful and is perhaps the most famous representation of an actor of all time.

Hogarth (1697–1764) received the sum of £200 for the painting, then a huge sum normally commanded by the works of Old Masters. Garrick had taken London by storm with his performance as Richard III at Goodman's Fields Theatre in 1741, and Hogarth's painting portrays him in this signature role. It depicts Richard in his tent on the night before the Battle of Bosworth (5.3), capturing the moment when he awakes from a nightmare, having dreamt that the ghosts of all his victims appeared in turn to formally curse him. The pieces of armour in the foreground were modelled on real examples borrowed from the Tower of London.

'Last night,' said Garrick of his first performance, 'I play'd Richard the Third to the Surprize of Every Body'.[1] His first biographer, the playwright Arthur Murphy (1727–1805), recalls how 'Mr Garrick shone forth like a theatrical Newton; he threw new light on elocution and action; he banished ranting, bombast and grimace; and restored nature, ease, simplicity and genuine humour':

> When he started from his dream he was a spectacle of horror. He called out in a manly voice 'Give me another horse', he paused, and with a countenance of dismay, advanced crying out in a tone of distress 'Bind up my wounds', and then, falling on his knees, said in a most piteous accent, 'Have mercy heaven'. In all this the audience saw an exact imitation of nature.[2]

Garrick (1717–1779) cultivated close relations with the artists of his day and had strong ideas about how he wanted to be portrayed, writing to the Royal Academician Francis Hayman (1708–1776) about a projected painting of Othello, which was never in fact realised:

> The Scene which in my Opinion will make the best Picture, is that point of Time in the last Act, when Emilia discovers to Othello his Error about the Handkerchief... [Othello] must be thunderstruck with Horror, his Whole figure extended, with his Eyes turn'd up to Heav'n & his Frame sinking, as it were, at Emilia's Discovery. I shall better make you conceive My Notion of this Attitude & Expression when I see You.[3]

With the exception of King George III, more paintings and sculptures were made of Garrick in his lifetime than of any other living person, with paintings of him in such Shakespearean roles as Romeo, Macbeth and King Lear.

1. *Letters of David Garrick*, ed. David M. Little and George M. Kahrl, vol. 1, p. 28.

2. Iain Mackintosh and Geoffrey Ashton, *Thirty Different Likenesses*.

3. *Letters of David Garrick*, ed. Little and Kahrl, vol. 1, pp. 82–3.

Philippe Jacques de Loutherbourg, sketch for the scenery of David Garrick's production of *Richard III* (*c.* 1775)

This sketch – one of three in the V&A's collection – is inscribed as having been made by Philippe Jacques de Loutherbourg (1740–1812) for David Garrick's production of *Richard III*, and later given to Henry Irving in 1874 by 'his old friend CR' (most probably the author Charles Reade). They represent the initial stage in producing a scenic model.[1] When de Loutherbourg came to London in 1771, he was already a French Academician and painter to the French King, described as 'one of those few geniuses that centuries only produce from time to time. All genres of painting are familiar to him and he treats them in a style so superior that even the least accomplished ones are worth the highest admiration.'[2] De Loutherbourg had asked the Director of the Opéra-Comique in Paris to write a letter of introduction to the great actor David Garrick (1717–1779) on his behalf: 'Mr de Loutherbourg,' it reads, 'one of our greatest painters and a very agreeable man, intends for his pleasure to make an excursion to London... I advise you strongly to let him paint three small pictures for you, one a sea piece, another a landscape... and thirdly a battle scene. He is delightful in all three genres.'[3] Garrick initially employed de Loutherbourg to design the set for a pantomime, *The Pigmy Revels*, which proved a great success. De Loutherbourg went on to be employed at the Drury Lane Theatre on a permanent contract for the considerable salary of £500 per year.

The sketches of *Richard III* may relate to stagings in 1772 or in 1775 when the play was last performed by Garrick, one year before his retirement. They show de Loutherbourg's ideas for Act Five. In the first, prior to the battle, there are orderly rows of tents and a trestle bridge beyond. The second sketch – shown here – depicts the field after the battle, with an overturned wagon in the foreground. The arched bridge in the background is of a different design from that in the first image, and the rows of tents can be seen in the far distance. The third sketch is more generalised, with neither bridge nor tents, and shows the battlefield, strewn with broken cartwheels, a discarded drum and an abandoned treasure chest. The bridges are described as 'practical', over which soldiers could march, reflecting contemporary stage practice, as found, for example, in Handel's *Radamisto* of 1720, a convention surviving well into the 1850s in Charles Kean's production of *Richard III*.

After Garrick's retirement from management, de Loutherbourg continued at Drury Lane under the management of Sheridan, but resigned in 1781 when threatened with a reduction in salary. His final theatre production was at the Covent Garden Theatre in 1785: the spectacularly successful *Omai, or, a Trip Round the World*, based on Captain Cook's South Sea voyages. Soon after leaving Drury Lane, he designed an illuminated Christmas masquerade for the novelist and collector William Beckford at Fonthill, which lasted for three days and three nights, transforming the whole property into a magically lit oriental wonderland. The artist also caused a sensation with his 'Eidophusikon' – a miniature theatre without actors, which he described as an imitation 'of Natural Phenomena, represented by Moving Pictures'. Visitors to his house in the winter of 1781 paid five shillings to view a series of scenes displayed in the theatre, measuring ten feet wide, six feet high, and eight feet deep: 'Aurora; or the Effects of the Dawn, with a View of London from Greenwich Park'; 'Noon; the Port of Tangier in Africa, with the distant View of the Rock of Gibraltar'; 'Sunset, a View near Naples'; 'Moonlight, a View in the Mediterranean, the Rising of the Moon contrasted with the Effect of Fire', concluding with 'a Storm at Sea, and Ship-wreck'. The exhibition continued for several short seasons, including diverse exotic locations, and a scene showing 'Satan arraying his Troops on the Banks of the Fiery Lake, with the Raising of Pandemonium'.[4]

As well as being a stage designer, de Loutherbourg was an RA, exhibiting regularly at the Royal Academy. It was not unusual for artists to combine painting with scene design for the theatre, and de Loutherbourg belongs in the prestigious company of Hogarth, Turner and Clarkson Stanfield in excelling in both disciplines.

1. Jane Martineau (et. al.), *Shakespeare in Art*, p. 134 (catalogue description by Christopher Baugh).

2. Rüdiger Joppien, *Philippe Jacques de Loutherbourg, RA, 1740–1812*, Introduction, [p. 2].

3. *Ibid.*

4. Richard D. Altick, *The Shows of London*, pp. 121–2.

original sketch made for "Richard the 3d" by de loutherbourg for Mr Garrick — the first practical Bridge on an old print &c Presented to H. Irving by J. W. Wilson

Mr. KEAN as RICHARD.   Mr. COOPER as RICHMOND.

Tinsel print of Edmund Kean as Richard III (*c.* 1850), hand-coloured and decorated (*c.* 1920)

This tinsel print depicts the epic moment in the last act of *Richard III* on the Field of Bosworth when John Cooper as the Earl of Richmond towered over the fallen Edmund Kean as Richard, before dispatching him in the final duel. Kean's swordsmanship was legendary. He loved to make much of his death in the play, one contemporary commentator noting that the sword fight lasted five or six minutes.[1]

Edmund Kean (1787–1833) had made his name in London at the Drury Lane Theatre in February 1814 with his performance of the crookbacked king, with Alexander Rae as Richmond, whom Kean chased 'round and round the stage' before finally letting Rae kill him.[2] He first played Richard to Cooper's Richmond at Drury Lane on Monday, 23 July 1821. That night was Kean's first performance at the Lane after a year's leave of absence to tour in America, and it was heralded earlier in the day by a triumphal procession into Covent Garden, masterminded by the theatre's manager, Robert William Elliston (1774–1831). Six costumed outriders led a procession followed by Elliston, Kean and Cooper in their own horse-drawn carriages. The theatre that night was crowded with a packed audience who so cheered Kean's performance as had 'never been heard before'.[3]

John Cooper (1793–1870), an actor from Bath, had first appeared at Drury Lane in November 1820, having been engaged as a leading tragedian, along with James William Wallack (1795–1864), to plug the gap of Kean's absence. Cooper was well received at the Lane in various roles, including Romeo, Othello and Edgar in *King Lear*. He had acted with Kean when Kean was a relatively unknown touring player, but *Richard III* was their first London appearance together.

Kean was portrayed in prints in all his major roles. The etched copper plates from which the images were printed were copied from drawings made by artists during performances. Plates often passed from publisher to publisher, so popular prints of Regency actors drawn during their lifetime were frequently reprinted and sold much later. This example is undated but was issued between 1846 and 1860 by the London print-seller and publisher William Spencer Johnson, who specialised in portraits. Johnson traded in Nassau Street, Soho, until 1846 when he moved to St Martin's Lane, the address which appears on the print. He operated there as sole trader until 1860. This particular image had been published earlier, however, by J. Fairburn in 1838, and by reprinting it Johnson shows the enduring fame of Kean.

Like cutting out and pasting scraps, making tinsel portraits was a popular Regency and Victorian pastime. Actors and actresses could gain celebrity overnight and command vast fees after triumphant performances, and print-sellers were quick to cash in, printing full-length engravings of actors in their latest roles. From 1811 to 1850 every major player, and many minor ones, appeared in these prints which were dubbed, according to their price, 'Penny Plain, Tuppence Coloured'. To make a tinsel portrait, the picture was glued with scraps of fabric representing clothing, and leather scraps for belts, boots and gauntlets, while specially stamped and embossed metallic pieces for items such as shields and helmets, breastplates and swords, could be bought for the corresponding print. Fragments of feathers could add a final flourish to a plumed helmet or dainty headdress. A maple frame was the most popular way to finish the work and display it at home. The chief producer of tinsel decorations was James Webb, a gunsmith, whose great-nephew H.J. Webb produced some of the best examples of tinsel prints in the 1920s, using James's stock of original prints and ornaments. This print was probably tinselled by H.J. Webb.

Kean's reputation as the most brilliant actor of his day, gained partly by his innovative and energetic portrayal of Richard III, was marred during his lifetime – by scandal about his personal life, his drinking, and his consequent inability to remember lines. 'The first step toward the Throne of Mercy is confession,' he avowed in a penitent interview in America in 1825, proceeding to regret his many 'errors and indiscretions, my loss of fame and fortune'.[4] None of this mattered, however, to those who bought this stirring image, either for their craftwork or ready-made years later. Kean was the stuff of legend, and a great subject for a dramatic tinsel portrait.

1. Étienne-Jean Delécluze, *Journal de Delécluze 1824–1828*, quoted in Jeffrey Kahan, *The Cult of Kean*, p. 112.

2. *Ibid.*, p. 111.

3. Giles Playfair, *The Flash of Lightning*, p. 98.

4. Interview published in the *Columbian Centinel*, quoted in Harold Newcomb Hillebrand, *Edmund Kean*, p. 263

Playbill advertising *Richard III* at Astley's Circus (1860)

White Surrey was the war horse everyone wanted to see when the last act of *Richard III* was presented at Astley's Circus for William Cooke's Farewell Benefit on 30 January 1860. It was not Richard's death but that of his charger that stole the show, and its advertisement – 'DEATH OF WHITE SURREY' – features in large font, midway down the playbill.

William Cooke (*c.* 1807–1886), equestrian and lessee of Astley's Amphitheatre from 1853 until 1860, originally presented William West's modified version of Colley Cibber's *Richard III* as a three-act equestrian drama at Astley's Circus on 4 August 1856. James Holloway from the Theatre Royal, Edinburgh, played Richard; and Henry Reeves played Richmond – but Cooke's trained horses were the stars. The horses were always the main attraction at Astley's and the playbill for the original production noted that extra locations had been added to the play to ensure as many opportunities as possible of featuring them, although none 'but what the original text of Shakespeare has given authority for'.[1]

Spoken drama was the sole preserve of the Theatres Royal before the Theatre Regulations Act of 1843, and no minor, lesser-denominated theatre could present such drama without including music, to circumvent the law. The situation had changed by 1856 when Cooke presented *Richard III* as a 'hippodrama', or entertainment featuring horses as actors, but stirring orchestral music still accompanied every equine entrance. As patrons were informed, 'Scarcely in any Play of Shakespeare's are there so many references made to the Noble Horse, as in *Richard III* – their introduction consequently necessitates Music more frequently than is ordinarily given, but its recurrence has been avoided as much as possible.'[2]

Circuses like Astley's were permanent buildings, incorporating both a traditional stage and a circus ring, with ramps connecting the two. During his tenure at Astley's, Cooke produced four of Shakespeare's plays as equestrian dramas – as well as *Richard III*, *Macbeth*, *Katherine and Petruchio* (Garrick's version of *The Taming of the Shrew*), and *Henry IV, Part One*. The last act of *Richard III*, as presented by Cooke, featuring the Battle of

Bosworth Field, was the most dramatic of all – a riot of equine action, clashing swords and martial music, ending with resounding cries of victory and a tableau of general carnage. The production was such a success that by October 1856 Cooke joined the prevailing fashion for so-called 'archaeological accuracy' in stage design and re-costumed it after paintings at Hampton Court.[3] Its influence even pervaded the West End, and when Charles Kean revived *Richard II* at the Princess's Theatre in March 1857, he included actual horses in his production.

Richard III ran at Astley's until 22 November 1856 for an uninterrupted run of ninety-seven performances, almost equalling the ground-breaking hundred-night run of Charles Kean's 1855 *Henry VIII* at the Princess's Theatre. In December 1856, Cooke alternated *Richard III* with his version of *Macbeth* for a week, revived it briefly in 1857 and 1858, and chose the last act for his Farewell Benefit. He would have wanted this playbill to be as eye-catching as possible because it marked his retirement from the management of Astley's, and his last appearance on his favourite charger, Raven. The larger the audience the playbill attracted, the more Cooke would receive personally as the recipient of the Benefit.

Printed with a medley of different letterforms, this playbill features two dramatic woodcut illustrations – especially useful for catching attention. The first image, originally published as an engraving in the *Illustrated London News* depicts the moment in Act Five when White Surrey falls in battle and Richard mercilessly continues setting about his enemies, two at a time.[4] The second shows the comic moment in the equestrian pantomime *Harlequin Tom Moody, or, Old Towler, the Huntsman and the Goddess Diana*, when a fox hunt and a field of Derby Day racehorses become embroiled in the Harlequinade, complete with shocked shopkeepers, a fainting customer, hunting dogs, Clown and Pantaloon. *Richard III* and a comic pantomime on the same bill may seem an unusual notion today but in the mid-nineteenth century it was typical circus fare that satisfied customers in overflowing houses.

1. Playbill in V&A Collection, Astley's Circus, 4 August 1856.
2. *Ibid.*
3. According to the *Theatrical Journal*, 8 October 1856.
4. *Illustrated London News*, 6 September 1856.

ASTLEY'S
AMPHITHEATRE.

EQUESTRIAN & DRAMATIC ATTRACTIONS
WITHOUT PARALELL.

MORNING PERFORMANCES!
PANTOMIME AND HORSEMANSHIP,
On SATURDAY, FEBRUARY 4th, and 11th, Each Day at TWO o'Clock.

MONDAY, JANUARY 30th, 1860.

☞ FAREWELL BENEFIT
OF

Mr. WILLIAM COOKE.

In announcing his Last Benefit as a Performer from the management of ASTLEY'S AMPHITHEATRE, Mr. COOKE craves with humble gratitude his sincere thanks to his NUMEROUS PATRONS and THE PUBLIC, for all favours during the seven years of his Lesseeship.

ON THIS NIGHT ONLY
MR. GEORGE HODGSON,
The POPULAR IRISH COMEDIAN SINGS and COMIC SINGER, has kindly volunteered his services, and will appear in his Extraordinary MEDLEY of COMICALITIES.

By particular request and by permission, the Last Act of Shakespeare's Tragedy of

RICHARD III.

FINELY ILLUSTRATED with a GRAND and STARTLING EQUESTRIAN EFFECTS,

BOSWORTH FIELD; The FIGHT; The SLAIN; and

DEATH of "WHITE SURREY."

THE GRAND PRODUCTIONS AND OLYMPIC CIRCLE SCENES

Illustrating the MASTER ALFRED COOKE Fantastic Reflexions on a very small School in

MARINER JACK, or the YOUNG MIDDY AFLOAT.

Followed by the superb exhibition

THE HIGH SCHOOL OF MANEGE,

By MISS MANDA COOKE in the RONDESVOUS WONDERFULL.

ENCHANTING EQUITATION

By MISS EMILY COOKE who will convey her unusual speed of the Manege to the most astonishing, highly toned and sweetest

SUPERIOR ILLUSTRATIONS IN RIDING

By Mr. WILLIAM COOKE, on his handsome Menage Charger, "Raven"

PHÆTON THE CHARIOTEER OF THE SUN !

The incredible Comedians and Comic Epitome of the CLOWNS and PRESTIDENES Messrs. FRÈRES and SYLVESTER, will contribute to the Arts in the Arena

THE GRAND EQUESTRIAN PANTOMIME Entitled HARLEQUIN

TOM MOODY,

⸸ Or, Old Towler, the Huntsman and the Goddess Diana,

Has not lost one particle of its great attraction, In scope of the Harlequinade, a representation of the DERBY DAY, or Horse Racing in reality, giving a vivid picture of all the scenes and exciting incidents of that truly English Sport and Pastime. ☞ The Characters are small bills. ☜ The whole concluding with

THE ASTONISHING ASBESTINE OR

SALAMANDER STEED

COMPLETELY ENVELOPED IN A SHOWER OF FIRE.

On TUESDAY JANUARY 31st, and During the Week,

RICHARD III.

New Features in the Circle and the Comic Pantomime.

Prices:—PRIVATE BOXES, £1 1s. and upwards. DRESS CIRCLE, 4s.
BOXES, 3s. PIT, 2s. LOWER GALLERY, 1s. GALLERY, 6d.
Stage Manager. Mr R. PHILLIPS. Equestrian Director; Mr W. COOKE.

DOORS OPEN at Half-past 6 ½. Commence to commence at 6½ o'clock.
BOX OFFICE OPEN DAILY, from ELEVEN till FOUR, under the direction of Mr. R. SMITH,
Where Parties Hiring the Boxes from 4 to 7 Tennets, and Places may be secured, also all the schemes listener, at the War or Back.
NO BOOKING FEES.

The Rival Richards or Sheakspear in danger!

William Heath, *The Rival Richards, or, Sheakspear in danger* (c. 1814)

William Shakespeare is the central figure in this satirical print, the human rope in a vicious tug of war between (left) Charles Mayne Young (1777–1856) and (right) Edmund Kean (1787–1833). Both actors are costumed as Richard III, and each calls out apposite lines from the play while struggling to gain supremacy over the unfortunate playwright.[1] Shakespeare cries 'Murder! Murder!' as he looks fearfully towards the lanky Young, but the diminutive Kean is winning.

Satirical prints sold well in the early nineteenth century, before the advent of illustrated newspapers. Print-sellers could react speedily to topics of public interest and scandal, and the issue here was the relative success of these actors as Richard III, following the overwhelming critical approval the twenty-six-year-old Kean had received when he first played the role on the London stage at the Theatre Royal, Drury Lane, on Saturday, 12 February 1814.

Richard was Kean's second major Shakespearean role at Drury Lane. On 26 January 1814 the then unknown actor had demonstrated a completely new style of emotional and energetic acting with his captivating portrayal of Shylock in *The Merchant of Venice*. When Kean played it again on 1 and 3 February, the critics were out in force to report rapturously on his fresh interpretation. Kean chose Richard III as his next major role to consolidate this success, and to demonstrate his mastery of the lengthy part that had been associated with the great David Garrick ever since he took London by storm with it in 1741.[2] The ecstatic reaction to Kean's Richard meant that Drury Lane had a bankable new star in their firmament, and a smash-hit production. After the debut of his next major tragic role, Hamlet, on 12 March, Kean appeared at the Lane in all three plays each week, but his Richard drew the greatest crowds, jostling outside the theatre to gain admittance. In a vain attempt to combat Kean's pulling power, Thomas Harris, the manager of the rival Covent Garden Theatre, presented Young as Richard III on 14 May.

173

Ten years Kean's senior, Young had a mellifluous voice and had already established himself at Covent Garden with roles including Mark Antony in *Antony and Cleopatra* and Othello. He had worked with the leading tragedian of the day, John Philip Kemble, and by 1814 was generally considered his successor, but like Kemble's icy portrayal of the villainous Richard, Mayne's interpretation of the part was considered too cerebral and restrained in comparison to Kean's fiery rendition. Harris, the despondent manager, features in this print, standing outside his theatre and complaining: 'they are too Kean for me & will Harris me to death.' In contrast, on Kean's side the brewer, MP, and major shareholder of Drury Lane, Samuel Whitbread, is seen capering delightedly outside his theatre, a pint of Whitbread's in hand. The legend on the façade of Covent Garden – 'the best Booth in the Fair… what's a Stage without Horses' – refers to its fondness for hippodrama, or plays with horses, to attract audiences; that on Drury Lane's – 'Real Home Brew'd' – to its associations with Whitbread's brewery.

William Heath's original etching of this subject was first published by the London publisher S. Knight on 18 May 1814, four days after Young's appearance as Richard at Covent Garden. Heath (*c.* 1795–1840) was a caricaturist and illustrator whose first satirical prints were published in 1809 when he was only fourteen. His earliest work was as an illustrator of books on military themes, but he also produced portraits, reverting to caricatures in the 1820s, published individually or in sets. In Heath's original, Kean is on the left and Young on the right, but this print is reversed since it is a mirror copy produced in Dublin by William McCleary, a print-seller who specialised in the early part of his career, from 1791 onwards, in publishing unattributed copies of English prints. His earliest premises were in Lower Ormond Quay, but by 1798 he had relocated to larger premises on Nassau Street overlooking College Green, one of Dublin's most fashionable shopping areas. The fact that McCleary chose to reproduce this subject for sale in Ireland says much about the amount of interest there was in the affairs of the London theatre in Dublin at the time.

1. In the version adapted from Shakespeare in 1700 by Colley Cibber (1671–1757).
2. At Goodman's Fields Theatre, 19 October 1741.

Papier mâché bust of Shakespeare, produced to advertise Flowers Ales (mid-twentieth century)

This likeness of Shakespeare was reproduced in large numbers in the twentieth century in a variety of colours, both in papier mâché and in ceramic form, and was used in inns and public houses to promote Flowers Ales, often with printed slogans such as 'Pick Flowers Keg Bitter'. The image is based on the memorial bust of Shakespeare in Holy Trinity Church, Stratford-upon-Avon, by Gheerart Janssen, erected following Shakespeare's death in 1616. The V&A cherishes this image of Shakespeare in recognition of the pivotal role of the Flower family in realising the dream of building a theatre dedicated to Shakespeare in the town of his birth. The founder of the brewery, Edward Flower, was a major financial contributor to the Shakespeare Tercentenary Celebrations held in Stratford in 1864. His son, Charles Edward Flower (1830–1892), who took over as head of the brewing firm after his father's death in 1883, bought up land on the waterside in Stratford close to the site of the Rotunda built for Garrick's 1769 Shakespeare Jubilee, and donated it to Stratford Town Council as a site for a Shakespeare Memorial Theatre. In addition to a cash sum of £22,700, he gave further land to create gardens around the theatre, together with the freehold of the nearby properties, whose rents could be used for maintenance of the building. Completed in 1879, the theatre opened with a production of *Much Ado About Nothing*. From then on, it was used for an annual Shakespeare Festival lasting for several weeks, with its facilities available for use by local residents for the rest of the year.[1]

A competition held to choose a design for the new theatre attracted twenty-five entries. The winning design by Dodgshun and Unsworth combined Tudor and Gothic styles, with pinnacles, turrets and ornamental chimneys, and featured ornamental striped red-and-white and chequered blue-and-red brickwork. The overall effect earned comparison with 'a German fairy-tale castle' and was in fact contemporaneous with Wagner's Bayreuth, completed in 1876. Although initially admired, the design of the building went out of fashion. The interior of the theatre was a horseshoe-shaped auditorium with orchestra stalls, a dress circle supported on pillars, and a gallery accessed from outside by a separate staircase. A library and art gallery were completed in 1881, linked to the dress circle of the theatre by a shallow arched bridge, and a tower housing offices and a water tank in case of fire was added in 1884. Unfortunately, the tower burned down before the water could be used to save the theatre when it was destroyed by fire in 1926. Only the library and art gallery were rescued and now provide access to the Swan, completed in 1986. The Swan occupies the space of the conference centre which had been created in 1932 from the burnt-out shell of the old theatre's auditorium.

Archibald Flower, nephew of the theatre's founder and Chair of the Governors, backed the Town Council's preference to keep the existing waterside site as the location for a new theatre, and launched an international competition for the design of the building. The winner was Elisabeth Scott (1898–1972), second cousin of Giles Gilbert Scott, architect of Liverpool's Anglican Cathedral, and great-niece of Sir George Gilbert Scott, who designed St Pancras Station and the Albert Memorial. In her acceptance speech, the architect declared herself to be a modernist, and the exterior of her building was uncompromisingly modern, softened only with patterns of pink and silver-grey bricks, the sole decoration being five carved stone panels above the main entrance. Materials of the finest quality were used throughout the interior, the only problem was the theatre itself: the fan-shaped auditorium created a distance between actors and audience which was very difficult to overcome. Many years later Festival Director W. Bridges-Adams wrote that Scott had created 'the theatre, of all theatres, in England in which it is hardest to make an audience laugh or cry'.[2]

1. See Marian J. Pringle, *The Theatres of Stratford-upon-Avon, 1875–1992.*
2. David Ward, *Transformation*, p. 9.

FLOWERS

Henry Dawe, engraving after John Greenhill's portrait (1664) of Henry Harris as Cardinal Wolsey in *Henry VIII* (1820)

This engraving of Henry Harris (*c.* 1634–1704) acting the role of Cardinal Wolsey in Shakespeare and Fletcher's *Henry VIII* is based on the earliest known image of an identified actor in role as a Shakespearean character. The engraving is from the oil painting now in the Garrick Club, which is a copy made by Horace Walpole from one of the chalk or pastel portraits by John Greenhill (1644–1676), now in the Ashmolean Museum and Magdalen College, Oxford. Henry Harris was a good friend of Pepys, who often mentions him in his diaries, and liked him so much that he commissioned a portrait of him from the painter John Hayls. The part of King Henry VIII was played by Thomas Betterton in the production, and there is a direct link from his performance that leads back to Shakespeare, as recorded by John Downes the prompter: 'The part of the King was so right and justly done by Mr Betterton, he being Instructed in it by Sir William [Davenant], who had it from old Mr Lowen, that had his Instructions from Mr Shakespear himself.'[1] Acting for the King's Men, John Lowin (1576–1653) had starred in the title role when *Henry VIII* was first performed in 1613. Henry Harris's performance as Cardinal Wolsey was highly rated by Downes, 'he doing it with such just State, Port, and Mien, that I dare affirm, none hitherto has Equall'd him'.[2]

Skilled in both music and acting, Harris performed the songs in many plays, including *The Tempest*, with Pepys recording that 'between two acts, I went out to Mr Harris and got him to repeat to me the words of the Echo, while I writ them down'.[3] Gossiping with Harris about the forthcoming production of Jonson's *Catiline* by the rival King's Company, Pepys learns that the King is giving £500 to make 'sixteen scarlett robes', but later Pepys hears from his friend Mrs Knepp that *Catiline* 'for want of the clothes which the King promised them, will not be acted for a good while', in the event not until almost a year later.[4] The success of a production depended greatly upon the fineness of the costumes: the Earl of Orrery's verse play *Henry V* was staged in 1664 by Davenant's Company in the actual Coronation robes lent by the King.

The revival of *Henry VIII* in 1663 was a spectacular success, particularly because, as Downes records, it was staged 'all new Cloath'd in proper Habits: The King's was new, [and] all the Lords, the Cardinals, the Bishops, the Doctors, Proctors, Lawyers, Tip-Staves... it continu'd Acting 15 Days together with general Applause.'[5] When Count Cominges saw the revival of the play three years later he was particularly impressed by the authenticity of the costumes: 'Cardinal Wolsey appears there with his bonnet, and Cranmer, Archbishop of Canterbury, with his rocket [vestment] and cape, and even, if I remember aright, his pallium [mantle].'[6] The trend towards authenticity in historical costume was so strong that Restoration actors sometimes discarded their wigs when playing leading roles; the illustration from Rowe's 1709 Shakespeare edition shows Henry VIII as he appeared in Holbein's portrait, with the minor characters wearing contemporary Restoration costume and wigs. When a production of *Pompey the Great* was staged entirely in then-modern dress, there was strenuous objection from the audience: 'Caesar was sent in with his feather & muff, till he was hiss'd off the Stage.'[7]

1. John Downes, *Roscius Anglicanus*, p. 55.

2. *Ibid.*, p. 56.

3. *Diary of Samuel Pepys*, vol. 9, p. 195.

4. *Ibid.*, vol. 8, p. 575; vol 9, p. 20.

5. Downes, *Roscius Anglicanus*, pp. 55–6.

6. Emmett L. Avery and Arthur H. Scouten, *The London Stage 1660–1700*, pp. xcii–xciii.

7. *Ibid.*, p. xciii.

66 Spirits of peace, where are ye? Are ye all gone? **99**
Henry VIII (4.2)

58

Henry Fuseli, *Queen Katharine's Dream*, detail (c. 1789)

Arriving in London from Switzerland in 1764, Henry Fuseli (Johann Heinrich Füssli, 1741–1825) became a lifelong enthusiast of Shakespeare, having seen David Garrick (1717–1779) acting the roles of Macbeth and Richard III. His painting of Queen Katharine's vision in Act Four of *Henry VIII* was exhibited at the Royal Academy in 1781. That version is now in the collection of Fylde Borough Council in Lancashire. Another, which only exists in fragmentary form, is held by the V&A. *Henry VIII* – among Shakespeare's final collaborations (with John Fletcher) – dramatises the fall of Cardinal Wolsey, the arrest of Archbishop Cranmer, and the sadness of King Henry's rejected Queen, whose death is foreshadowed in the dream. The detailed stage direction in the play's unique Folio text describes a procession and a dance to music by six white-robed figures wearing golden masks and carrying garlands, which they hold over the Queen's head, then vanish. The Queen on awaking says:

> Saw you not, even now, a blessed troop
> Invite me to a banquet; whose bright faces
> Cast a thousand beams upon me, like the sun?
> They promis'd me eternal happiness,
> And brought me garlands…

> (4.2.87–91)

Fuseli imagined the spirits as naked female figures who carry crowns rather than garlands, to suggest that the Queen's lost role as the King's consort will be made up to her in Heaven. He was the first artist to paint this scene, and his paintings became the basis for the staging of the play by the Kemble family and their successor, Charles Kean, well into the mid-nineteenth century, though their spirits were decorously clad. Advancement in lighting and stage technology enabled the apparitions to be shown descending from Heaven in a wide shaft of light, an effect made possible by 'limelight' (in use from 1837), in which a block of lime was burned in a mixture of oxygen and hydrogen, producing brilliant illumination which could be directed in a hand-held spotlight. The scene was a favourite with Queen Victoria, who saw Charles Kean's performance at the Princess's Theatre in 1855. She recorded in her diary the splendour of Queen Katharine's dream, 'with the angels descending on a sunbeam, waving palm branches and holding out to her a crown of the same', and she commissioned artists to make watercolour sketches of the plays she most enjoyed, with her album in the Royal Library at Windsor preserving numerous highlights from Shakespeare's plays.[1]

Charles Kean's 1850s productions were acclaimed for their gorgeous pageantry and beautiful spectacle, based on meticulous historical research. One of the stream of angels floating in limelight in Queen Katharine's vision was the young Ellen Terry, who recalled:

> in *Henry VIII* I was 'top angel' in the vision, and I remember that the heat of the gas at that dizzy height made me sick at the dress-rehearsal!... The production of *Henry VIII* at the Princess's was one of Charles Kean's best efforts... which I have never seen surpassed... Wolsey [was] his best part after, perhaps, his Richard II. Still, the lady who used to stand ready with a tear-bottle to catch his tears as he came off after his last scene rather overdid her admiration.[2]

Henry Irving mounted a spectacular production of *Henry VIII* in 1892, which rivalled Kean's in scenic grandeur. Designed by Hawes Craven (1837–1910), it featured a magnificent Tudor hall, and a splendid Gothic setting for the final baptism scene.[3] Herbert Beerbohm Tree's 1910 production strove to outdo even this, particularly in the tableau of Queen Katharine's dream, where:

> illuminated angels... crowned with wreaths or garlands, passed down from hand to hand a crown of gold leaves... the last angel doubtless holding it in the air in a tableau; from the audience it would have seemed as if she were holding it over the Queen's head.[4]

An American critic, finding the style of the production outmoded, remained unimpressed, declaring that the vision 'had a pronounced resemblance to an Easter card on sale in a drug store in Kansas City', especially when 'the white-robed angels began to wave their arms at the dying Queen'.[5]

1. George Rowell, *Queen Victoria Goes to the Theatre*, p. 56.

2. Ellen Terry, *The Story of My Life*, p. 20.

3. George C.D. Odell, *Shakespeare from Betterton to Irving*, vol. 2, pp. 444–6.

4. Michael Booth, *Victorian Spectacular Theatre*, p. 151.

5. *Ibid.*

Louis François Roubiliac, terracotta model for a statue of Shakespeare (1757)

Louis François Roubiliac (1702–1762), a Huguenot, who came to London around 1730, achieved fame with his statue of Handel in Vauxhall Gardens, now in the V&A. He was also a prolific sculptor of Shakespeare, and the studio sale after his death included more than a dozen busts and figures of the dramatist, who was increasingly becoming recognised as the nation's favourite poet. The great actor David Garrick (1717–1779) commissioned Roubiliac in 1757 to carve a statue of Shakespeare for his 'Shakespeare Temple' beside the Thames at his home in Hampton. The terracotta figure pictured here is the model for the original, which now stands in pride of place in the entrance foyer of the British Library, having been acquired by the British Museum in 1823 after the death of the actor's ninety-eight-year-old widow the previous year. A laser copy of the statue made of resin today stands in the Temple itself.

The likeness of Shakespeare is taken by Roubiliac from the Chandos portrait, of which he owned a copy, and it is believed that Garrick modelled for the figure. The original portrait, thought to have been painted by Shakespeare's fellow actor John Taylor between 1600 and 1610, formed part of the collection of the third Duke of Chandos in the late-eighteenth century. It was the first painting presented to the National Portrait Gallery in the year of its founding, 1856. The design of Garrick's Shakespeare Temple, with its circular dome and classical pillars, is modelled on the Roman temple built by Lord Burlington in his grounds at Chiswick House. Garrick's temple was the first building ever to be dedicated to Shakespeare, placing the dramatist on a level with the classical gods and muses to whom temples were customarily dedicated. In 1762, Garrick commissioned Zoffany, then working as the assistant to the artist Benjamin Wilson, to paint portraits of himself taking tea with his wife and friends by the River Thames, and conversing with his wife on the steps of the temple accompanied by their dogs.

The steady rise of Shakespeare to the position of national poet is witnessed by the erection of the memorial to him in Westminster Abbey in

1741. The statue by Peter Gaspar Scheemakers shows Shakespeare leaning on a pedestal framed by classical pillars. At the foot of the pedestal are the carved heads of Henry V and Richard III, together with the head of Elizabeth I. *Richard III* was extremely popular in the eighteenth century and *Henry V* had become synonymous with patriotism and was played regularly during the Seven Years War (1754–1763).

Garrick presented a statue of Shakespeare cast in lead to the town of Stratford-upon-Avon in 1769, which is still in place over the entrance to the Town Hall. The statue, by John Cheere (1709–1787), is a reworked version of a marble statue at Wilton House, itself based on the Westminster Abbey memorial. In return, Garrick was given a document conveying the freedom of the town in a box made of wood from a mulberry tree said to have been planted by Shakespeare himself, which had been cut down in 1756. The Corporation of Stratford commisioned Garrick's friend Thomas Gainsborough (1727–1788) to paint a portrait of Garrick communing with a bust of Shakespeare, which hung in the Town Hall. Although the picture was destroyed by fire in 1946, a fine mezzotint by Valentine Green (1739–1813) captures the charm of the original painting, of which Gainsborough wrote to Garrick that he intended to take the form of Shakespeare 'from his pictures and statues, just enough to preserve his likeness… and supply a soul from his works'.[1]

1. *The Private Correspondence of David Garrick*, ed. James Boaden, vol. 1, p. 328.

Tragedies

66 O excellent motion! O exceeding puppet! 99
The Two Gentlemen of Verona (2.1)

60

Still from the National Video Archive of Performance recording of Gregory Doran's puppet production of *Venus and Adonis* (2004)

The V&A is home to the National Video Archive of Performance, which was launched in 1992. This recording of the narrative poem *Venus and Adonis*, performed as a puppet play, is part of a growing collection of recordings made by the museum for educational and research purposes. Directed by Gregory Doran, the play was devised by the RSC in conjunction with the Little Angel Theatre, based in Islington, where the production had its initial run in October and early November 2004, before transferring to The Other Place at Stratford-upon-Avon. Doran describes how he was inspired to perform Shakespeare's poem with puppets after visiting the Bunraku Puppet Theatre in Osaka, Japan, when touring with the RSC. There he saw masked puppet-masters dressed in black, working one-third-life-sized puppets, acting out a narrated poem to the accompaniment of music. In *Venus and Adonis*, Doran uses Bunraku-style puppets for the main narrative, but with the faces of the puppeteers visible to the audience. Smaller, stringed puppets are used for the entrance and departure of Venus in a chariot in the form of a seashell, pulled by silver doves, drawing inspiration from Jacobean court masques, with animal shadow puppets enhancing the hunting scenes. The figures of Venus and Adonis are created from wood, leather, and foam rubber, and Gregory Doran paid tribute to the skill of the puppet-makers drawn from across the world: 'Czech-born maker Jan Zalud shaping the classical lines of Adonis's fine features; Stefan Fichert from Munich, creating the capricious half-life-size horses and the shadow puppets; South African John Roberts expertly honing and stringing the limbs of the marionettes; and Simon Auton carving the wild boar.'[1]

The production revived a long tradition of puppet plays performed for adult audiences: the story of the classical lovers Hero and Leander is performed as a puppet play in Ben Jonson's *Bartholomew Fair* (1614), while Charlotte Charke, daughter of Colley Cibber (the playwright and actor manager at the Drury Lane Theatre), set up a company in 1738 to perform theatre in miniature as puppet plays, a venture that required a licence from the Lord Chamberlain. *Henry IV* and *Richard III* were in her repertory, and *Henry VIII*, *Romeo and Juliet*, *As You Like It* and *Julius Caesar* regularly featured in the repertoire of eighteenth- and nineteenth-century puppeteers.[2]

Published in 1593, when the theatres were closed due to plague, *Venus and Adonis* went through sixteen editions before 1640, and was by far the most popular of Shakespeare's works in this period. In Doran's hour-long performance, Shakespeare's abridged poem is narrated by Michael Pennington, to a guitar accompaniment by Steve Russell. Taking place within a miniature gilded proscenium, the play is prefaced by a prologue, in which a balding Shakespeare attempts to present a bound copy of *Venus and Adonis* to the poem's dedicatee, the golden-haired Earl of Southampton, whose attention is engaged elsewhere with a beautiful, richly dressed lady. Shakespeare addresses the young Earl in the words of his Sonnet 26, sending a 'written embassage' to the 'Lord of my love', so linking Venus's wooing of Adonis with the love expressed for an unresponsive young man by Shakespeare himself in so many of his sonnets.

All the reviewers, even those confessing to a prejudice against plays performed by puppets, were enchanted by the production. J.D. Atkinson writes: 'The smallest gestures of the puppets are so beautifully observed and imitated that it is hard to believe these little people aren't real. Venus uses her superhuman strength to drag Adonis off his horse, he primly removes her wandering hand from his thigh, she faints theatrically and sneaks a peek to make sure Adonis is paying attention... when Pennington lists the sterling qualities of Adonis's stallion, the creature shows off outrageously, beaming at the audience and flicking his tail.'[3] When Adonis finally gives in to Venus, the entwined couple levitate into the air in ecstasy, but Adonis's continuing preference is for hunting rather than love, and the mood of the poem rapidly changes to tragedy. Adonis is killed by the boar, the sun appears in the sky as a golden skull, and Venus finds herself trapped in Death's huge, bony hands. The death of her Adonis leads to the Goddess of Love's chilling prophecy that 'Sorrow on love hereafter shall attend' and to her curse: 'Sith in his prime death doth my love destroy / They that love best their loves shall not enjoy.'[4]

---

1. *Guardian*, 13 October 2004.

2. George Speaight, *The History of the English Puppet Theatre*, pp. 102–8.

3. J.D. Atkinson, British Theatre Guide Review (2004): <www.britishtheatreguide.info/reviews/venusadonis-rev>, accessed 14 October 2013.

4. *Venus and Adonis*, lines 1136, 1163–4.

Tyrone Guthrie's *Troilus and Cressida*, Old Vic (1956)

Certain names recur throughout the V&A Theatre and Performance Department's collections. The career of director Tyrone Guthrie (1900–1971) is represented by a wide range of objects, including headdresses, drawings, designs and photographs. Guthrie was never afraid to experiment, and his inventive approach to Shakespeare delighted and infuriated audiences in equal measure. For the Old Vic he directed twenty-one productions, notably a celebrated pastiche Victorian staging of *A Midsummer Night's Dream* in 1937 and a modern-dress *Hamlet* in 1938, famous for the umbrellas carried at Ophelia's funeral. His four productions at Stratford-upon-Avon included a 1959 *All's Well That Ends Well* that mixed Edwardian aristocrats with 1940s soldiers. Guthrie worked on both sides of the Atlantic and, in 1953, was responsible for the first productions of the Shakespeare Festival at Stratford, Ontario, on a permanent open stage which he had co-designed. In 1963, his *Hamlet*, again set in the twentieth century, opened a similar theatre in Minneapolis, which was named after him. A fervent champion of the open stage, Guthrie disliked the divide between actors and audience in conventional proscenium-arch theatres, but some of his best-regarded work was presented on proscenium stages at London's Old Vic and the Shakespeare Memorial Theatre in Stratford-upon-Avon.

In 1956, Guthrie directed *Troilus and Cressida* for the Old Vic. Though the theatre had an impressive record of presenting the lesser-known plays of Shakespeare, this was only its second *Troilus*. Guthrie's production, staged as the Suez Crisis loomed, was a witty anti-war satire that set the action immediately before the First World War. Designer Frederick Crooke (1908–1991) dressed it in 'the trappings of the last epoch which thought war glamorous'.[1] The Greeks wore Prussian helmets and greatcoats, the Trojans were Ruritanian cavalry officers in canary yellow, and Paul Rogers as Pandarus was first seen dressed for Ascot in grey top hat and tails and carrying binoculars. Wendy Hiller's Helen of Troy, a faded beauty in shocking pink, was summed up by *The Times* as 'the sort of Edwardian actress who sips champagne from her dancing shoe'.[2] Helen's one scene took place in a small conservatory where she was discovered 'sitting at a highly decorated piano, smoking through a long black holder and playing sentimental ditties to Paris.'[3] Pandarus joined them and sang at the piano while the tipsy lovers drank and flirted. Audiences laughed, and the futility of a war fought over a foolish woman was neatly conveyed.

The scene is captured here by photographer Houston Rogers (1901–1970), whose archive of 45,000 negatives, covering plays, operas, ballets and portraits from the early 1930s to the year of his death, was acquired by the V&A in 1980. Although he was not a prolific photographer of drama, averaging about twenty plays each year, Rogers photographed many London productions of Shakespeare, including Gielgud's 1937 *Richard II* at the Queen's Theatre and *Romeo and Juliet*, directed by Franco Zeffirelli, at the Old Vic in 1960. Rogers preferred to light his own photo sessions on stage, creating clear and detailed images. His photographs of *Troilus and Cressida* are the most widely reproduced pictures of this production.

1. Kenneth Tynan, *Observer*, 8 April 1956.

2. *The Times*, 4 April 1956.

3. Mary Clarke, *Shakespeare at the Old Vic: 1955–6.*

Thomas Lawrence, portrait of John Philip Kemble as Coriolanus (*c.* 1800)

John Philip Kemble (1757–1823), and his sister Sarah Siddons, were the two leading actors of their generation, although John Philip Kemble initially trained for the priesthood. He epitomised a dignified, statuesque acting style which is captured in this famous portrait by Thomas Lawrence (1769–1830), who was from childhood an ardent friend of the Kemble family. The painting, which was bequeathed to the museum by the Reverend Alexander Dyce, is a scaled-down version of the life-sized portrait in Tate Britain, which hangs alongside Lawrence's painting of Kemble in the role of Hamlet, holding Yorick's skull. Kemble's stately, classical style of acting led to him being described as 'an icycle on the bust of tragedy', in contrast with the dynamic style of Edmund Kean, whose acting was famously likened by Coleridge to 'reading Shakespeare by flashes of lightning'.[1] Kemble was especially successful in his portrayal of Coriolanus, a character preoccupied with his own nobility, and Kemble's biographer James Boaden describes how Kemble in majestic mood remonstrated with Drury Lane proprietor Richard Brinsley Sheridan: '"I am an EAGLE, whose wings have been bound down by frosts and snow; but now I shake my pinions, and cleave into the general air, unto which I am born." He then deliberately resumed his seat, and looked as if he had relieved himself from insupportable thraldom.'[2] As well as being an actor, Kemble was a gifted stage manager and designer, who was interested in historical accuracy in costumes and settings. His fondness for early playtexts led to his being nicknamed 'black-letter Jack' on account of the close gothic type of early printed books. He was appointed stage manager at Drury Lane by Sheridan in 1788 but the two men did not see eye to eye, and Kemble left in 1802 and bought a holding in the Covent Garden Theatre in 1803.

He first starred in *Coriolanus* at Drury Lane in 1789, and it was this role he chose as his final performance before his retirement from the stage thirty years later. Hamlet was also a role to which he repeatedly returned, although he was censured by Hazlitt for the rigidity of his interpretation: 'He played it like a man in armour, with a determined inveteracy of purpose, in one undeviating straight line.'[3] The arrival of Edmund Kean upon the acting scene led inevitably to comparisons between his and Kemble's very different styles:

> The fineness of Mr Kemble's figure may be supposed to have led to that statue-like appearance, which his acting was sometimes too apt to assume: as the diminutiveness of Mr Kean's person has probably compelled him to bustle about too much... If Mr Kemble were to remain in the same posture for half a hour, his figure would only excite admiration: if Mr Kean were to stand still only for a moment, the contrary effect would be apparent.[4]

Coriolanus's elitist politics bring out the radical in Hazlitt: 'The whole dramatic moral of Coriolanus is, that those who have little shall have less, and that those who have much shall take all... The people are poor, therefore they ought to be starved. They are slaves, therefore they ought to be beaten. They work hard, therefore they ought to be treated as beasts of burden.' Hazlitt mischievously punctures Kemble's patrician posturing by remarking that 'Kemble's supercilious airs and *nonchalance* remind one of the unaccountable abstracted air, the contracted eye-brows and suspended chin of a man who is just going to sneeze.'[5]

1. Cited in Geoffrey Ashton and Iain Mackintosh (eds.), *Royal Opera House Retrospective 1732–1982*, p. 80; Samuel Taylor Coleridge, *Table Talk*, entry for 27 April 1823.

2. Ashton and Mackintosh (eds.), *Royal Opera House Retrospective 1732–1982*, p. 80.

3. William Hazlitt, *A View of the English Stage*, p. 457.

4. *Ibid.*, p. 459.

5. *Ibid.*, pp. 392–3.

Motley (Margaret Harris), set design for *Coriolanus* (1952)

The design team Motley (sisters Margaret and Sophia Harris and their friend Elizabeth Montgomery) had their first success in 1932 when John Gielgud (1904–2000) asked them to create sets and costumes for the production of *Romeo and Juliet* that he was directing for the Oxford University Dramatic Society. It was the beginning of a long association with Gielgud and of highly successful careers for all three of the Motley team. They designed over 300 productions in Britain and America, their theatre work encompassing new drama and the classics, opera, musicals and ballet, and including Shakespeare at Stratford, the Old Vic, and in the West End. The Harris sisters and Montgomery worked in a very cooperative way with no one taking credit for individual designs, and the Motley name became something of a brand, used by all three women whether working alone or in collaboration. Professor Michael Mullin, who established the Motley Collection at the University of Illinois Library, considered that 'In the best sense, theirs was the art that concealed art – not a flashy "concept" stamped on the play, but sets and costumes that helped the performers to give it shape and meaning.'[1]

In 1940, Elizabeth Montgomery (1902–1993) and Margaret Harris (1904–2000) went to work in New York, where Montgomery remained and married, developing a career as a Broadway costume designer under the Motley name. Harris returned to Britain, and continued to design as Motley, with and without her sister Sophia (1900–1966). In 1946, Margaret designed *Antony and Cleopatra* at the Piccadilly Theatre for director Glen Byam Shaw, and this began a working relationship which continued throughout the 1940s and 1950s, and included twelve Shakespeare productions. Byam Shaw, who was to become the Memorial Theatre's co-director in 1953, first directed at Stratford in 1952 with Margaret Harris designing his productions of *Coriolanus* and *As You Like It*. *Coriolanus*, which featured the theatre's Artistic Director, Anthony Quayle, in the title role, was a typical example of 1950s Stratford Shakespeare, with attractive period settings and good solid performances. Philip Hope-Wallace called it 'a sturdy if not a very deep interpretation, handsomely mounted and most intelligently produced'.[2]

Quayle (1913–1989) had become the Memorial Theatre's director in 1948, when many metropolitan critics regarded Stratford as a provincial backwater, staging hastily prepared productions which did not stand up to comparison with the Old Vic's. Quayle aimed to change all this and put Stratford on the theatrical map. He brought in star names to attract audiences, and designers, like Motley, who could work to West End standards. Though not as star-studded as some productions, *Coriolanus* included Mary Ellis (1897–2003), well known as a leading lady of musical theatre, in her Stratford debut as Volumnia, Laurence Harvey (1928–1973), on the verge of film stardom, as Aufidius, and Michael Hordern (1911–1995) as Menenius. Margaret Harris put the Romans in classically inspired costume and the Volscians in Cretan dress. Her set, described as 'historically austere and dramatically suggestive' by *Theatre World*, comprised a permanent feature of steps leading to an arched gateway, and a wall running across the rear of the stage.[3] When open, the gate represented Rome, and when closed, with a row of spikes added along the top of the wall, it became Corioli. The tall tents, shown here, were placed in front of the fortifications to form Coriolanus's camp outside Rome in Act Five, where Volumnia pleads for her city.

1. Michael Mullin, *Design By Motley*, p. 1.

2. *Manchester Guardian*, 15 March 1952.

3. H.G. Matthews, *Theatre World* 330 (July 1952), p. 18.

SHAKESPEAR

Sketch of Stratford Jubilee Booth or Amphitheatre.

The Rotunda for David Garrick's Shakespeare Jubilee (1769)

The Jubilee at Stratford-upon-Avon in 1769, which missed the bicentenary of Shakespeare's birth by five years, had its inception when David Garrick (1717–1779) was given the freedom of the town in 1768, having promised to give a memorial statue in lead by John Cheere to adorn the exterior of the new town hall, with the interior graced by Gainsborough's idealised portrait of Garrick himself leaning against a pillar supporting a bust of Shakespeare. Gainsborough's portrait was destroyed by fire in 1946 but survives in the engraving by Valentine Green.

The Jubilee celebrations devised by Garrick lasted for three days. Performing actual works by Shakespeare formed no part of his plans; instead, the projected celebrations included a pageant, fireworks and horse races, with 'Catches, Glees, & ballads, all New after dinner'.[1] The high point was the performance by Garrick of his specially composed 'Ode of Dedication' to the statue of Shakespeare, which was extremely well received. This engraving shows the circular wooden structure built on the banks of the River Avon near the site of the present main theatre. Modelled on an earlier Rotunda in Chelsea's Ranelagh Gardens, it accommodated an audience of a thousand people, in addition to singers and musicians. Garrick threw himself into the preparations, driving the composer Charles Dibdin (1745–1814) to distraction: 'I was a slave to it for months,' he complained, 'I set and reset songs to it till my patience was exhausted... He really had not an idea of how to write for music... Matters went on in this train, till at last I was so palpably insulted that I declared I would not go to Stratford.'[2] In the event he relented, arriving at the last minute, waking Mr and Mrs Garrick at five in the morning with a surprise performance of the dawn serenade Garrick had penned, set to the music of guitars and flutes. Then followed a firing of cannon, the ringing of church bells, and a military parade with fife and drums, all before breakfast.

The proceedings of the first day went reasonably to plan, with processions and a performance of Thomas Arne's *Judith*, conducted by the composer. At night there were transparencies of scenes from Shakespeare back-lit by lamps, and a fireworks display. But by the second day, heavy rain had set in; the pageant could not take place and it was too wet for the fireworks. Garrick nevertheless performed his Ode with great success: James Boswell, who appeared in Corsican dress to mark the very successful publication of his travel memoirs, danced until dawn, with water over shoe top, after which the Rotunda was abandoned to the rising flood waters. On the third day the horse racing went ahead despite the water-logged ground: the rain stopped at midday and fireworks and dancing rounded off the celebrations.

Garrick had promised that any profit on the investment of an estimated £50,000 would be given to Stratford Council; in fact he sustained a loss of £2,000, which had to be paid back in instalments. These losses were offset by the spectacular success of the restaging of the rained-off pageant at the Drury Lane Theatre in London, playing over ninety times in 1769–70 to packed houses. One enthusiastic German tourist saw the pageant twenty-eight times and described it in his memoirs:

> In *Macbeth* one saw the big witches' cauldron; in *Coriolanus*, this general's tent, ornamented with weapons, and in *Romeo and Juliet*, Juliet's tomb. When the characters approached the proscenium arch they acted out an important scene from their play in pantomime, whereby everything came wonderfully alive.[3]

The pageant appeared to far better effect on stage than it could ever have done outside in daylight, due to the wizardry of the stage technician James Messink, who used gauzes, lighting and stage machinery to create a mood and atmosphere otherwise unattainable.

1. *Letters of David Garrick*, ed. David M. Little and George M. Kahrl, vol. 2, p. 658.

2. Johanne M. Stochholm, *Garrick's Folly*, p. 34.

3. *Ibid.*, p. 167.

Rudolf Nureyev's tunic as Romeo in his *Romeo and Juliet* for London Festival Ballet (1977)

The costume created for Romeo in Rudolf Nureyev's *Romeo and Juliet* is typical of many theatre costumes in that it presents the illusion of a slashed brocade doublet while in reality comprising a single piece: a light-green silk velvet tunic decorated with silver braid, paint, appliquéd fabrics, and a few sequins. The apparent undershirt is simply two white silk sleeves and a gathered collar attached to the main garment, and the whole is unlined. The doublet is only slightly shaped at the waist, indicating that it is one of the originals made for London Festival Ballet (the company for which Nureyev created the production in 1977), rather than a later remake for other companies. Nureyev (1938–1993) always liked to keep costumes as brief as possible to allow complete freedom of movement. The photograph shows the back of the doublet.

While Romeo's costume is basic, those worn by dancers in less strenuous roles were more elaborate. Visual inspiration came from paintings of the fourteenth and fifteenth century. Fabrics were specially printed in Italy, with designs copied from canvases and frescoes. While Romeo's costume is fastened with Velcro and hooks and eyes (for quick changes), others featured traditional lacings and ties. Some of the women, most notably Rosaline and her friends, wear balzi – high, rounded headdresses worn on artificially high foreheads, which were fashionable in early quattrocento Italy.

As with many ballet productions of *Romeo and Juliet*, the costumes for the opposing factions were colour-coded, with the Montagues appearing in green and white, and the Capulets in shades of red and pink with white. Thus when Romeo gatecrashes the Capulets' ball he covers his green tunic with a red *farsetto* or doublet. The colour-coding goes further, as Rosaline and friends wear blue while Prince Escalus and his attendants wear black *gonnelli* or gowns and high flat hats.

The production was designed by Ezio Frigerio, who was assisted by Franca Squarciapino for the costumes. Like the costumes, Frigerio's sets are inspired by the Italian Renaissance, with the setting for Verona's marketplace based on Piero della Francesca's *The Ideal City*. The Capulets' garden evokes a view of Assisi through the morning mist, and Juliet's balcony is replaced by an *altana* (a covered terrace at the back of a Renaissance house used for sleeping in hot weather). The set itself is made up of sliding panels through which the cloths are revealed, enabling the production to have a cinematic quality with the scene being transformed without pauses.

Just as the designs show a careful study of paintings, Nureyev's interpretation displays a very close reading of Shakespeare's text and an appreciation of life in Renaissance Italy. He recognised that society was frequently divided by feuds and bloody riots, and that whole communities could be suddenly devastated by plague. The production opens and closes with gamblers throwing dice and there are repeated images of Fate. While much of the production suggests the darker side of life, the Capulets' ball is a magnificent affair and the background for Act Two is the pageantry of the *sbandierata*, or flag-throwing, which survives in hill towns such as Siena as part of the 'Corsa del Palio'.

Initially Nureyev considered using period music, but recognised that Sergei Prokofiev's famous score carried the drama along – though he rearranged some sections to support his choice of action. He also briefly toyed with the idea of an all-male cast, but recognised that would not be a popular move with a ballet company in which more than half the dancers were women. Although Nureyev created Romeo for himself, the choreographic honours are shared among the characters. Juliet is determined and passionate, taking her cue from her description of herself as 'too fond; / And therefore thou mayst think my 'haviour light' (2.2.98–9). Juliet's friends are lively adolescents. Lady Capulet, as in the play, is considerably younger than her husband, and Tybalt is no stage villain but a real friend of Juliet. Mercutio has much of the best choreography – from the start Nureyev was creating an alternative role for himself (much as Olivier and Gielgud had famously shared the role in the 1930s) – and a brilliant death scene which, true to the play, juxtaposes jokes and reality to play up the horror of the situation.

Nureyev created his production as London Festival Ballet's contribution to the Queen Elizabeth II Silver Jubilee celebrations at the London Coliseum. The ballet became more elaborate when restaged for larger companies at La Scala, Milan, and the Paris Opéra, but the principles of the production remained the same and the original went on to receive the Society of West End Theatre Award for Dance.

Laura Knight, drawing of Gwen Ffrangcon-Davies as Juliet, backstage at the Regent Theatre (1924)

Gwen Ffrangcon-Davies's friends presented this picture to the V&A to mark the actress's 100th birthday in 1991. In 1992, a few months before her 101st birthday, she appeared with Jeremy Brett in *The Master Blackmailer*, a dramatisation of a Sherlock Holmes story for Granada Television, of which reviewer Nancy Banks-Smith wrote: 'There is a certain playfulness about her performance which suggests that she is, perhaps, too young for the part.'[1] A few years earlier, in 1988, the BBC received great numbers of enthusiastic letters from viewers who had watched her directing an *Omnibus* masterclass on acting for aspiring Juliets, the role in which she is here portrayed over sixty years before by Laura Knight. The actress received the utmost praise for her interpretation of Juliet, 'as near flawless as any Juliet has ever been or is likely to be', which delivered the love scenes 'exactly as we have lived love in our dreams'.[2] In her quest to capture the vitality of the theatre, Laura Knight (1877–1970) spent many hours drawing in cramped conditions backstage, and she was especially satisfied with the work she produced at the Regent Theatre in 1924. 'Some of these drawings were the best I did. I lived in the theatre, I knew it all inside out; I could have gone on for ever, if the run had not come to an end.'[3]

This production of *Romeo and Juliet* established the reputations of Gwen Ffrangcon-Davies and her co-star, the twenty-year-old John Gielgud. Although Gielgud chose Peggy Ashcroft rather than Ffrangcon-Davies as Juliet in his next two productions of *Romeo and Juliet* in 1932 and 1935, their stage partnership was to last for a further thirty years, playing together in *Macbeth* in 1942, and in *Much Ado About Nothing*, *Julius Caesar* and *Henry VIII* at Stratford in 1950. Ffrangcon-Davies went on to become a founder member of Peter Hall's Royal Shakespeare Company and appeared in its first London season at the Aldwych in 1960–1.

Laura Knight employs artistic licence in this picture, depicting Juliet in a ginger-coloured dress instead of the actual yellow dress worn in the production, with hair restrained in a headpiece invented by the artist.[4]

The contrasting presence of the dresser in the background is key to the composition, and the artist explains the importance of contrast when writing of her experience working backstage with Anna Pavlova's ballet company at the Drury Lane Theatre in 1920, where she saw:

> Half stripped and half costumed fairy-like creatures, their flesh all dipped in the gilt of electric light – greater contrast than the two Cockney dressers, stout and solid ladies, who 'weren't going to stand any nonsense whatever happened', could not be imagined, nor could a greater contrast in colour have existed than their plain dresses… with the rich coloured silk and satin costumes and tarlatan skirts hanging on the wooden rack.[5]

Laura Knight explores in her art the dingy backstage world of the theatre which is not meant to be on show, and depicts the unglamorous circumstances in which illusions are created: 'The world is full of undiscovered beauty,' she wrote, 'no petty scene but can be glorified in the eyes of him who can see it truly!' For her, 'the manure heap or the battered ash-bin' were perfectly worthy artistic subjects, and in relation to Shakespeare she observed: 'Could we sympathise with the mean and vulgar if Shakespeare had never drawn Shylock or Falstaff?'[6]

1. Martial Rose, *Forever Juliet*, p. 188.

2. *Ibid.*, pp. 38–9.

3. Laura Knight, *Oil Paint and Grease Paint*, p. 261.

4. Timothy Wilcox, *Laura Knight at the Theatre*, pp. 66–9.

5. Laura Knight, *The Magic of a Line*, p. 159.

6. Knight, *Oil Paint and Grease Paint*, p. 391.

Edward Gordon Craig, sketch for a set design for *Romeo and Juliet* (1891)

Edward Gordon Craig (1872–1966) was enormously influential as an innovator in modern European stage design, despite the fact that the number of plays he actually staged was very small. His ideas were widely disseminated in his book *The Art of the Theatre*, first published in German in 1905, and in his periodical *The Mask*, published between 1908 and 1929. In addition, he staged many exhibitions of his woodcuts and drawings which made him famous throughout Europe.

This early drawing of the Friar's cell in *Romeo and Juliet* shows light streaming through the window upon a crucifix on an otherwise bare wall. Craig preserved the sketch by pasting it on a page from an 1893 diary. It dates from his days working as an actor at the Lyceum Theatre with Henry Irving (1838–1905) and illustrates his ambition to create a new kind of staging, using space and light. While enjoying considerable success as an actor, he remained dissatisfied, saying: 'I could either be content for the rest of my life to follow Irving and become a feeble imitation of him, or discover who I was and be that'.[1] His idea for Friar Lawrence's cell was adapted for the church scene in his production of *Much Ado About Nothing* at the Imperial Theatre, London, in 1903: 'except for the curtains there was only one strong ray of sunlight, falling on the stage in a thousand colours through an invisible stained-glass window.'[2] His earlier productions of Purcell's *Dido and Aeneas* (1900) and *The Masque of Love* (1901) were admired for their use of colour. W.B. Yeats recalled the 'purple backcloth that made Dido and Aeneas seem wandering on the edge of eternity'.[3] Yeats later used sketches and set models provided by Craig for productions at the Abbey Theatre.

Although Yeats experienced no difficulty in making full-sized sets from Craig's models, Herbert Beerbohm Tree (1852–1917) abandoned his projected production of *Macbeth* designed by Craig after discussing Craig's set model with his chief designer Joseph Harker:

> Tree said he could not quite make out, apart from their obvious
> ugliness, exactly what was wrong with the models produced for his

approval, and asked me to examine them and enlighten him on their defects… we found that if the scenery were made to the scale of the models it would have risen through the roof of His Majesty's and overtopped the Carlton Hotel. 'Better tell him to take it to New York, where the skyscrapers are,' I said.[4]

It was the Moscow Art Theatre that provided Craig with his most successful collaboration, when Stanislavsky invited him to work on a staging of *Hamlet*. The production was three years in preparation but caused a sensation when staged in 1912. It featured Craig's 'simple convex screens which could be placed on the stage in endless combinations. They hinted at architectural forms, corners, niches, streets, aided by the imagination of the spectator'.[5] The court scene 'was visualised as a glittering cloth of gold streaming down stage from the thrones of the King and Queen. The figures of the courtiers protruded through slits in the cloth.'[6]

Although the production proved to be a landmark in the history of European theatre, neither Stanislavsky nor Craig felt that it fully realised Craig's vision. Craig's writings show him to be in pursuit of an ideal theatre, in its extremest form 'without either a written play or actors'. When Count Kessler remarked, 'I would feel that the instrument I was playing had some strings missing', Craig laughed and retorted that this was an experiment in playing on two or three strings 'with the rest of the piano left out'.[7] He nevertheless succeeded sufficiently in realising his vision for those who experienced his work to be convinced of his genius. The artist and writer Filiberto Scarpelli wrote to his friend, the actor Giovanni Grasso:

Craig is a great painter, a great architect, a great poet. He paints with light, he constructs with a few rectangles of cardboard, and with the harmony of his colours and of his lines he creates profound sensations, as only the fathers of poetry knew how to create…[8]

1. Edward Gordon Craig, *Ellen Terry and Her Secret Self*, p. 122.

2. Harry Kessler, quoted in Janet Leeper, *Edward Gordon Craig*, p. 8.

3. Leeper, p. 7.

4. Joseph Harker, *Studio and Stage*, pp. 175–6.

5. Constantin Stanislavsky, *My Life in Art*, p. 511.

6. George Nash, *Edward Gordon Craig*, p. 13.

7. Harry Kessler, *The Diaries of a Cosmopolitan*, p. 194.

8. Leeper, pp. 19–20.

Sunday, April 2

Idea for Romeo & Juliet
Friare Cell : GC : 1891 :

Lyceum
influence.

my first style !

Benjamin Wilson, portrait of David Garrick and George Anne Bellamy as Romeo and Juliet (1753)

One of three surviving versions, this painting by Benjamin Wilson (1721–1788) of the 1750 production of *Romeo and Juliet* reflects David Garrick's acting and staging of the play at the Drury Lane Theatre.[1] The scene depicted (from Act Five) is set in a moonlit churchyard, with the moon in this era most likely simulated by a glass vessel containing coloured liquid lit from behind by a lamp. In later practice the lamp was suspended in a polished metal pan. The action takes place in the area at the rear of the stage, reserved for 'discoveries' and sensational scenic effects. The stage directions for the 1763 acting version of the play describe how Romeo enters the churchyard and breaks open the doors to the Capulets' tomb. This stage practice survived well into the nineteenth century, and James Boaden recalls in his *Memoirs of Mrs Siddons* (1827) how 'our stage Romeo batters a couple of doors fiercely with the crow[bar] in his grasp, which very naturally fly open outwards'.[2] In Wilson's painting the battered doors open into an illuminated tomb as Juliet awakes from her drugged sleep. Garrick seized the opportunity to heighten the pathos by adding his own lines to allow the fated lovers to say their final farewells, an embellishment to Shakespeare's text that continued in performance for over a century. The production also included a funeral procession, showing Juliet lying 'on a state bed with a canopy over her, guarded by girls who strew flowers and by torch bearers with flaming torches'.[3]

Garrick's original leading actors in *Romeo and Juliet*, Spranger Barry and Mrs Cibber, had defected from his management at Drury Lane to the rival Covent Garden Theatre. Not to be outdone, Garrick himself took over the role of Romeo at Drury Lane, opposite George Anne Bellamy (*c.* 1731–1788), and the two theatres proceeded in head-on competition to stage the play for twelve successive nights, until Covent Garden conceded defeat on the thirteenth. Despite Barry's advantages in height and matinee-idol looks, and the music by Thomas Arne in the rival funeral procession, Garrick won the day through the energy of his acting in the tomb scene and the pathos of his final farewell to Juliet. The added stage business of the funeral procession remained popular with playgoers despite the reservations of the critic Francis Gentleman: 'Though not absolutely essential, nothing could be better devised than a funeral procession, to render this play thoroughly popular; as it is certain, that three-fourths of every audience are more capable of enjoying sound and shew, than solid sense and poetical imagination.'[4] A fervent disciple of Shakespeare, Garrick restored many lines of Shakespeare's texts that had been lost or mangled in adaptation, but as a man of the theatre, he also took the opportunity to improve on Shakespeare, with this scene of his own devising remaining popular with audiences until the original text was restored by Henry Irving in 1882. Garrick's lines are designed to maximise the dramatic pathos of the lovers' last meeting:

> ROMEO. She speaks, she lives: and we shall still be bless'd!...
> Quick! let me snatch thee to thy Romeo's arms,
> There breathe a vital spirit in thy lips
> And call thee back to life and love.
>
> JULIET. Bless me! how cold it is! Who's there?[5]

In contrast to the success of his adaptation of *Romeo and Juliet*, Garrick's later alterations to *Hamlet*, which among other things omitted the gravediggers, were strenuously resisted by audiences: 'the spectators of *Hamlet* would not part with their old friends the Grave-diggers. The people soon called for *Hamlet* as it had been acted from time immemorial.'[6]

1. Other copies are at Stourhead and the Yale Centre for British Art.

2. Cited in *The London Theatre World, 1600–1800*, ed. Robert Hume, p. 80.

3. James Fowler, 'Picturing *Romeo and Juliet*', p. 111.

4. George C.D. Odell, *Shakespeare from Betterton to Irving*, vol. 1, p. 419.

5. *Romeo and Juliet: A Tragedy, by Shakespeare*, Theatre-Royal, Drury-Lane (1774), Act Five (sig. H2^v).

6. Odell, *Shakespeare from Betterton to Irving*, vol. 1, p. 388.

François-Antoine Conscience ('Francis'), lithograph of Charles Kemble and Harriet Smithson as Romeo and Juliet (1827)

This lithograph, by the French artist known as 'Francis' (1795–1840), records the performance of Charles Kemble as Romeo and Harriet Smithson as Juliet, which took Paris by storm in 1827. The lovers have just emerged from the tomb to say their final farewells, in the scene that ends the adapted version of Shakespeare's play which held the stage at that time. The humorous tone of the print suggests the artist, at least, did not give way to the hysteria that swept Paris in the wake of the production. A member of a great theatrical dynasty, Charles Kemble (1775–1854) was the younger brother of Sarah Siddons (1755–1831) and John Philip Kemble (1757–1823), and like them reached the top of his profession. Born the eleventh child of provincial theatre manager Roger Kemble and his wife Sarah, Charles started out as an actor on the northern circuits before joining his brother John Philip on the London stage in 1794. Harriet Smithson (1800–1854) grew up in Ireland, the daughter of a theatre manager: she made her debut on the London stage at Drury Lane in 1818, but it was when she travelled to Paris ten years later with actors from Covent Garden that she achieved the highest acclaim for her performances as Juliet and Ophelia opposite Charles Kemble. 'She was barely twenty, she was called Miss Smithson, and she conquered as of right the hearts and minds of that audience on whom the light of the new truth shone.'[1] Charles had already acted on the Continent in Brussels, Calais and Boulogne when, in 1827, he travelled to Paris with members of the Covent Garden Company to act in English plays at the Théâtre de l'Odéon. When *Othello* was performed in Paris five years before, the actors had been pelted with rotten fruit, but earlier in the year of the company's visit, Victor Hugo's attack on the constraints of classical drama in his famous preface to *Cromwell* had signalled a new mood of Romanticism that was more receptive to Shakespeare.[2] Hector Berlioz was at the first night of the company's *Hamlet*:

> In the role of Ophelia I saw Henriette [sic] Smithson, who five years later became my wife. The impression made on my heart and mind by her

extraordinary talent, nay her dramatic genius, was equalled only by the havoc wrought in me by the poet she so nobly interpreted. That is all I can say. Shakespeare, coming upon me unawares, struck me like a thunderbolt. The lightning flash of that discovery revealed to me at a stroke the whole heaven of art, illuminating it to its remotest corners. I recognised the meaning of grandeur, beauty, dramatic truth, and I could measure the utter absurdity of the French view of Shakespeare... and the pitiful narrowness of our own worn-out, academic, cloistered traditions of poetry. I saw, I understood, I felt... that I was alive and that I must arise and walk.[3]

He purchased a stalls seat for *Romeo and Juliet*, where he was observed in the audience, his eyes 'fixed on Juliet with the expression of ecstasy that pre-Renaissance painters gave their saints and angels. Body and soul were entirely absorbed in that gaze.'[4] Shakespeare was to prove an enduring inspiration to Berlioz's music: he composed *Fantaisie sur la Tempête* in 1830, the overture *King Lear* (1831), the dramatic symphony *Romeo et Juliette* (1839), a funeral march for *Hamlet* (1844), the ballad *La Mort d'Ophelie* (1848), and the opera *Béatrice et Bénédict* (1862). Although Harriet was the inspiration for *La Symphonie Fantastique* (1830), she had been unresponsive to his written declarations of love, and Berlioz became engaged to another woman while writing the symphony, then left for a two-year trip to Italy. He returned to Paris on hearing his fiancée had become engaged to another man, intending to kill her, her intended husband, and her mother, but his rage dissipated on the journey home, and when he met Harriet for the first time on his return, he proposed to her, and they were married in 1833. The story did not end happily: the couple separated in 1844 after Harriet's descent into alcoholism.

1. *Berlioz and the Romantic Imagination*, ed. Elizabeth Davison, p. 44.

2. John Pemble, *Shakespeare Goes to Paris*, p. 11.

3. *The Memoirs of Hector Berlioz*, trans. and ed. David Cairns, p. 95.

4. David Cairns, *Berlioz: Volume One: The Making of an Artist*, p. 251.

KEMBLE et MISS SMITHSON,

Nicholas Georgiadis, preliminary set design for Kenneth MacMillan's ballet *Romeo and Juliet* (c. 1964)

'Sumptuous' was the adjective with which most critics welcomed the designs by Nicholas Georgiadis (1923–2001) for the Renaissance-style *Romeo and Juliet* by Kenneth MacMillan (1929–1992) that was first performed by The Royal Ballet on 9 February 1965. *The Times* maintained his designs for this ballet secured a place for Georgiadis 'by the side of such ballet immortals as Bakst and Benois', while Charles Spencer in the *Weekend Telegraph* added that 'the brooding, gorgeous colours of Georgiadis's designs... are imbued with a sense of Greek fateful tragedy and complement the psychological atmosphere of the dance'.[1] In spite of its constructed set, the stage seemed as large as it ever did for ballet, and the designs for *Romeo and Juliet* looked as happy in the vast Metropolitan Opera House in New York as they did at Covent Garden.

It has been said that in the early 1960s Georgiadis, as a set designer, was going through an 'architectural period'.[2] This peaked with the creation of his set for Minos Volanakis's chilling production of Shakespeare's *Julius Caesar* for the Old Vic in 1962. Georgiadis had been inspired by forums in the ruins of Roman cities to create an open colonnade on two levels. For the play, this structure could be placed towards the front of the stage but any architectural setting for a ballet is always required to leave a clear area for dancing. Working on the same principle for *Romeo and Juliet*, Georgiadis repeated his idea of a colonnade with an upper arcade as his permanent setting for Verona. It remained in place throughout the ballet but with a squat tower it became Verona's piazza, or marketplace; a balustrade was proposed for the Capulets' ballroom but was only ever used for the section, stage left, when it serves as Juliet's balcony under which Romeo may lurk. To create other locations, set cloths and furniture were added, with carved angels to decorate Juliet's tomb.

British theatre design in the 1960s saw a significant move away from using painted cloths to constructed elements, but it is said that Georgiadis's set designs presented something of a challenge to the technical department at Covent Garden. Georgiadis emphasised that three-dimensional sets created a more effective and convincing environment for the ballet and the production was built at the Royal Opera's workshops at Killick Street, King's Cross.

When MacMillan began creating *Romeo and Juliet*, he intended the ballet for his protégés Lynn Seymour and Christopher Gable, and even choreographed a 'Balcony pas de deux' for them to dance on Canadian television. The television pas de deux had been designed by the Australian artist Kenneth Rowell, and it was Rowell who expected to design the full production. The Board at Covent Garden did not approve this choice, however, and MacMillan turned to his long-time collaborator. MacMillan was happy to work on his ninth ballet with Georgiadis and its success led to repeated collaborations on multi-act ballets: *Manon* (1974), *Mayerling* (1978), *The Sleeping Beauty* (1987) and *The Prince of the Pagodas* (1989).

When MacMillan approached Georgiadis, the designer had a busy schedule but found he could devote twenty days to designing the three-act ballet, and the preliminary design in the V&A's collection was presumably made at this time. The design suggests an arrangement for the urban exterior of Verona's marketplace but with discrete balconies (rather than having a practical, separate upper arcade). In the design the steps appear to run upstage but in the set as realised there is a main, curved staircase in the centre with others running downstage at the sides. For the costumes both MacMillan and Georgiadis studied quattrocento paintings, costumes and poses, not treating them literally but through the filter of mid-twentieth-century theatre and fashion.

The creation of *Romeo and Juliet* proved somewhat traumatic, not least as the company's American impresario, Sol Hurok, insisted that the premiere in both London and New York should be given to Margot Fonteyn and Rudolf Nureyev. This upset MacMillan and his chosen cast, selected for their youth and acting abilities, as well their dancing – his production having been inspired by the youthful Judi Dench and John Stride as the lovers in Franco Zeffirelli's recent production at the Old Vic (1960–1961). The production was nevertheless an enormous success, receiving a forty-minute ovation, with forty-four curtain calls on its opening night. Obviously the presence of Fonteyn and Nureyev contributed to this, but Georgiadis's designs were among the stars of the show.

1. 'Sumptuous Spectacle at Covent Garden', *The Times*, 10 February 1965; Charles Spencer, 'Building a Ballet', *Weekend Telegraph*, 9 April 1965.

2. Evgenia Georgiadis, *Nicholas Georgiadis: Paintings, Stage Designs*, p. 87.

'J.B.', *The Theatrical Caesar! Or Cassius and Casca in Debate* (1804)

Shakespeare's characters, and the actors who portrayed them, are central to this print. It features the well-known Shakespearean actors John Philip Kemble (left) and his brother Charles (right) as characters from *Julius Caesar*, and satirises their attitude to the unconscionably popular child star 'Master Betty' (top, centre), who astonished audiences in challenging lead parts, including Romeo, Hamlet, Richard III and Macbeth.

This 'infant phenomenon' was William Henry West Betty (1791–1874), whose earliest appearances at the Theatre Royal, Belfast, in August 1803, at the age of eleven, were an unlikely success. Managed by his spendthrift father and coached by the Belfast prompter William Hough, interest in the boy quickly took hold. Advertisements for his performances as those of 'A Young Gentleman' were soon replaced by playbills for 'the Infant Roscius', likening him to the celebrated Ancient Roman actor Quintus Roscius Gallus, and by association to the great David Garrick, on whom the name had also been conferred. At Dublin, Betty's performances 'Drenched the audience in tears'.[1] At Cork, he broke box-office records and netted the theatre £100 nightly instead of its usual £10. Subsequent engagements proved equally successful, his father negotiating ever more lucrative fees. Despite the occasional backlash – the spectacle of Betty's Romeo to Mrs Knighton's Juliet striking one critic as resembling 'an overgrown girl and her doll' – when he reached Edinburgh in August 1804, *The Times* compared his 'premature genius' to that of Mozart.[2]

'Bettymania' soon ran rife in England. Betty opened on 13 August at the New Theatre, Birmingham, engaged by its manager William Macready (1755–1829), father of the actor William Charles Macready.[3] While in Birmingham, negotiations took place with Master Betty's father to engage the Infant Roscius for both patent theatres in London that autumn. Macready suggested that Drury Lane should pay fifty guineas a night for twelve performances, plus the takings from one 'benefit' performance – more than had been paid to any other actor in the history of the stage.

When Richard Sheridan, proprietor of Drury Lane, realised that Thomas Harris, the proprietor of Covent Garden, also wished to engage the boy, he accused Harris of violating the 'first come, first served' agreement usually observed between the two theatres. Harris was adamant that his discussions with Betty's father had started earlier in Edinburgh, but since the contract he had negotiated was not exclusive, Sheridan engaged Betty for Drury Lane, to play between engagements at Covent Garden.

While Master Betty was astounding the Irish with his mastery of Hamlet, the more mature actor John Philip Kemble (1757–1823) was doing the same in London. He had played Hamlet, Richard III, Macbeth and Othello at Drury Lane, but when his relationship with the manager Sheridan soured at the end of the 1801–2 season, Kemble bought a share of Covent Garden and made his debut there as Hamlet on 24 September 1803. His attitude to the engagement of the boy wonder at Covent Garden must have involved mixed emotions. As a lessee he would profit financially from Betty's success; as the hitherto leading exponent of Shakespeare he was mortified by the prospect of being supplanted by a child.

When Betty arrived in London on 25 November 1804 he was mobbed by crowds. Medals were struck in anticipation of his arrival dubbing him 'Not yet mature but matchless'. His first appearance at Covent Garden on 1 December caused near hysteria and Charles Kemble's prologue spoken on stage was drowned by the shouts of the audience longing for their wunderkind.

The fame of the boy was such that the educated public who saw this print, issued on 15 December 1804, would have appreciated its satirical references. They knew their Shakespeare and would have realised why the speech about Caesar's power that Cassius makes to Brutus in *Julius Caesar* (1.2.135–8) is adapted to become a speech to the 'envious' Casca – or envious Charles. They would have known that Betty was appearing at both leading theatres. Indeed, he is depicted whip in hand, riding Covent Garden and Drury Lane like a trick rider astride two horses at Astley's Circus.[4]

1. According to a journalist in the *Dublin Evening Post*, quoted in Giles Playfair, *The Prodigy*, p. 33.

2. John Wilson Croker, *Familiar Epistles*, p. 37; *The Times*, 8 August 1804.

3. Giles Playfair, *The Prodigy*, pp. 49–50.

4. The watchman's rattle in Master Betty's left hand is the type that audience members used to make a noise at the theatre, and was to be a feature of the Old Price Riots at Covent Garden Theatre five years later.

The Young Roscius.

Drury Lane

Covent Garden

Why Man – he doth bestride
the narrow way like to a colossus
and we petty mortals crawl while
his huge legs, and peep about to find
Ourselves dishonourable Graves

Tragedy
Comedy
Opera
Farce
Pantomime
&c &c&c &c

J.B.

Pub. Dec 15 1804 b S.W. Fores
No 50. Piccadilly London

Folios of Caracatures lent out for the Evening.

The Theatrical Cæsar! or Cassius and Casca, in Debate.

Ernst Stern, illustration of the assassination scene in *Julius Caesar*, the Players' Shakespeare edition (1925)

The Players' Shakespeare *Julius Caesar* was published in two limited editions: the V&A's National Art Library holds one of 100 copies signed by the illustrator Ernst Stern (1876–1954), and by Harley Granville-Barker, whose introduction formed the basis for his text on *Julius Caesar* in his *Prefaces to Shakespeare*. The Theatre and Performance Department's library has two copies of an unsigned edition of 450. Both editions contain Ernst Stern's black-and-white drawings of stage settings and costumes, along with coloured illustrations of scenes from the play. Stern had designed Max Reinhardt's spectacular 1920 production in which Caesar was assassinated at the top of a staircase and rolled down step by step, stabbed by the conspirators until he reached the bottom. Stern's interest in Shakespeare had been stimulated in childhood by the German edition of the plays, with illustrations by John Gilbert, especially the pictures of battles on horseback in *Julius Caesar*, although he later claimed to have been disappointed when he first saw the play performed, because 'there wasn't a sign of a horse from beginning to end'.[1]

Ernst Stern settled in England in the early 1930s to escape Nazi Germany. Born in Romania, he was sent to be educated in business studies in Vienna, but soon found he was more interested in going to see plays in the Imperial Theatre. From there he went to Munich to study art, and then to Berlin, where he was employed as a cartoonist on a weekly newspaper, when Max Reinhardt (1873–1943) invited him to design his production of *Orpheus in the Underworld*. The article Stern wrote about the production led to an invitation to become Costume and Scene Director of the Reinhardt theatres, a post he retained from 1906 to 1921.

Reinhardt's productions made use of the latest innovations in lighting and stage technology, and he invited leading artists and designers, including Edvard Munch and Edward Gordon Craig, to collaborate with him. The productions initially caused shock waves among the critics, although Stern stresses that it was not their aim to be innovative for its own sake:

Reinhardt never consciously played the role of innovator and iconoclast, and neither did I... The mere fact that I was a newcomer to the stage was apparently guarantee enough for him that I would avoid the rut.[2]

Stern describes being initiated by Reinhardt into the psychological importance of colour, such that Iago was imagined in green, 'glistening like a reptile', and Tybalt was costumed in red 'like a fighting cock'.[3] When Stern came with Reinhardt to England in 1911 to stage *Sumurum* at the Coliseum, he was nicknamed 'Whitewash' on account of his feat of creating huge expanses of white background contrasting with black to recreate the effect of the Berlin production: 'the colours of the costumes, which were carefully chosen and ordered, combined in a logical harmony against the white of the wall to produce a most striking effect'.[4] His most amazing achievement was transforming the inside of London's Olympia into a vast cathedral to stage *The Miracle* in 1911 with a cast of 1,500, for which he designed 2,000 costumes.[5]

Stern was briefly interned at the outbreak of the Second World War, but protests were made on his behalf, and his internment fortunately proved of short duration. He continued his work as a theatre designer during the war, designing the set of Wolfit's famous performance of *King Lear* in which 'an appropriate variation on Stonehenge was devised for touring purposes'.[6] The production was heralded as 'the greatest tragic performance... seen on the British stage since the death of Irving', containing 'all imaginable fires of agony and all the light of redemption'.[7] Stern spent his remaining years in England; he bequeathed his personal archive to the V&A on his death in 1954.

1. Ernst Stern, *My Life My Stage*, p. 9.

2. *Ibid.*, p. 82.

3. *Ibid.*, p. 75.

4. *Ibid.*, p. 89.

5. Charles B. Cochran, *The Secrets of a Showman*, pp. 167–78.

6. Robert Speaight, *Shakespeare on the Stage*, p. 229.

7. *Ibid.*

**Still from the National Video Archive of Performance
recording of Phyllida Lloyd's Donmar Warehouse production
of *Julius Caesar* (2012)**

In 2012, the Donmar Warehouse staged an 'extraordinarily bold' production of *Julius Caesar*, set within a women's prison.[1] Directed by Phyllida
Lloyd, the all-female cast starred Frances Barber in the title role, with
Cush Jumbo and Harriet Walter as Mark Antony and Brutus. The production ran from 30 November 2012 to 9 February 2013. Lloyd, best
known for such film work as *Mamma Mia!* and *The Iron Lady*, deliberately
chose *Julius Caesar* to demonstrate that female actors could portray its
weighty masculine roles, and to give a group of women the chance to
speak the great, challenging speeches of the male leads.

The production was well timed, coinciding with four all-male productions of Shakespeare's plays, by Propeller and Shakespeare's Globe,
and sparking the current debate about the lack of women in British theatre. As the *Financial Times* noted, watching a group of women 'enact the
traditionally male roles of statesman and military tactician, one notices
more than usual how the women in the play are sidelined by the men'.[2]
There was, however, nothing feminine about the production, which was
set in a stark and brutal world inspired by Holloway Prison. Lloyd and
Walter workshopped a number of key scenes at Holloway before
rehearsals began, and talked to prisoners about how they could relate to
the play.

Lloyd's production was firmly rooted in this prison setting, which provided a framing device for the action of the play itself, as *Julius Caesar*
was performed as a play-within-a-play by a group of inmates within the
prison yard. This device provided a reason for the all-female casting, and
gave the audience a brilliant new perspective on the play. The world of
the prison was constantly felt and infiltrated the action, as when the staging of the killing of Cinna the poet got out of hand, prompting the prison
guards to step in hastily to intervene; or when the guards removed one

of the actors for her 'meds', and another prisoner had to take her place. The prisoners used only the props which they could have accessed for a prison production, such as plastic knives, used in the fight scenes.

Bunny Christie's cold, bleak set design seeped off the stage and into the auditorium, where the audience sat on rows of plastic chairs. The Donmar, usually so intimate and cosy, was stripped back to a cold, menacing space, with a high brick wall, clanking metal walkway and staircase. The action was played out in close proximity to the audience, as actors frequently used paths through the auditorium to enter and exit. Indeed, the murder of Caesar took place in the front row of the stalls, as 'he' was forced down and made to drink from a bottle of prison bleach, before being stabbed.

Although the production was set in a modern landscape, where hoodie-wearing prisoners shouted over a thrash-metal band, symbolic of warfare, there was a strict adherence to the verse of Shakespeare's play, which kept it on track. As Lloyd said, they expected to come under fire for many of their production choices, but she was determined that the way they dealt with Shakespeare's language would not be one of them. The production felt dangerous and anarchic throughout. It was designed to unsettle. As the *Evening Standard* noted in its review, every element 'abounds with weirdness, thuggery and horror'.[3] The V&A filmed this production for the National Video Archive of Performance (NVAP) on 22 January 2013. Using five cameras located around the auditorium, the recording aimed to capture the spirit and ambience of the production, as well as the action onstage.

1. Henry Hitchings, *Evening Standard*, 5 December 2012.

2. Sarah Hemming, *Financial Times*, 5 December 2012.

3. Hitchings, *Evening Standard*, 5 December 2012.

William Dawes, *The Downfall of Shakespeare Represented on a Modern Stage* (1765)

This painting satirises the growing popularity of opera, pantomime and popular music which, it was feared, might drive Shakespeare's works off the stage. It was acquired by the V&A in 2006 from the widow of Allardyce Nicoll, to whose collection the painting belonged, then attributed to the artist Philip Dawes.[1] The painting was exhibited in 1765 at the Free Society of Artists by Philip Dawes, though it has been persuasively argued by Iain Mackintosh that the picture is actually by Philip's father, William Dawes, a pupil of Hogarth, and exhibitor of other works at the Society.[2] The prostrate figure of Shakespeare lies at the feet of the two singers who trample upon the scattered pages of his plays. Shakespeare has been stabbed by the tenor, who holds a dagger in his hand, in a parody of the killing of King Xerxes in the opera *Artaxerxes* (in which the same singers starred) by Thomas Arne, who is here pictured in the foreground leading the orchestra from his harpsichord. The murderous tenor is in fact a portrait of the celebrated John Beard, who sang the role of Macheath in *The Beggar's Opera*, and the female singer beside him is Charlotte Brent, who starred in the same production as Polly Peachum. Beard's feathered headdress may look absurd to us, but is in fact of the type actually worn by lead singers in the operas of the day, while the theatre being depicted accords in many respects with the Covent Garden Theatre. John Beard (*c*.1717–1791) was the son-in-law of Covent Garden's manager, John Rich, who popularised opera and pantomime, and was famous for his portrayal of Harlequin. After Rich's death in 1761 John Beard succeeded him as manager.

The cartouche above the stage reads 'Vox et Praeterea Nihil' (*Voice and nothing else*), and the satire continues in the grotesque satyr depicted on the left-hand pedestal, who ridicules opera with his bagpipes, while the popularity of pantomime is satirised by the figure of Scaramouche on the pedestal to the right. These figures occupy the same positions as the statues of the Muses of Comedy and Tragedy which stood on the actual stage at the Covent Garden Theatre, while the decoration on the front of the theatre's boxes substitutes asses' heads. The pillar behind the satyr is decorated with a set of scales in which the tragic crown and sceptre are outweighed by musical instruments, and the opposite pillar has scales in which the works of Beaumont and Fletcher, Shakespeare, Jonson and Congreve weigh lighter than papers inscribed with the words 'Pantomime' and 'The Favourite Song'. Serious opera is represented in the scenery by an ancient Roman obelisk, while comic opera is represented by a windmill. Charlotte Brent (1734–1802) played the leading role in the light opera *The Maid of the Mill* in 1765, and a windmill had also featured prominently in the famous pantomime created by John Rich in 1723, *The Necromancer, or, Harlequin Dr. Faustus*, in which he had excelled in the role of Harlequin.

The ladies in the audience seem entranced by the performance in different ways, one studying the libretto intently, another staring fixedly at the actors, while a third looks upwards in rapturous enjoyment. The dark-skinned gentleman on the right has been variously identified as the Moroccan Ambassador (who visited London in 1756) and the King of the Cherokee Indians, Ostenaco, whose portrait was painted by Reynolds in 1762 (when he was introduced to George III). Ostenaco and his companions are reported to have been greatly entertained at the Sadler's Wells Theatre, 'the activity of the performers, and the machinery of the pantomime, agreeing best with their notion of diversion'.[3]

1. Allardyce Nicoll, *The Garrick Stage*, ed. Sybil Rosenfield, frontispiece.

2. Iain Mackintosh, 'Deciphering *The Downfall of Shakespeare Represented on a Modern Stage* of 1765', *Theatre Notebook* 62 (2008). This account is indebted to his interpretation.

3. Henry Timberlake, *The Memoirs of Lieutenant Henry Timberlake* (London, 1765), cited in Mackintosh, p. 46.

Mezzotint of Barton Booth and John Mills (as Brutus and the Ghost of Caesar) in *Julius Caesar* (c. 1715)

Prints of actors in role on stage are scarce before Hogarth realised the potential for marketing prints of his own paintings on theatrical subjects, most famously with his series of prints of John Gay's *The Beggar's Opera*. This very rare mezzotint published by Pierce Tempest (1653–1717) came to the V&A in a collection of over 10,000 English and European prints, drawings and paintings on theatrical subjects assembled by opera singer and author Harry Beard, which was donated to the museum by Beard's family in 1970. It is now part of the Theatre and Performance Department's collection. This illustration shows Barton Booth (1681–1733) as Brutus and John Mills (d. 1736) as the ghost of Caesar, in the production of *Julius Caesar* performed at the Drury Lane Theatre. The play was enduringly popular, with Barton Booth inheriting the lead role of Brutus from Betterton in 1709 and continuing to play it for the next twenty years. John Mills started to play opposite him as Caesar in 1713, the beginning of a long association in which he later exchanged the role of Caesar for Cassius.

The mezzotint shows the scene detailed by Shakespeare, where Brutus is seated in his tent at his writing desk, lit by a single candle, when Caesar's ghost appears to him, making Brutus's hair stand on end:

> How ill this taper burns! Ha! who comes here…
> That mak'st my blood run cold and my hair to stare?
> Speak to me what thou art.

> (4.3.273–9)

Brutus wears armour as if already dressed for the next day's battle; Caesar wears a laurel crown and carries a torch illuminating the many stab wounds on his bare torso. The antique Roman costumes with decorative armour and ornate sandals are carefully recreated and illustrate the delight in classicism which overtook England in the early-eighteenth century.

In this era, the Drury Lane Theatre was run by a triumvirate of actor-managers, comprising Thomas Doggett, John Wilkes and Colley Cibber, with the young Barton Booth replacing Doggett in 1714. Booth acted in no less than thirty-five roles, including King Lear, Brutus, Banquo and the Ghost in *Hamlet*. He excelled in stately and majestic parts, and the actor Charles Macklin, on entering the theatre during Booth's performance as Pyrrhus in Ambrose Philips's tragedy, *The Distrest Mother*, was so impressed by 'the grandeur and dignity of his manner' and his 'air of majesty' that he 'stood fixt with amazement; nor could he take his seat till Pyrrhus left the audience chamber'.[1] John Mills also had an astonishing range of roles, excelling, unlike Booth, in both comic and tragic parts. In the 1721–2 season at Drury Lane, he played fifty different roles in the seventy plays offered, acting on 160 of the 192 nights on which the house was open. He is credited by the early theatre critic Benjamin Victor with being 'the *most useful Actor* that ever served a Theatre'.[2]

1. Philip H. Highfill (et al.), *A Biographical Dictionary of Actors... 1660–1800*, vol. 2, p. 222.
2. Emmett L. Avery, *The London Stage 1700–1729*, p. cxxviii.

'Twas Cæsar's spirit Brutus did affright,
It wrapt it selfe ith' terrors of the night,
I'le meet thee at Philippi. Say y.e Spright.
I'le meet thee there, Ingth' there,
With such a voice & such a Frowne,
As put y.e trembling Ghost to sudain Flight.

P. Tempest ex

The Spirit of Shakspere appearing to his Detracters

Tremble, thou wretch.
That hast within thee undivulged crimes.
Unwhipped of justice.

Shakspere.
Ah me, Ah me, O dear. O dear.
What Spectres this approaching here.

Surely the Shakspeares injured shade.
It fills my soul with so much dread
It is it is thus on our knees.
Let's strive his anger to appease.
O Father of the British Stage.
Whose wit has charm'd from age to age.

Pardon the base unworthy flame.
That durst to rob thee of thy fame.
But now this solemn mockrys o'er
Thy gracious mercy wee implore.
We'll never more disgrace thy page.
Our Brains were gone a pilgrimage.

"Which of you have done this?"
Macbeth (3.4)

76

Silvester Harding, *The Spirit of Shakspere appearing to his Detracters* (c. 1796)

Samuel Ireland was a respected publisher and collector, with a passion for Shakespeare which his teenaged son, William Henry (1775–1835), endeavoured to satisfy by forging documents and letters, freely inventing details to cover inconvenient gaps in Shakespeare's biography. The younger Ireland soon progressed to fabricating whole plays. The forgeries took in many people who should have known better, much as the 'Hitler diaries' fiasco would reel in distinguished dupes in the 1980s. The Theatre Royal, Drury Lane, signed up the 'new' Shakespeare play *Vortigern and Rowena*, with predictably disastrous consequences on its sole outing (2 April 1796).

William Ireland was apparently inspired by Thomas Chatterton, the 'marvellous boy' who passed off his own forgeries as the works of a medieval monk, Thomas Rowley, and committed suicide at the age of seventeen.[1] Chatterton at least had the wit to invent a poet, but Ireland's bolder and reckless choice of Shakespeare as his model was bound to attract more rigorous scrutiny and a wide degree of scepticism. The scholar Edmond Malone comprehensively demonstrated that the documents could not possibly be genuine in his *Inquiry into the Authenticity of Certain Miscellaneous Papers* (1796).

The Spirit of Shakspere appearing to his Detracters [sic] (c. 1796), engraved by Silvester Harding (1745–1809), pictures the Ireland family cowering from the encroaching and reproachful shade of Shakespeare, resurrected in full Elizabethan fig, while leaves of text are scattered in the foreground, each containing satirical digs at the forged output. There are discarded papers alluding to the wretched *Vortigern* and a gibe at Ireland's clumsy and inauthentic orthography: 'Tributary lines to Ireland Irelande or Irlaunde for I could not spell his name W Shakspere'. Its humorous attribution to William Hogarth, 'found by somebody in an old chest', playfully echoes Ireland's parodies of a greater talent, and his cover story of an anonymous benefactor as the source of the Shakespeare cache.

Jonathan Bate elucidates the accompanying verse:

Among the couplets after the apposite quotation from *Lear*
('...Undivulged crimes, / Unwhipp'd of justice' [3.2.52–3]) we find
the line 'But now this Solemn mock'ry's o'er'. It had been [John
Philip] Kemble's repetition of the unfortunate line 'And when this
solemn mockery is ended' that had brought the house down in the
final Act of *Vortigern*.[2]

Samuel Ireland died in 1800, having unsuccessfully attempted to combat
in print Malone's debunking of the forgeries. He appeared to uphold his
belief in the legitimacy of the archive, not least because he believed his
son incapable of the workmanship. In 1805, William Ireland published
his *Confessions*, fell into debt, and lived for a time in France, dying in
London in 1835.

---

1. William Wordsworth, 'Resolution and Independence' (1802), stanza 7.

2. Jonathan Bate, 'Shakespearean Allusion in English Caricature in the Age of Gillray', p. 204.

François Boitard, illustration of *Macbeth* (1709)

Thomas Betterton (1635–1710) was the leading actor of the Restoration stage and this image from *Macbeth* in Rowe's edition of 1709 shows him in the title role, dressed in contemporary Restoration costume, such as 'Marlborough might have worn'.[1] Macbeth was one of his many celebrated Shakespearean roles, and Pepys complained that when Betterton was temporarily incapacitated from playing the title role, the production was 'mightily short of the content we used to have when Betterton acted'.[2] He was equally renowned for his acting of Hamlet, and Pepys judged his portrayal 'the best part, I believe, that ever man acted'.[3] Betterton was at the forefront of innovation on the Restoration stage and made several visits to France to research advances in scene design and stage technology. He was Davenant's deputy manager at the Duke's Company, initially based at a converted tennis court in Lincoln's Inn Fields, later leading the company in 1671 to their new base at Dorset Garden, a purpose-built theatre designed to stage spectacular productions using movable scenery arranged in perspective and lit by candlelight. Betterton and his wife lodged in a flat above the portico and he took credit for twice saving the theatre from burning down.

In addition to achieving the greatest possible acclaim in the roles of Macbeth and Hamlet, he appeared in an astonishing variety of Shakespearean roles, including King Lear, Angelo, Henry VIII, Hotspur, Mercutio, Thersites, Timon, Prospero, Brutus, Othello, Sir Toby Belch and Falstaff. Betterton believed that an actor 'must transform himself into every Person he represents' and he succeeded so well that, in Colley Cibber's view, 'Betterton was as an actor, as *Shakespear* was an Author, both without Competitors!'[4] As an actor, Betterton was famous for being able to enforce 'universal Attention, even from the *Fops* and *Orange-Girls*', and his encounter as Hamlet with his father's ghost won universal acclaim, with Cibber noting: 'he made the Ghost equally terrible to the Spectator as to himself!'[5] His performance was still being recalled, decades after his death, in *The Laureate* (1740):

I have been lately told by a Gentleman who has frequently seen Mr Betterton perform this Part of *Hamlet*, that he has observ'd his Countenance (which was naturally ruddy and sanguin)... turn instantly on the Sight of his Father's Spirit, as pale as his Neckcloath... with a Tremor inexpressible; so that, had his Father's Ghost actually risen before him; he could not have been seized with more real Agonies; and this was felt so strongly by the Audience, that the Blood seemed to shudder in their Veins likewise.[6]

At the end of the performance 'the whole Audience hath remain'd in a dead Silence for near a Minute, and then – as if recovering all at once from their Astonishment, have joined as one Man, in a Thunder of universal Applause.'[7]

Betterton's *Macbeth* was the play as reworked by Davenant to give opportunites for spectacle and music. According to John Downes, who worked as prompter for Betterton's company, the production staged at Dorset Gardens was 'drest in all it's Finery, as new Cloath's, new Scenes, Machines, as flyings for the Witches; with all the Singing and Dancing in it... being all Excellently perform'd, being in the nature of an Opera, it Recompenc'd double the Expence; it proves still a lasting Play.'[8]

1. George C.D. Odell, *Shakespeare from Betterton to Irving*, vol. 1, p. 210.

2. *Diary of Samuel Pepys*, vol. 8, p. 521.

3. *Ibid.*, vol. 9, p. 296.

4. Philip H. Highfill (et al.), *A Biographical Dictionary of Actors... 1660–1800*, vol. 2, p. 95.

5. *Ibid.*, pp. 93 and 95.

6. *Ibid.*, p. 95.

7. *Ibid.*

8. John Downes, *Roscius Anglicanus*, pp. 71–2.

Ruskin Spear, oil sketch for a portrait of Laurence Olivier as Macbeth (1955)

This oil sketch, donated to the museum by Dr Anna Schönholzer, is one of at least two preparatory studies made by the artist for the portrait of Laurence Olivier (1907–1989) as Macbeth, which hangs in the RSC Gallery, and was commissioned by the governors of the Shakespeare Memorial Theatre in 1955 in recognition of Olivier's brilliance in the role. A second sketch was presented by Dr Schönholzer to the actor's son, Tarquin Olivier, and was for a while on loan to the museum. Ruskin Spear (1911–1990) completed many portraits of eminent figures, including Ralph Richardson in the role of Falstaff (commissioned by the National Theatre in 1984), Winston Churchill and Harold Wilson.

Due to Olivier's work schedule, the Macbeth portrait was painted partly from photographs specially taken at Stratford by John Underwood, and partly from studio sittings. Spear recalled: 'He was always late, and always charming. When he first stood in front of me with his Macbeth kit over a pin-stripe suit – glimpses of which I could see – the whole thing worried me. He looked like a whisky advert!'[1] However, Olivier proved an excellent subject, happy to stand for hours, though he did have a tendency to fall asleep after a long day.

Olivier had first starred in the title role of *Macbeth* at the Old Vic Theatre in its 1937–8 season, to mixed reviews, in a production jinxed by the cancellation of the first night due to technical problems with lighting, and by the death of the theatre's founder, Lilian Baylis, the day before the postponed opening. His performance was generally agreed to lack strength and maturity, and it was in the Stratford production twenty years later that he really came into his own in the role. 'My voice was infinitely stronger and more powerful,' he recalled, 'and the greater experience of life I had had since I first played the part really made a difference... It was my moment... and I understood the play. Not that I didn't understand it before, but somehow I had grown into it.'[2] Now regarded as one of Britain's finest Shakespearean actors, Olivier took time to develop confidence in his verse-speaking. Emlyn Williams recounts a meeting in 1935 in a Lyons Corner House, when a depressed Olivier lamented that reviewers had found him 'dull' in his most recent play, *Golden Arrow*, adding: 'now there's talk of me alternating Romeo and Mercutio with Johnnie G., imagine me speaking verse next to that one, I'll sink without trace.'[3] Olivier's fears over having to compete with John Gielgud were not unfounded, and his delivery of Shakespeare's poetry was duly found wanting in some quarters. 'His blank verse is the blankest I've ever heard,' wrote one critic; 'He played Romeo as if he was riding a motorbike,' wrote another.[4] But Olivier also found admirers of his portrayal of Romeo – notably the production's Juliet, Peggy Ashcroft, who wrote: 'to me, Larry's was the definitive Romeo – gauchely graceful, awkward, ardent – a complete characterisation of an impulsive adolescent.'[5]

Ruskin Spear paints Olivier during Macbeth's great fifth-act soliloquy ('Out, out, brief candle!'). 'He looked fiercely beautiful,' wrote Sally Beauman of Olivier's performance, 'like Masefield's conception of Macbeth, as "Not a hangman... but an angel who has fallen",' going on to link Olivier's Macbeth with Hazlitt's likening of Kean in the same role to a snared lion.[6] It is indeed difficult to read Hazlitt's description of Kean without thinking of Laurence Olivier:

> He runs a-tilt with fortune, and is baffled with preternatural riddles. The agitation of his mind resembles the rolling of the sea in a storm; or he is like a lion in the toils – fierce, impetuous, and ungovernable... The two finest things that Mr Kean has ever done, are the recitation of the passage in *Othello*, 'Then, oh, farewell the tranquil mind,' and the scene in Macbeth after the murder... as a lesson in common humanity, it was heart-rending... It was a scene, which no one who saw it can ever efface from his recollection.[7]

1. Mervyn Levy, *Ruskin Spear*, p. 48.

2. Laurence Olivier, *On Acting*, pp. 75–6.

3. Emlyn Williams, 'Brief Encounters', in Garry O'Connor (ed.), *Olivier: In Celebration*, pp. 153–63 (p. 158).

4. Harry Andrews, 'Companions in Arms', in *ibid.*, pp. 63–8 (p. 65).

5. Peggy Ashcroft, 'Salad Days', in *ibid.*, pp. 21–5 (p. 24).

6. Sally Beauman, *The Royal Shakespeare Company*, pp. 221–2.

7. William Hazlitt, *A View of the English Stage*, pp. 64–6.

George Clint, oil sketch for a portrait of Edmund Kean as Sir Giles Overreach (1820)

When Edmund Kean (1787–1833) played Richard III in his first season at the Drury Lane Theatre in 1814, David Garrick's ninety-year-old widow went to see every performance. The young actor accepted her invitation to visit, and she presented him with Garrick's stage jewels, insisting that he sat in her husband's chair, as nobody had done since her husband's death, because no one before was found worthy of the honour. (A comparably magnanimous honour was later bestowed by John Gielgud in 1944, when he presented the sword Kean had worn in the same production to Laurence Olivier 'in appreciation of his performance of Richard III'.)[1]

It was not, in fact, Kean's first appearance on stage at Drury Lane, which had been at the age of seven as an imp in *Macbeth* under the tutelage of his Aunt Charlotte, who was a supporting actress in the company. Hearing a noise in the green room one night, Mrs Charles Kemble had been informed that 'It is only young Kean reciting Richard III... he's acting after the manner of Garrick. Will you go and see him? He is really very clever.'[2] He was soon hailed as a prodigy, publicised in 1801 as 'The Celebrated Theatrical Child' for his recitation of the whole of *The Merchant of Venice*, but still spent long, impoverished years acting in the provinces before being invited back to London to become leading actor at Drury Lane. He joined a theatre in financial difficulties, struggling to meet the debts incurred by its manager, Sheridan, as well as the massive cost of rebuilding following the disastrous fire of 1809. It was also losing out in the constant rivalry with Covent Garden, where John Philip Kemble reigned supreme, the Drury Lane management eventually hiring Kean almost in desperation, after a number of other actors had failed to revive the theatre's fortunes.

Despite the house being half-empty, Kean's debut as Shylock in *The Merchant of Venice*, in January 1814, caused a sensation. The audience is reported to have risen to their feet in excitement: 'his hatred of all Christians, generally, and of Antonio in particular... his alternations of rage, grief, and ecstasy... in all this, there was such originality, such terrible force, such assurance of a new and mighty master.'[3] William Hazlitt, in the audience as theatre critic for the *Morning Chronicle*, recognised at once that something extraordinary was happening: 'Mr Kean's appearance was the first gleam of genius breaking athwart the gloom of the Stage'.[4] For George Henry Lewes, Kean was 'incomparably the greatest actor I have seen'.[5] Kean's restless energy and unpredictable emotional outbursts epitomised the new Romantic style of acting, in contrast to the restrained classicism perfected by John Philip Kemble. Paradoxically, however, every detail of Kean's performance was carefully premeditated, as Alexander Dyce records:

> When he and Mrs Kean were alone together of an evening, he would place the candles on the floor, in imitation of the stage lights; and after going through a speech, or a portion of a scene, in more ways than one, he would ask 'Well, Mary, which of these do you prefer?' and was generally guided by her opinion. Having once fully made up his mind about the best mode of giving certain passages, he, as it were, stereotyped them, and never deviated into any other manner.[6]

Kean's reputation was based upon a limited number of mainly Shake-spearean roles, with Shylock, Richard III and Othello deemed his masterpieces, along with the role of Sir Giles Overreach in Massinger's *A New Way to Pay Old Debts* (c. 1625), in which the mad scene in Act Five (where this domineering villain attempts to kill his own daughter for marrying beneath her) gave full rein to Kean's dramatic genius. This painted sketch of him in the role by George Clint (1770–1854) captures his mercurial acting style, 'fitful, flashing, abounding in quick transitions... carrying you along with its impetuous rush and change of expression'. George Vandenhoff, the fellow actor who made this observation, goes on to wonder at Kean's delivery of Othello's 'farewell' speech (3.3.351–61): 'it ran on the same tones and semi tones, had the same rests and breaks, the same *forte* and *piano*, the same *crescendo* and *diminuendo*, night after night, as if he spoke it from a musical score. And what beautiful, what thrilling music it was! the music of a broken heart – the cry of a despairing soul!'[7]

1. Jonathan Croall, *Gielgud*, p. 322.

2. Raymund FitzSimons, *Edmund Kean*, p. 4.

3. *Ibid.*, p. 54.

4. *Ibid.*, p. 55.

5. George Henry Lewes, *On Actors and the Art of Acting*, p. 1.

6. *The Reminiscences of Alexander Dyce*, ed. Richard J. Schrader, p. 60.

7. George Vandenhoff, *Dramatic Reminiscences*, p. 21.

Sword presented to Edmund Kean for his performance as Macbeth (1819)

Edmund Kean (1787–1833) first played Macbeth in 1814 and, although critics did not regard it as his best role, it proved popular with audiences. His nineteenth-century biographer, F.W. Hawkins, wrote:

> the sternest heart was taken captive; and the sympathy awakened by his performance was indicated by the solemn stillness which pervaded the whole house while *he* was before it, and by the earnest and irrepressible acclamations which followed his different exits.[1]

Kean kept the role in his repertoire, playing it at Edinburgh in April and October 1819, when he was seen by the politician, agricultural reformer, and prolific author Sir John Sinclair of Ulbster (1754–1835). A painting by Henry Raeburn shows Sinclair resplendent in scarlet jacket and Gordon tartan trews and plaid, the dress uniform, designed by himself, of his own regiment, the Rothesay and Caithness Fencibles. It is the epitome of the eighteenth-century 'swagger portrait'.[2]

Having somehow found time to visit the theatre, Sir John was hugely impressed by Kean's Macbeth: 'it was one of the most perfect specimens of acting I had ever witnessed', he later wrote.[3] He and a group of like-minded friends decided to present Kean with a sword 'as a proof of the high idea we entertained of his theatrical abilities.'[4] Sinclair, who was familiar with swords – he wears one in Raeburn's portrait – commissioned the weapon from George Hunter and Co., an army supplier with premises in Edinburgh, which was to become famous when it provided tartan for the Highland dress worn by George IV on his visit to the Scottish capital in 1822. The sword was dispatched to Kean with a letter, dated 16 November 1819, in which Sinclair explained that 'having witnessed the very superior manner in which you performed the character of "Macbeth"', some friends had resolved 'to present you with "*A Sword of State*," to be worn, when you appear upon the stage in that tragedy, as "*The crowned King of Scotland*".'[5] Kean replied on 27 November, assuring Sir John and the unknown patrons that 'their kindness has not been lavished, where it is not duly appreciated' and declaring that he was happy to receive the sword 'as at once a record of national liberality, and Scottish patronage of the stage.'[6]

The sword is a basket-hilted broadsword of the type carried by early-nineteenth-century infantry officers. The grip, covered in shagreen, as was common with military swords of the period, is protected by an elaborate guard decorated with jewelled thistles. This is attached to a blade which appears to be older than the hilt and is of the type known as an 'Andrea Ferrara'. Ferrara is said to have been a maker active in Scotland in the sixteenth century. This may be apocryphal, but the name has become associated with wide-bladed broadswords renowned for their flexibility and strength, and was, according to Walter Scott, inscribed 'on all the Scottish broadswords which are accounted of peculiar excellence.'[7] Although the original inscription has been ground out, the name is faintly visible on the blade of Kean's sword, one word on each side.

For safety's sake the sword is unsharpened, but it is still a formidable weapon, though whether Kean actually wore it in performance is uncertain. A satirical piece in *Blackwood's Magazine* mocked both the donors and the recipient by claiming that the sword was too big for the actor (who stood just under 5ft 7ins), likening him to a beetle 'transfixed by a huge corking-pin', but this reads like journalistic mischief-making.[8] The engraved silver plaques attached to the scabbard give it the appearance of a display item rather than a practical stage property.

1. F.W. Hawkins, *The Life of Edmund Kean*, vol. 1, p. 270.

2. The portrait is held by the National Gallery of Scotland.

3. Published in *The Correspondence of the Right Honourable Sir John Sinclair*, vol.1, p. 454.

4. *Ibid.*

5. *Ibid.*

6. *Ibid.*, p. 456.

7. Walter Scott, *Introductions, and Notes and Illustrations*, vol.1, p. 116.

8. *Blackwood's Magazine* 16 (July–December 1824), p. 277.

Ellen Terry as Lady Macbeth (1889)

By the time Ellen Terry (1847–1928) played Lady Macbeth in this production at the Lyceum Theatre, she had been on the stage for over thirty years, and was well known for her Shakespearean roles. She had joined Henry Irving's company at the Lyceum in 1878, and, until his death in 1905, was closely associated with him, both professionally and in her private life. Although, as reflected in her letters at the time, she was racked by doubts about her ability to play the role of Lady Macbeth successfully, the production opened to great acclaim in December 1888. Critics were divided over her portrayal and hotly debated both her and Henry Irving's interpretations of their leading roles, but on 3 January 1889 Ellen Terry wrote excitedly to her daughter, Edie Craig:

> It is a most tremendous success, and the last 3 days booking forward has been greater than ever was known... at the Lyceum. – It is a great success and I am a great success!! Which amazes me. For never did I think I should be let down so easily. Some people hate me in it – some (Henry amongst them) think it my best part – and the critics differ, or discuss it hotly, which in itself is my best success of all!!! Those who don't like me in it, are those who don't want, and don't like to, read it fresh from Shakespeare, and who hold by the *fiend* reading of the character... I shall not budge an inch in the reading of it, for that I know is right... By no means do I make her 'a gentle lovable woman'... she was nothing of the sort, altho' she wasn't a 'fiend'.[1]

Terry had prepared by studying modern criticisms of the play, but regardless of how she chose to portray Lady Macbeth, she still had to overcome the public's view of her as a charming and much-loved actress whom they were accustomed to seeing in gentler roles. As the critic of the *Illustrated London News* wrote in the week after the show opened, 'It is impossible to enter a club, or sit down to a dinner-table, or take a seat in a train, without facing the inevitable discussion as to the true Macbeth and the new Lady Macbeth.'[2]

Aside from issues of characterisation, there was no disagreement about the success of the production. It reflected the highest standards of artistic taste, and Irving was careful to exclude any inadvertently comic interludes, such as in the visualisation of the three Witches and of other supernatural elements in the play, which had undermined productions of *Macbeth* earlier in the century and inspired ridicule. The costumes designed for Ellen Terry were particularly admired, most famously the robe she wore in Act One, the so-called 'beetle-wing dress', hand-crocheted in green tinselled yarn, and encrusted with the iridescent wing cases of the jewel beetle. John Singer Sargent attended the first night and immediately asked to paint her; Terry's letters refer to sitting for him as early as January 1889. The finished painting was purchased from the artist by Irving himself, and was later donated to the Tate Gallery.

The costume in this photograph was worn in the banquet scene (3.4) and, like the beetle-wing dress, this robe, the cloak and the headdress are preserved at the National Trust's Smallhythe Place, Ellen Terry's rural retreat from 1899 until her death in 1928. The splendour of Terry's costumes was famously commented upon by Oscar Wilde: 'Lady Macbeth seems to be an economical housekeeper, and evidently patronises local industries for her husband's clothes and servant's liveries; but she takes care to do all her own shopping in Byzantium.'[3]

1. V&A, Ellen Terry Archive, THM/384/1/4.

2. *Illustrated London News*, 5 January 1889.

3. Roger Manvell, *Ellen Terry*, p. 198.

**❝I have of late – but wherefore I know not –
lost all my mirth…❞**
Hamlet (2.2)

82

Sarah Bernhardt as Hamlet (1899)

Sarah Bernhardt (1844–1923) was arguably the most celebrated actress ever to have lived, her appearances throughout Europe and the Americas earning for her the title 'The Divine Sarah'. Her fame was also enhanced by her bohemian lifestyle, fiery temperament, and by her appetite for self-publicity.

This photograph was taken in the Lafayette Studio at 179 New Bond Street, London, in 1899, while she was appearing in her controversial production of *Hamlet* at the Adelphi Theatre. The production had transferred from her native Paris, where it had generated passionate debate and divided opinions. The new translation of *Hamlet* Bernhardt commissioned moved away from the adaptations to which French audiences were accustomed: here at last was a text directly translated from Shakespeare's, and not in the rhyming alexandrine couplets required by the orthodoxies of French tragedy. French audiences also expected to see Hamlet portrayed as a romantic, indecisive character, whereas Bernhardt played him as a man of action, carefully planning his strategy for revenging his father's murder. The production of *Hamlet* Bernhardt brought to London was presented in French; performances lasted four hours.

The colourful stories surrounding Bernhardt (the coffin which she travelled with and claimed to sleep in, her menagerie, her tradition of bedding her leading men) can sometimes distract attention from her legendary abilities as an actor and manager, her professional energy, and her attention to detail. When London critics attacked her characterisation of Hamlet, she wrote a letter to the editor of the *Daily Telegraph* justifying her approach to the play:

> Some wish to see in Hamlet a womanish, hesitating, flighty mind. To me
> he seems a manly, resolute, but thoughtful being. As soon as Hamlet
> gathers what is in his father's mind and learns of his murder, he forms
> the resolution to avenge him; but as he is the opposite of Othello – who
> acts first and thinks afterwards – Hamlet thinks before he acts, which is
> the sign of great strength and power of mind.[1]

Although some critics questioned Bernhardt's decision to take on the role of Hamlet, she was certainly not the first major actress to do so. Since the late-eighteenth century, the complexity and ambiguities of Hamlet's character had attracted actresses, beginning in 1775 with the great tragedienne Sarah Siddons, who played the role nine times over a thirty-year period. Sarah Bernhardt played many male roles throughout her career, and was noted for them. 'It's not that I prefer male roles,' she had remarked when challenged on her repertoire, 'it's that I prefer male minds.'[2] The duel scene from *Hamlet* was filmed in 1900 (accessible via YouTube) and demonstrates her skill, as a fifty-six-year-old actress, in portraying a nimble and masculine young Prince of Denmark.

Sarah Bernhardt was one of the most frequently photographed actresses of the nineteenth century, sitting for the best studios in Paris and in the cities to which she toured. The Irishman James Stack Lauder founded the Lafayette Studio in Dublin in 1880, and specialised in photographing an elite clientele, having risen to fame by photographing Alexandra, Princess of Wales, in 1885. Two years later, Lauder was invited to Windsor Castle to photograph Queen Victoria, and the resulting surge in business led to the opening of Lafayette's London studio in Bond Street. The clients who sat for their portraits there largely comprised the aristocracy, statesmen and visiting royalty. After the Lafayette Studio went into liquidation in 1952, the archive lay forgotten in an attic in Fleet Street until 1988, where it was discovered by builders hired to clear the space. Thanks to the actions of their foreman, Terry Thurston, the collection was saved, and approximately 3,500 early glass-plate negatives were acquired by the V&A.

1. *Daily Telegraph*, 17 June 1899.
2. Robert Gottlieb, *Sarah*, p. 142.

William Telbin, preliminary set design for *Hamlet* at the Lyceum Theatre (1864)

William Telbin's superbly atmospheric sketch, with its looming expanse of moonlit sky, is one of several preliminary set designs the artist executed for Augustus Harris's production of *Hamlet* at the Lyceum Theatre in May 1864. Starring Charles Fechter as Hamlet and Kate Terry (elder sister of Ellen) as Ophelia, the production was due to open on Saturday, 14 May, but was postponed for a week 'in consequence of the Extraordinary Scenic Preparations', as the playbills announced.[1]

Telbin's design depicts the moment in Act One, Scene Five when Hamlet first sees his father's ghost. Unlike more conventional settings for the scene where the Ghost and Hamlet remain on the battlements, Telbin envisages the characters at a distance from the castle, by the sea, with Hamlet on the steps advancing towards the translucent Ghost, who features as the central figure, arresting the viewer's attention. Telbin may have visited Kronborg Castle at Helsingør (Shakespeare's Elsinore) in order to ensure that his designs were as accurate as possible.

By 1864, Telbin was an extremely well-established and respected landscape painter and scenic artist. His earliest major stage commission was for Macready's 1842 production of *King John* at the Theatre Royal, Drury Lane, where his unusual design for the throne room included flats set diagonally across the stage grooves. In the 1850s, he and the scenic artist Thomas Grieve (1799–1882) painted a large number of landscape views on giant canvases for exhibitions of diorama, or moving panoramas with commentary, at the Gallery of Illustration in London's Lower Regent Street that they leased from 1850 to 1860. The same decade saw Telbin designing for Charles Dickens's ambitious amateur productions, with the scene designer Clarkson Stanfield. Their work included Act One of Wilkie Collins's *The Frozen Deep*, which was staged at Dickens's London home, Tavistock House, in January 1857, and repeated in July of that year at the Gallery of Illustration. There was obviously a competitive element in the brilliance of the effects that each man envisaged since Dickens lamented that:

Nothing could induce Telbin… to explain what he was going to do before Stanfield; and nothing would induce Stanfield to explain what he was going to do before Telbin. But… each said that he would make a model in card-board, and see what I 'thought of it'.[2]

In 1856, Telbin (1813–1873) joined Charles Kean's team of scenic designers at the Princess's Theatre. Kean specialised in spectacularly pictorial productions of Shakespeare, emphasising in his playbills the amount of historical and archaeological research undertaken to create the scenery. The complex settings took an army of stagehands to change, and frequently meant delays between the scenes that were regretted by the critics and often overwhelmed the productions. Telbin's work at the Princess's included productions of *The Winter's Tale* (1856), *The Tempest* (1857) and *The Merchant of Venice* (1858), alongside Thomas Grieve and William Gordon, who specialised in landscapes, and Frederick Lloyds and Henry Cuthbert, who worked on the architectural scenes and the historical research.

The decision to use Telbin for the 1864 *Hamlet* at the Lyceum was well received by the critics. They praised it for being 'so beautifully illustrated by Mr. Telbin's magnificent scenery', noting how the production comprised 'a series of pictures', and how the Ghost gradually disappeared 'by an ingenious accumulation of gauze media', evidently a unique effect created by Telbin.[3]

This design, and others, were presented to the V&A in 1925 by Telbin's younger son William Lewis Telbin, himself a successful scenic artist, especially well known for the work he executed for Henry Irving's lavish productions at the Lyceum. Telbin's eldest son Henry was also a scenic artist but his career was tragically cut short in 1866; he died, aged twenty-five, after falling over a precipice in Switzerland while on a sketching tour in preparation for a production of Rossini's *William Tell*.

1. Playbill advertising *Hamlet* at the Lyceum Theatre on 21 May 1864.

2. Charles Dickens to Wilkie Collins, 1 November 1856, *Letters of Charles Dickens to Wilkie Collins*, ed. Laurence Collins (1892), available on <jr.digitalpixels.org/wc/letters/letters.html>, accessed 2 October 2013.

3. *Illustrated London News*, 28 May 1864; *The Times*, 26 May 1864; *ibid*.

> **66** And let those that play your clowns speak no
> more than is set down for them...**99**
> *Hamlet* (3.2)

Lez Brotherston's costume design for a Tragedian in Tom Stoppard's *Rosencrantz and Guildenstern Are Dead*, National Theatre (1995)

Tom Stoppard's absurdist play *Rosencrantz and Guildenstern Are Dead* uses two minor characters from *Hamlet* as its protagonists and turns the main action of Shakespeare's tragedy into the play's backdrop. As the Player explains: 'We do on stage the things that are supposed to happen off. Which is a kind of integrity if you look on every exit being an entrance somewhere else.'[1] Stoppard's Rosencrantz and Guildenstern are often likened to Elizabethan versions of Vladimir and Estragon from Beckett's *Waiting for Godot*; the pair amuse themselves by playing probability games and tossing coins, which always land on 'heads'.[2] They neither control nor understand their fate, and die without knowing why. The *Sunday Times* labelled Stoppard's play 'the most important event in the British professional theatre of the last nine years'.[3] Initially staged by the Oxford Theatre Group at the Edinburgh Festival Fringe in 1966, the play premiered in 1967 at London's Old Vic in a production presented by the National Theatre. In 1990, Stoppard directed the film of his own adaptation, starring Tim Roth and Gary Oldman.

This costume design by Lez Brotherston, for the National Theatre's 1995 revival, was for the actor Clive Llewellyn's role of a Tragedian – one of the six travelling players specified in the text, whose morals may be gauged by their 'spokesman', the unnamed Player:

> Now for a handful of guilders I happen to have a private and uncut
> performance of the Rape of the Sabine Women – or rather woman, or
> rather Alfred – (*Over his shoulder.*) Get your skirt on, Alfred – (*The Boy
> starts struggling into a female robe.*)... and for eight you can
> participate.[4]

The production was directed by Matthew Francis, designed by Brotherston, and starred Adrian Scarborough as Rosencrantz, Simon Russell Beale as Guildenstern, and Alan Howard as the Player.

Lez Brotherston trained at the Central School of Art and Design and is one of Britain's most well-known stage designers. He has designed for theatre, opera, ballet and film; however, he is best known for his collaborations with Matthew Bourne and the dance company Adventures in Motion Pictures, for which he designed the award-winning *Swan Lake* (1995). Brotherston places focus on the costumes by using a few standard poses for his figures and giving them all similar features. The ragged costume in this design is Elizabethan in style, and consists of a red shirt worn under a brown waistcoat. Black breeches are tucked into brown lace-up boots and a dark-blue scarf is tied around the waist. The figure holds suitcases in both hands and wears a rucksack on his back. The National Theatre's 'NT' logo has been drawn in black crayon in the lower left-hand corner. In 2002, Brotherston donated an extensive collection of his designs, including those for *Rosencrantz and Guildenstern Are Dead*, to the V&A Theatre and Performance Collections.

1. Tom Stoppard, *Rosencrantz and Guildenstern are Dead*, p. 21.

2. *Ibid.*, p. 7.

3. Harold Hobson, *Sunday Times*, 16 April 1967.

4. Stoppard, *Rosencrantz and Guildenstern are Dead*, p. 19.

François Boitard, illustration of *Hamlet* (1709)

The actress Elizabeth Barry (*c.* 1658–1713) was more than twenty years younger than Thomas Betterton when she played Gertrude to his Hamlet, as shown in this illustration from Rowe's 1709 edition of Shakespeare's play. Apprenticed to the stage at an early age, under the protection of Thomas Betterton and his wife, Mrs Barry failed to achieve immediate success as an actress. Edmund Curll recounts that the libertine poet, the Earl of Rochester, wagered that he could make an actress of her within six months, forcing her to 'Rehearse near 30 times on the Stage, and about 12 in the Dress she was to Act in.'[1] Despite her lack of musical ability, she went on to become one of the most successful actresses of her day, and a star of the Duke's Company, excelling particularly in tragic roles. Cibber describes the power she exerted over her audience:

> a Presence of elevated Dignity, her Mein [sic] and Motion superb and gracefully majestick; her Voice full, clear, and strong, so that no Violence of Passion could be too much for her: And when Distress or Tenderness possess'd her, she subsided into the most affecting Melody and Softness. In the Art of exciting Pity she had a Power beyond all the Actresses I have yet seen, or what your Imagination can conceive.[2]

Mrs Barry acted all the leading female roles across the repertoire of the Duke's Company, although in later years she concentrated on tragedy, with comic parts taken by her younger contemporary, Mrs Bracegirdle (1671–1748). One of her most admired performances was as Cordelia in Nahum Tate's adaptation of *King Lear*, with her other Shakespearean roles including Mistress Ford in *The Merry Wives of Windsor*, Calphurnia in *Julius Caesar*, Queen Katharine in *Henry VIII* and Lady Macbeth.

Although she never married, she bore a daughter to the Earl of Rochester, and later became romantically involved with the playwrights Thomas Otway and George Etheredge, taking the principal female roles in their plays. Her unconventional beauty attracted the close attention of the men of her day, with one observing: 'She was not handsome, her mouth opening most on the right side, which she strove to draw t'other way, and at times composing her face, as if sitting to have her picture drawn – she was middle-sized and had darkish hair, light eyes, dark eyebrows, and was indifferent plump... She could neither sing nor dance.'[3] Another male observer, Edmund Curll, noted that she had 'a peculiar Smile... which made her look the most genteelly malicious Person that can be imagined.'[4]

Led by Betterton, she and Mrs Bracegirdle rebelled against the management of the Rich family at the Drury Lane Theatre, leaving to form the United Company at Lincoln's Inn Fields, along with members of the King's Company. At the risk of being labelled parsimonious, and perhaps because of having to make her own way in the world from an early age, she managed to save enough to be able to retire from the stage in 1710, when she was in her early fifties. Unfortunately, she did not live to enjoy her retirement, dying of rabies in 1713 after being bitten by her lap dog. Aware of the precarious financial future awaiting actresses who had lost their youth and looks, she nobly left Mrs Bracegirdle £220 in her will to preserve her 'harmless from any debt of the Playhouse'.[5]

Boitard's engraved illustration shows Mrs Barry's Gertrude reacting in horror as Hamlet sees his father's ghost. The overturned chair in the foreground reflects a famous piece of Betterton's stage business – in anger his Hamlet violently overturned the furniture. In the later edition of Rowe's Shakespeare (1714), the chair was omitted from the picture, possibly because it upset the composition or perhaps on the ground of decorum.[6] The illustration is of further interest for its depiction of Old Hamlet's ghost in the 'complete steel' (1.4.52) of his first appearance – before the discovery of the 1603 First Quarto of *Hamlet*, which specifies the Ghost's entrance 'in his night gown' in this scene.

1. Philip H. Highfill (et al.), *A Biographical Dictionary of Actors... 1660–1800*, vol. 1, p. 314.

2. *Ibid.*, p. 324.

3. *Ibid.*, p. 325.

4. *Ibid.*

5. *Ibid.*, p. 323.

6. Geoffrey Ashton, 'The Boydell Shakespeare Gallery: Before and After', p. 37.

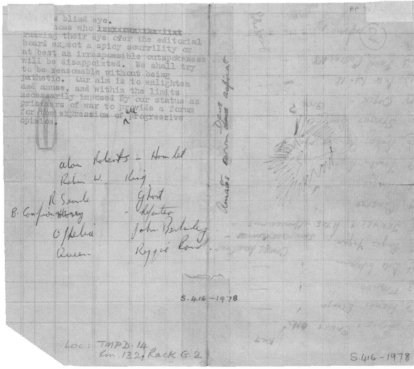

Ronald Searle, costume designs for 'Hamlet Goes Hollywood' (1944)

Shakespeare's works have been performed all over the world in all kinds of spaces and circumstances. The 'Robben Island Bible' (the edition of the complete works of Shakespeare used by African National Congress members imprisoned on Robben Island in the 1970s) is perhaps the most famous example of people in adversity drawing inspiration from Shakespeare's plays. The set of costume designs shown here, sketched on a scrap of paper, are another – first and foremost a testimony to the endurance of the human spirit, and secondly to the ensuring legacy of Shakespeare. The designs were made by Ronald Searle (1920–2011) during his time as a prisoner of war in Changi Jail in Singapore. The POWs wrote and performed revues and put on plays as a form of distraction, performing them in a number of locations across the jail, Searle variously contributing. This design is for the Barn, in the Sime Road section of the camp, where Searle helped to write sketches, designed costumes and sets, and drew makeshift 'programmes' for the many shows performed there.

'Hamlet Goes Hollywood' was a sketch performed in the *Rag Bag Revue* on 21 March 1944. A portion of the script survives in one of Searle's notebooks held by the Imperial War Museum, and it seems that the governing conceit of the sketch was exactly as the title suggests: Hamlet gets the Hollywood-movie treatment. Hamlet greets the Ghost's revelation with the words, 'No kidding! So it was moider, huh? Well, what do you know about that!'[1] The design shows us Horatio was dressed as a hardboiled Hollywood detective in a trench coat and trilby, while Searle played the part of the Ghost in a costume consisting of '2 Sheets'. He weighed around six stone at this point, so would indeed have made an effective ghost. He and his fellow prisoners must have related only too well to Old Hamlet's agonies, their lives indeed comprising a living hell: 7,000 men, in a camp built for 1,000, and crammed six or seven to a cell, were daily marched through the jungle to undertake heavy labour, while subsisting on fewer than 500 calories a day.

Given such unimaginable privations, two remarkable things about this design might be noted: that it is sketched in colour, and that the circumstances were no bar to Searle's imagination in mixing modern and period costume. The colour is explained by an episode the artist recounted in his memoir, *To the Kwai and Back: War Drawings 1939–45*. Searle was evidently approached by a Captain Takahashi, 'the prison administrator, lord of life and death', who asked to see his sketchbook. When Searle handed it over, Takahashi drew a sketch and confided that he had been an artist studying in Paris when war broke out. He gave Searle a handful of coloured pencils and wax crayons, an action Searle described as 'a quiet, unsoldierly gesture of solidarity between artists'.[2]

Appropriately, considering the revue's title, the production's costumes are a ragbag of styles. Hamlet (left, skull in hand) is shown in a green shirt, and blue-and-white-striped pyjama trousers poking out from beneath khaki shorts, with a long black gown over the top – not too difficult to find, perhaps, in a POW camp. But he is also wearing yellow stockings, a red cummerbund and a ruff. The King (third from left) looks like Macbeth, resplendent in a large skew-whiff crown, kilt and woollen jerkin. There is a question mark above his huge puffed sleeves, as if Searle were wondering how they could be achieved. The fact that Gertrude and Ophelia (third and second from right) are shown in full Tudor dress is perhaps overambitious – though Searle's sketchbooks suggest that such theatricals regularly issued a call-out to prisoners for donations for the manufacture of period costumes and props.[3]

By his own admission, Searle was a 'troublemaker' in the eyes of the British authorities in the camp, and in his memoir he suggests that he and his friends were deliberately given the hardest and most dangerous jobs because of this. The typed note on the back of the sketch seems to be aimed squarely at those he accused and is a powerful, if understated, testimony to his belief in the free expression of artists whatever their situation:

> Those who running their eye over the editorial board expect a spicy scurrility or at best an irresponsible outspokenness will be disappointed. We shall try to be reasonable without being pathetic. Our aim is to enlighten and amuse, and within the limits necessarily imposed by our status as prisoners of war to provide a forum for the expression of all progressive opinion.

1. Ronald Searle, Sketchbook: Theatre Notes and Stage Designs, The Barn Theatre, Spring Season 1944, Sime Road Prison Camp. Catalogue number IWM ART 15748 (p. 24).

2. Ronald Searle, *To the Kwai and Back*, p. 173.

3. Searle, Sketchbook, p. 2.

66 Not one now to mock your own grinning –
quite chap-fall'n? **99**
Hamlet (5.1)

87

Yorick's skull (1980)

This skull is a property from the 1980 production of *Hamlet* at the Royal Court Theatre directed by Richard Eyre, one of the few Shakespeare plays staged at the theatre since it was taken over by the English Stage Company in 1956. Hamlet was played by Jonathan Pryce, who drew on his father's recent death to bring a sense of heightened emotion and dangerous madness to the role. He and Eyre made the decision to cut the character of Old Hamlet and have his son deliver the lines in a deep, spectral voice as if possessed by his father's unquiet spirit. The museum has the prompt book recording these cuts.

Almost every production of *Hamlet* uses an image of the prince with the skull of Yorick the jester in his hand for some of its publicity shots, and this production was no exception. In the press photographs, the skull has considerably more teeth than it does now, perhaps a result of the 'childish glee' with which Pryce's Hamlet approached the graveyard scene and in which the skull was 'knock'd about the mazard with a sexton's spade' (5.1.87–8).[1]

The V&A has been the Royal Court's official repository for archival material since the 1960s and routinely acquires prompt books, show reports, and associated theatre correspondence. The skull shown here came to the museum by a more unusual route, however. It was anonymously donated and arrived with a note explaining that, as the donor was 'quite superstitious', they would rather it formed part of the V&A's collections than stayed in their home.

The skull has been signed by a number of the company members: 'Kevin Quarmby' (Player); 'Will Knightley' (Guildenstern); 'Simon Chandler' (Laertes); 'David Neville 1980' (Rosencrantz); 'Colum Gallivan' (Marcellus); 'Jude K' (Jude Kelham, ASM); 'Harriet Ophelia' (Harriet Walter); 'Jill Bennett' (Gertrude); 'Geoffrey C. with love' (Geoffrey Chater, Polonius); 'Rick Cottan xx' (Richard Cottan, Reynaldo); 'OSRIC' (David Sibley); 'ANNA'; 'Katrin x'; 'Bo' (Bo Barton, SM); 'ELPHICK' (Michael Elphick, Claudius).

This is one of two human skulls held by the Theatre and Performance Department. The other was given to legendary French actress Sarah Bernhardt by the great poet, novelist and Shakespearean, Victor Hugo (1802–1885), inscribed by him with a verse that reads (in translation):

> Skeleton, what have you done with your soul?
> Lamp, what have you done with your flame?
> Empty cage, what have you done with
> The beautiful bird that used to sing?
> Volcano, what have you done with your lava?
> Slave, what have you done with your master?

Both skulls play their ancient role as a memento mori – yet each also functions as a specific souvenir of a set of particularly memorable performances.

1. Francis King, review of *Hamlet*, *Sunday Telegraph*, 6 April 1980.

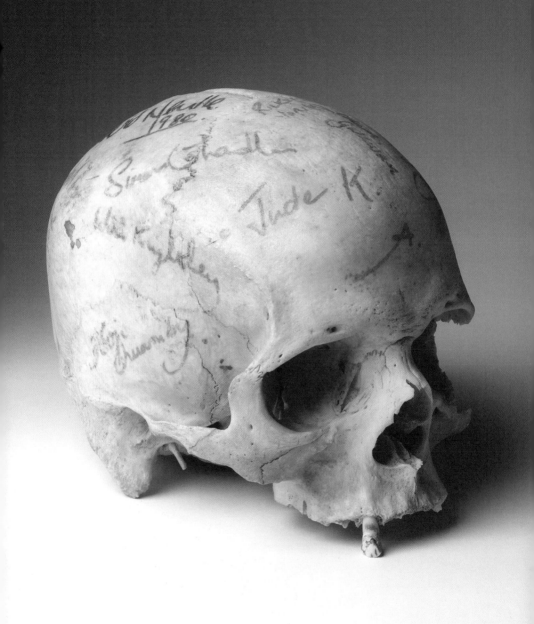

66 Let her paint an inch thick, to this favour
she must come; make her laugh at that. **99**
Hamlet (5.1)

88

Leslie Hurry, headdress for the Gravedigger in Robert Helpmann's *Hamlet*, Sadler's Wells Ballet (1942)

The jester's cap in dull red and yellow, trimmed with ivy, morphs into a grinning skull at the back, and indicates a great deal about Robert Helpmann's ballet of *Hamlet*. The production was created for the Sadler's Wells Ballet at the New Theatre (now the Noël Coward), London, on 19 May 1942. The premiere was presented to raise money for Mrs Churchill's Aid to Russia Fund.

An actor as well as a dancer, Helpmann (1909–1986) chose to choreograph *Hamlet* (playing the lead himself) to convince director Tyrone Guthrie (1900–1971) that he would be well cast in Shakespeare's play – an ambition he went on to achieve two years later. Helpmann worked out the ballet's synopsis with the assistance of the theatre director Michael Benthall (1919–1974), together contriving its structure to represent the confused recollections of the dying prince. Helpmann also consulted the composer Constant Lambert over the score, eventually choosing Tchaikovsky's *Hamlet Fantasy Overture*. The eighteen-minute production opened and closed with the dying Prince being carried off by four captains, the ballet's central inspiration deriving from Hamlet's famous line 'For in that sleep of death what dreams may come…' (3.1.66). This almost cinematic presentation distilled the essence of the play rather than telling it as a linear narrative, and included a then fashionable Freudian element as Hamlet confused his mother, Queen Gertrude (Celia Franca), with Ophelia (Margot Fonteyn).

This sense of confused identity, and duality, telescoping two characters into one person, was also evident in the role of the Gravedigger (initially performed by Leo Kersley), a 'Clown' in Shakespeare's texts, whose headdress also evokes Yorick, the late King's dead jester, whose skull he unearths. There is a similar sense of transience and change in the remainder of the Gravedigger's costume, of which one half appears to be an artisan's dress, the other a fantastically rich outfit. As the ballet critic and historian Cyril Beaumont wrote, this was 'a suggestion perhaps that Death knows no distinctions.'[1]

The headdress of papier mâché, plastic and paint was made by Hugh Skillen, and, like the whole production, designed by Leslie Hurry (1909–1978). Helpmann had been looking for a designer when his attention was captured during a visit to an exhibition of Hurry's paintings at the Redfern Gallery in London. Hurry was recovering from depression and the somewhat disturbing quality and colouring of the paintings captured the mood Helpmann hoped his dream-ballet would express in terms of dance and mime. Initially nervous, and having extracted the promise that he could pull out of the production if the designs did not work, the ballet established a second career for Hurry as a stage designer.

According to Helpmann in his funeral address for Hurry, having studied the music, Hurry designed the production in a week, creating a powerful set, predominantly in reds, oranges and crimson, with a deliberately distorted perspective. Barley-sugar columns forming a doorway stage right metamorphosed into a poisoned chalice and dagger-carrying hand, agents of destruction in the play, while the figure of a murderous warrior heralded doom and destruction. For this ballet the unusually detailed, overpowering set worked surprisingly well, and it was a deliberate choice that the dancers should appear dwarfed by their surroundings.

Within a month of the ballet's premiere, Hurry exhibited his designs for *Hamlet* at the Redfern Gallery (4 June – 4 July 1942), bringing the creative process full circle. After this ballet Leslie Hurry designed many stage productions, including two versions of Shakespeare's *Hamlet* – directed by Tyrone Guthrie and Michael Benthall (1944) for the Old Vic Company, and by Peter Wood (1961) for the Royal Shakespeare Company – and Humphrey Searle's opera of the play for Covent Garden (1969).

1. Cyril W. Beaumont, *Leslie Hurry*, p. 9.

George and Isaac Cruikshank, *The O.P. and N.P. Spectacles* (1809)

It is rare to witness a riot at a play by Shakespeare. When, on 18 September 1809, John Philip Kemble, manager of the newly rebuilt Covent Garden Theatre, stepped on stage in the costume of Macbeth to welcome the audience to the first production to be staged in the new theatre, he was met with a barrage of shouting, hissing and hooting, which continued throughout the performance. Although magistrates were summoned, and some protesters arrested, the disturbance did not end until two in the morning, when the audience only left after singing 'God Save the King' and 'Rule Britannia'. The riots, which continued for a further ten weeks, were known as the 'Old Price [or O.P.] Riots', because the principal objective of the protesters was for the management to restore the old system of pricing, and to abolish the higher prices introduced after the rebuilding of the theatre. The rebuilding cost was £300,000, and even with the £76,000 raised by public subscription, a gift of £10,000 from the Duke of Northumberland, and the insurance settlement of between £44,000 and £60,000, there remained a large shortfall. To increase revenue, the management had therefore reconfigured the one-shilling seats in the upper gallery, with these now condemned as no more than 'pigeon holes' by the audience. The price for a seat in the pit was raised from 3s. 6d. to four shillings, and the admission to the public boxes raised from six to seven shillings. Outrage was caused by the conversion of a whole tier of boxes into private boxes, which could be hired by the season, in theory bringing in an extra £15,000, although in the first six months after opening, only eleven boxes had been so leased.

A new version of the National Anthem was composed as a street ballad, which was sung nightly in the theatre, invoking the figure of John Bull to uphold the audience's rights as Englishmen:

> Oh, JOHNNY BULL be true,
> Oppose the Prices New,
> And make them fall.

> Curse Kemble's Politicks,
> Frustrate his Knavish Tricks,
> On thee, our Hopes we fix,
> Confound them all.[1]

The theatre was closed for a week and a committee appointed to look into the price rises, but their findings, that the increases were justified, were not accepted by the audience. The unrest was exacerbated by the management's decision to hire professional boxers for crowd control. The discontent escalated still further when the doorkeeper, James Brandon, arrested the barrister Henry Clifford, a well-known champion of radical causes. Released without charge, Clifford brought an action of false arrest against the doorkeeper which was upheld by the courts.

The mounting expenses of legal fees, the bouncers' wages, and free passes for allies paid to chant 'N.P.' (for 'New Price') meant that by December the management were losing £300 per night. After sixty-seven nights of rioting, Kemble capitulated on terms worked out with Henry Clifford: Kemble was to make a public apology, the private boxes would be thrown open for public use, and the prices in the pit would be reduced to 3s. 6d., the price for a box seat remaining at seven shillings. The deal was sealed by the resignation of James Brandon as 'box keeper', but did not include improving the cheapest seats, and the 'pigeon holes' remained. Kemble's apology was received by loud cheers from the audience, and a large placard was raised in the pit with the legend: 'We Are Satisfied'. The playwright Mrs Inchbald, however, writing to a friend in 1809, complained that 'If the public force the managers to reduce their prices, a revolution in England is effected.'[2]

1. *Theatrical Street Ballads: Some Nineteenth-Century Street Ballads About the Theatre*, ed. J.W. Robinson, pp. 42–3.

2. *Plays by George Colman the Younger and Thomas Morton*, ed. Barry Sutcliffe, p. 7.

The **OP** SPECTACLES.

The **N.P.** SPECTACLES

dark
indigo blue →

2.   Gloucester.   basic & jerkin, sleeves, armour, cloak (N),
                        hat.

George Devine

"Through tatter'd clothes small vices do appear...
King Lear (4.6)

Isamu Noguchi's costume design for Gloucester in George Devine's production of *King Lear* (1955)

Productions of Shakespeare are usually remembered by the name of an actor or director – think of Olivier's *Richard III* or Brook's *A Midsummer Night's Dream* – but the designers who created the settings and costumes for these performances, and who brought their directors' interpretations to life, tend to get a much lower billing. The cast of the Shakespeare Memorial Theatre's 1955 production of *King Lear*, which toured in Europe before coming to London's Palace Theatre and, briefly, to Stratford, was headed by John Gielgud, playing Lear for the fourth time, and included, as Cordelia, Peggy Ashcroft in Europe and Claire Bloom in London. The director, also playing Gloucester, was George Devine (1910–1966), who founded the English Stage Company at the Royal Court the following year. But the production has passed into theatre history by virtue of its design by the Japanese-American artist and sculptor Isamu Noguchi.

Noguchi (1904–1988) had a long and wide-ranging career, during which he created gardens, lighting, furniture and ceramics, as well as art works. His work is well represented in the V&A, which holds an example of his three-sided glass-topped coffee table (designed in 1947 but still in production in the twenty-first century), a paper table lamp, and a Bakelite baby monitor, as well as a set model and costume designs for *King Lear*. The costume designs are works of art in their own right. Instead of sketching and painting, Noguchi made paper and card figures. Though subsequently mounted on paper with the makers' notes and instructions added, the figures were designed to stand upright, and the wire strut that supported each one is still attached.

This unusual way of presenting costume designs caused problems for the makers. Experienced costumiers Carl Bonn and Colin Mackenzie, who dressed the production, were puzzled by a representation that reduced everything to a flat plane, giving no indication of the weight or drape of the fabrics. Such practicalities did not concern Noguchi, who had never designed costume before and did not supervise the manufacture. Though he had worked in the theatre in New York and was the designer of choice for modern dance pioneer Martha Graham, he had always been responsible for the decor, not the dress. A cloak and mask for Graham's 1940 work *El Penitente* were the only costume pieces that he had previously created. Devine and Gielgud were apparently aware of this but, impressed by Noguchi's sculptural designs for Graham's company, had developed the idea of a stylised staging of *King Lear*. They explained in a programme note that their object was 'to find a setting and costumes which would be free of historical or decorative associations so that the timeless, universal and mythical quality of the story may be clear.'

The reality turned out rather differently from the intention. Instead of being free of association, Noguchi's settings and costumes drew attention to themselves. They 'continue to paralyse with either ecstasy or horror', commented Devine when the production played at the Holland Festival.[1] In London, the words 'baffling' and 'science fiction' recurred in reviews, the majority of critics finding the design distracting and inappropriate. The geometric forms which made up the set reminded Philip Hope-Wallace of 'huge portions of Cheddar cheese'.[2] 'The women are hideously wrapped, while the men wear deck-tennis rings for hats and variations on the cellular bathmat over space suits in heavy leather,' wrote the critic of *Punch*.[3] Gielgud stood by his designer in public but later confessed that 'my costumes destroyed any chance of my giving an effective performance'.[4] However, he discovered that the novelty and notoriety did no harm to the audience figures – 'we are packed to standing room notwithstanding,' he wrote in a letter of 28 July that year.[5]

1. Quoted in the Peterborough column of the *Daily Telegraph*, 9 July 1955.

2. *Manchester Guardian*, 28 July 1955.

3. *Punch*, 10 August 1955.

4. John Gielgud with John Miller, *Shakespeare: Hit or Miss?*, p. 98.

5. Letter to Hugh Wheeler, *Gielgud's Letters*, p. 183.

Roger Furse's costume design for John Gielgud as King Lear (1940)

Roger Furse (1903–1972) was one of the leading British stage and screen designers of the mid-twentieth century. He frequently worked for the Old Vic, in productions which featured some of the great names of British theatre, and was particularly known for his collaborations with Laurence Olivier, for whom he designed the films of *Henry V*, *Hamlet* and *Richard III*. *Hamlet* (1948) won him Academy Awards for Art Direction and Costumes, the first time an Oscar had been awarded in the costume design category. *The Times* obituary writer summed up his work as 'always discreet, sensitive to the dramatic requirements of the play or film, and beautifully finished.'[1] A Roger Furse costume design would convey character as well as clothing. Those for the Old Vic's 1950 *Twelfth Night*, held by the V&A, group together Olivia's household, Sir Toby and his associates, and laughing villagers, all with their personalities caught by stance and gesture. This design for John Gielgud's 1940 King Lear is annotated 'Mr John Gielgud – 2nd costume', but without the note it could equally be the artist's interpretation of an Old Testament prophet.

John Gielgud (1904–2000) had played Lear at the Old Vic in 1931 when he was only twenty-seven, and he was still a young Lear when he again took the role in 1940. The production marked the reopening of the Old Vic after the enforced closure of London's theatres at the outbreak of the Second World War, and was keenly anticipated. Ostensibly the production was directed by Lewis Casson, who also played Kent, but a programme note stated that the production was based on Granville-Barker's *Preface to King Lear*, 'and his personal advice besides.'[2] Harley Granville-Barker had given up the stage to concentrate on writing, most notably his series of *Prefaces to Shakespeare* (1927–1947). He had not directed Shakespeare in Britain since his influential trio of productions at the Savoy Theatre (1912 and 1914). Gielgud persuaded him to be the co-director of *King Lear*, but Granville-Barker only agreed as long as he remained uncredited. Now living in Paris, he briefly visited London to plan the production with Casson, Furse and Gielgud, and then left Casson and his actors to work on it themselves, basing their interpretation on the published *Preface to King Lear*. Returning, he 'scrapped nearly everything' and conducted an intensive ten days of rehearsal.[3] Granville-Barker was 'a relentless but amazingly brilliant taskmaster', and Gielgud admired him greatly, observing that:

> Although he had a very strong conception of how every character should be played, he did not at first try to force his views upon the actors or attempt to discourage their ideas, though he frequently corrected them… no detail could escape his fastidious ear, his unerring dramatic instinct, and his superb sense of classic shapeliness of line.[4]

Furse gave the play a Renaissance setting. Describing the first scene in her book *Old Vic Drama*, Audrey Williamson noted that the 'glowing satins and jewelled earrings bespoke a Court decked in splendour, a living witness to the King's passion for pomp and power'.[5] Gielgud, she wrote, had 'the regal poise of one accustomed to rule without question, and the voice held possibilities of thunder'.[6] Several reviewers commented on the actor's lack of years, but his interpretation of the role was acclaimed. For the critic of *The Times*, Gielgud

> was acting with a nervous force which, though it seemed at times to fall something short in physical toughness, yet enabled him to trace with a brilliant exactness Lear's progress from worldly to spiritual authority. The Olympian grandeur, the frets, the rages, the madness lit with flashes of savage irony and broken in upon by spiritual illumination – all these phases of the part he succeeded in treating as though they were a spontaneous product of the mind, but the simplicities at the end he surrounded with a stillness of beauty which is rarely achieved on the stage.[7]

1. *The Times*, 21 August 1972.

2. *The Preface to King Lear*, originally written for The Players' Shakespeare edition of the play (London: Ernest Benn, 1927), was re-published in the first series of Harley Granville-Barker's *Prefaces to Shakespeare* (London: Sidgwick & Jackson, 1927).

3. Jonathan Croall, *John Gielgud: Matinee Idol to Movie Star*, p. 273.

4. Letter to Hugh Walpole, dated April 1940, in *Gielgud's Letters*, p. 59; John Gielgud, *Stage Directions*, p. 53.

5. Audrey Williamson, *Old Vic Drama: A Twelve Years' Study of Plays and Players*, p. 133.

6. *Ibid.*, p. 134.

7. *The Times*, 16 April 1940.

Paul Robeson and Peggy Ashcroft as Othello and Desdemona (1930)

Director Tony Richardson decided to travel to America to invite Paul Robeson (1898–1976) to perform Shakespeare at Stratford, because, he explained, 'Robeson had been ostracised, maligned and discriminated against for years'.[1] It was 1958 and Robeson's passport had only recently been returned to him, having been confiscated for eight years by the US State Department, which had placed him under surveillance on account of his political beliefs. To Richardson, his lunch appointment with Robeson at the fashionable Algonquin restaurant in New York seemed in itself 'almost a revolutionary gesture' in defiance of the colour bar still in operation.[2] Richardson initially asked Robeson to play Gower in *Pericles*, with the aim of setting Gower's narration to music, which would have been an ideal vehicle for Robeson's powerful bass voice. Although unable to accept the offer, Robeson agreed to come to Stratford the following year to play Othello.

Opposite Robeson's Othello, Richardson cast as Iago the American actor Sam Wanamaker, who had also been targeted by the US State Department for his political views. The audiences warmed to Robeson, but the production was not a success with the critics. Richardson himself acknowledged that the excellence of Robeson's long narrations in Act One were not matched by his performance in later scenes of the play. Robeson was over sixty years old, and had suffered a recent serious illness, but as Richardson saw, he also lacked a measure of experience and technical expertise. Robeson told Richardson that when he had last appeared in *Othello* on Broadway in 1943, the only direction he received from director Margaret Webster was 'Be a black panther and stalk'.[3] The Broadway production had nevertheless been hugely successful: Robeson's appearance on stage was greeted with applause from the audience lasting for twenty minutes and it was recognised as the moment when 'the doors of the American theatre opened for the Negro people'.[4] The play had over 280 performances, a record for Shakespeare on Broadway and went on tour visiting forty-five American cities. The critic Robert

Garland considered that 'in all my nights of attendance on the world of make-believe, there has been nothing to equal it'.[5]

Margaret Webster later confessed that she had not been overly impressed when she first saw Robeson play Othello at the Savoy Theatre in London in 1930, opposite Peggy Ashcroft (shown here), and Robeson himself admitted that he had felt unprepared for the role then. Sybil Thorndike, who played Emilia in that production, recalled:

> It was very interesting working with Paul. He was such a dear person – and how he worked! He was potentially a fine actor, but he hadn't the technique of acting, so he had to do everything *really*. He poured with sweat with the effort of it all. He was very courteous... And modest too. In our big scene together I used to have to go on saying, 'This is your scene. Take the stage.'[6]

The chemistry between Robeson's Othello and Peggy Ashcroft's Desdemona was nevertheless electrifying. 'How could one not fall in love in such a situation with such a man?' admitted Ashcroft, who, with Sybil Thorndike, received hate mail for appearing with a black actor.[7] The experience awakened her to the issues of racism: 'The fact that Paul Robeson, who was acclaimed as a great singer and a great artist in this country, was not welcome in the Savoy Hotel was enormously shocking and surprising to me... I think my first feelings about racism were aroused in that play.'[8] As the six-week London run progressed, Robeson gained in confidence in the role, with excited audiences standing on chairs and cheering his performance. Talking to a journalist, he expressed the tremendous sense of liberation and transformation that he found in playing the role: 'Othello has taken away from me all kinds of fears, all sense of limitation, and all racial prejudice. Othello has opened to me new and wider fields; in a word, Othello has made me free.'[9]

1. Tony Richardson, *Long Distance Runner*, p. 100.

2. *Ibid.*

3. *Ibid.*, p. 101

4. Paul Cope, *Let Paul Robeson Sing!*, p. 28.

5. *Ibid.*

6. Elizabeth Sprigge, *Sybil Thorndike Casson*, p. 193.

7. Michael Billington, *Peggy Ashcroft*, p. 41.

8. *Ibid.*

9. Martin Bauml Duberman, *Paul Robeson*, p. 137.

Portrait of Ira Aldridge as Othello (*c.* 1848)

This oil painting of Ira Aldridge (1807–1867) as Othello, by an unknown artist, came to the V&A in 1958 as a gift from Aldridge's co-biographer Herbert Marshall, who found the museum's theatre collections a valuable resource for researching his subject, the first black Shakespearean actor to win international recognition. Born in New York in 1807, Aldridge began his acting career at an inauspicious time in America. Although slavery had been abolished in New York by 1799, racial segregation was still enforced in the theatres, with gallery seats only reserved for 'Negroes', who were not admitted into any other part of the house. Audiences were not receptive to Shakespeare's plays being performed by black actors; when *Richard III* was presented by the African Grove Theatre in 1822, with white members of the audience segregated to the back of the theatre, a closure order was issued, and when this was defied, the police entered the auditorium to shut the performance down and arrest the actors.[1] There appeared to be better prospects for black performers in England: Aldridge's fellow actor James Hewlett, the former servant of the English actor George Frederick Cooke, was offered work at the Coburg Theatre (the Old Vic) in London. At the age of seventeen, Aldridge left America for good, and never performed his signature role of Othello in his native land.

On his arrival in England, he assumed the stage name of Mr Keene, probably on the basis of having seen Edmund Kean perform in America in 1820. As well as playing Othello at the Coburg Theatre in 1825, he acted in an adaptation of *Oronooko*, a play based on the novel by Aphra Behn about an African prince kidnapped into slavery, a real-life figure whom she had met on her travels in Surinam. Despite being well received by the public, Aldridge's performance as Oronooko attracted hostility from the reviewer in *The Times*: 'owing to the shape of his lips,' he wrote, it was 'utterly impossible for him to pronounce English in such a manner as to satisfy even the unfastidious ears of the gallery.'[2] Aldridge was never

287

able to escape prejudice of this kind from certain quarters, although it is more than balanced by the extraordinary honour and praise he received from others. In 1827, aged twenty, he was given his first international recognition, from the Republic of Haiti, which awarded him an honorary commission in the army as 'the first man of colour in the theatre'.[3] He went on to receive honours from the courts of Prussia, Austria, Saxe-Coburg, Switzerland, and the cities of Riga and St Petersburg. He became a British citizen in 1863.

When Edmund Kean saw Aldridge play Othello in Dublin in 1832, he admired his 'wondrous versatility', and recommended him to the theatre manager in Bath.[4] Kean saw that Aldridge was the natural successor of Garrick in excelling in comedy as well as tragedy. Nevertheless, Aldridge did not succeed in establishing himself upon the London stage, despite being well received in other parts of Britain, especially in Hull, home of the abolitionist William Wilberforce, where he played Shylock, Macbeth, King Lear and Richard III to an enthusiastic reception.

Aldridge found on the Continent the recognition that eluded him in his adopted country. When Aldridge's forthcoming appearance in Zurich was advertised, Richard Wagner wrote to Mathilde Wesendonck: 'For your attention: Wednesday, Othello with Ira Aldridge. Tickets should be secured well in advance.'[5] As a kind of itinerant missionary of art, Aldridge brought Shakespeare to remote areas of Russia, and he was feted in the major cities. The French poet Théophile Gautier, who saw him play Othello in St Petersburg in 1863, was full of admiration, describing the performance as 'quiet, reserved, classic, majestic' and 'Othello himself, as Shakespeare has created him', even though Aldridge performed his role in English, with the rest of the cast speaking German.[6] *Red Velvet*, a play by Lolita Chakrabarti based on Aldridge's life and starring Adrian Lester, was staged at the Tricycle Theatre in Kilburn in 2012 to sold-out houses, with Lester's own Othello following at the National Theatre in 2013, to equal acclaim.

1. Kim C. Sturgess, *Shakespeare and the American Nation*, p. 156.

2. Herbert Marshall and Mildred Stock, *Ira Aldridge*, p. 62.

3. *Ibid.*, p. 79.

4. *Ibid*, p. 103.

5. *Ibid.*, p. 191.

6. Martin Bauml Duberman, *Paul Robeson*, p. 275.

MRS BRACEGIRDLE AS "THE INDIAN QUEEN"

Mrs Bracegirdle as the Indian Queen in Aphra Behn's *The Widow Ranter* (*c.* 1690)

Like Mrs Barry, Anne Bracegirdle (*c.* 1671–1748) was one of the actresses trained for the stage by Thomas and Mary Betterton. Admired for her comic gifts and for her singing, she was not, according to her fellow actor Colley Cibber, conventionally beautiful, but nevertheless a great favourite with the male members of the audience, and the more she resisted their desires, the more irresistible she became:

> tho' she might be said to have been the Universal Passion, and under the highest Temptations, her Constancy in resisting them served but to increase the number of her Admirers... [yet] she had no greater Claim to Beauty than what the most desirable *Brunette* might pretend to. But her Youth and lively Aspect threw out such a Glow of Health and Chearfulness, that... few Spectators that were not past it could behold her without Desire. It was even Fashion among the Gay and Young to have a Taste or a *Tendre* for Mrs *Bracegirdle*.[1]

The passions she excited led to an abduction attempt in 1692 by the army officers Captain Richard Hill and Lord Mohun, who, assisted by six soldiers, ambushed her as she and her mother left their friend Mr Page's house and were walking home. The attempt failed partly because she could not be separated from her mother, who clung to her tightly, and partly because their friend Mr Page raised the alarm and beat Hill off with his stick. The attack was provoked by Captain Hill's jealousy of Mrs Barry's fellow actor William Mountfort, with whom he suspected she was involved. Meeting Mountfort, who happened to be on his way to the Bracegirdle home a little while later, unaware of the attempted abduction, Hill ran him through with his sword and Mountfort later died. Hill escaped justice, and although Mohun stood trial, he was acquitted. Both eventually met violent ends; Hill was killed in a brawl five years later and Mohun died in a duel in 1712.

Mrs Bracegirdle's Shakespearean roles were Lady Anne in *Richard III*, Desdemona in *Othello*, Ophelia in *Hamlet*, Portia in *Julius Caesar*, and Isabella in Gildon's version of *Measure for Measure*. She played Angelica in the premiere of *Love for Love* and Congreve created the part of Millamant in *The Way of the World* especially for her. This engraving shows her as Semernia, the Indian Queen in *The Widow Ranter* by Aphra Behn (*c.* 1640–1689). Although in the illustration she appears demure, fashionably bedecked in feathers, the part was a breeches role, in which she dresses as a man and shoots with a bow and arrow. The stage direction for Act Five, Scene Three reads: '*Enter* Queen *dress'd like an* Indian *Man, with a Bow in her Hand.*' Set in the American Colonies, the play is described as a tragicomedy, because although the Indian Queen appears to have been fatally wounded in battle by mistake by the English General Bacon, she emerges unscathed in the final scene in order to triumphantly marry him.[2]

The premiere of Behn's play is likely to have been a posthumous production, since the author died in 1689. The first female professional playwright, ranked by Daniel Defoe with the Earl of Rochester and Milton as among the 'great wits' of her era, Behn had been employed as an undercover agent overseas for the British Secret Service by Thomas Killigrew, although forced to sell off her jewels and borrow money because the government failed to pay her wages.[3] The playwright had recently returned from Surinam and brought back large quantities of feathers, which were much in demand for fashionable dress and for stage costumes. As may be seen from the exotic costume in the illustration, the Indian Queen wears a feathered headdress and carries a bunch of feathers in her hand, attended by two small native children clothed in feathers, one holding her train and the other holding a parasol over her head. The fashion for exotic feathers could be taken to extremes on the Restoration stage, and when the trend reached Ireland, it was reported: 'We have Plays here [in Dublin] in the newest Mode... only the other Day when Othello was play'd, the Doge of Venice and all his Senators came on the Stage with Feathers in their Hats, which was like to have chang'd the Tragedy into a Comedy.'[4]

---

1. Philip H. Highfill (et al.), *A Biographical Dictionary of Actors... 1660–1800*, vol. 2, p. 271.

2. Aphra Behn, *The Widow Ranter*, in *Five Plays*, ed. Maureen Duffy, p. 283.

3. Paddy Lyons and Fidelis Morgan (eds.), *Female Playwrights of the Restoration: Five Comedies*, Introduction, p. xv.

4. George C.D. Odell, *Shakespeare from Betterton to Irving*, vol. 1, p. 206.

Ronald Cobb's costume design, inspired by *Antony and Cleopatra*, for the Eve Club, London (1970s)

When Ben Jonson described Shakespeare as 'not of an age, but for all time', he was probably not thinking of a time, 450 years on, when Shakespeare's work would form the inspiration for a floor show featuring scantily clad showgirls.[1] Nevertheless, in the 1970s, that's exactly what happened. Helen O'Brien (1925–2005), the owner and proprietor of the Eve Club, a private members' club in Regent Street, had a talent for devising interestingly themed floor-shows to entertain the politicians, legal professionals, royalty, celebrities, and other establishment figures who frequented the club. O'Brien and designer Ronald Cobb produced elaborate and ingenious costumes that referenced a variety of popular culture sources.

Eve's clientele appreciated the spectacular and witty nature of the floor shows which were performed on one of the first illuminated glass floors in London. The show was the high point of the 'journey into fantasy' that O'Brien envisaged for her clients.[2] But there was also a more serious side to the club, which was 'a honeypot for espionage', as O'Brien was employed by MI5 and MI6 to pass on the information that guests shared with the hostesses.[3]

The costume design shown here is for *Antony and Cleopatra*, and is one of six Shakespeare-inspired costumes from the 'Bibliotheque' show in which the girls represented a range of literary genres, including Drama. Shakespeare represented the theatre and Cobb reduced six of his plays – *Macbeth*, *Romeo and Juliet*, *Antony and Cleopatra*, *The Merchant of Venice*, *A Midsummer Night's Dream* and *Hamlet* – to their bare essentials to form the basis of the costumes. So *Antony and Cleopatra* describes the clash of cultures between Rome and Egypt via a Roman soldier's breastplate (but with breasts on display), an Egyptian motif on the G-string, a helmet with a ship and tower atop it (representing the Battle of Actium), and an asp coiled round the performer's right arm. This is actually one of the more tasteful costumes. The G-string for the *Hamlet* costume features the head of the drowned Ophelia, while the *Merchant of Venice* G-string shows the head of a Jewish man, complete with yarmulke and peyots. The V&A has a number of costume designs and costumes from the Eve Club donated by the O'Brien family, including all the Shakespeare designs and the *Hamlet* headdress. Although the plays featured are among the most frequently represented of Shakespeare's works, the Eve Club material remains among the most unusual of our Shakespeare holdings.

1. From Jonson's dedicatory poem in the First Folio (1623).

2. Helen O'Brien obituary, *Daily Telegraph*, 20 September 2005.

3. Helen O'Brien obituary, *Guardian*, 29 September 2005.

Ronald Cobb.

Madam Elinora Gwynne,

S Couper pinx.   G Valck Sculp. et ex.

Gerard Valck, engraved portrait of Nell Gwyn (*c.* 1670)

This rare engraving by Valck was published in Nell Gwyn's lifetime (*c.* 1651–1687), when her beauty and popularity were immortalised in countless images and reproductions. Her sister Rose was an associate of Henry Killigrew, whose father Thomas was patentee of the King's Theatre, and on the strength of this connection, Nell started to work as an orange-seller for the King's Company, soon graduating to become a member of the acting troupe in 1664. The patent issued by Charles II to Thomas Killigrew on 25 April 1662 allowed actresses onto the public stage for the first time, in line with the practice on the Continent. The sudden demand for actresses at first exceeded supply, with men continuing to star in women's roles. According to Pepys, the young actor Thomas Kynaston, who played the Duke's sister in *The Loyal Subject*, 'made the loveliest lady that ever I saw in my life'.[1] Nell Gwyn soon became the mistress of leading actor Charles Hart, and then of Charles, Lord Buckhurst, before capturing the interest of the King himself, whom she accordingly called 'Charles III'. She became the most famous of all the King's mistresses, due in part to the homage to her recorded by Pepys in his diary, which was decoded from shorthand and made available to the public from 1825:

> Thence to Westminster, in the way meeting many milk-maids with
> their garlands upon their pails, dancing with a fiddler before them, and
> saw pretty Nelly standing at her lodgings door in Drury-lane in her
> smock-sleeves and bodice, looking upon one – she seemed a mighty
> pretty creature.[2]

Perhaps on account of her lowly origins, she captured the public imagination. The V&A has a painting dating from 1920 of the actress Julia Neilson as Nell in Paul Kester's *Sweet Nell of Old Drury*, and another play of the same era, *English Nell*, starring Marie Tempest, became a firm favourite in provincial repertory theatre. Although it is not certain that Nell played any Shakespearean parts, she did go to see his plays: the accounts of the Royal Exchequer record payments for her, and groups of her friends, for seeing *The Tempest* (four times), *Macbeth*, and *Hamlet* in the space of three months in late 1674, and for seeing *King Lear* in 1675.[3] The leading poet and dramatist of the day, John Dryden, created the character of Florimell especially for Nell in *Secret Love*, a role which helped establish the Restoration convention of the fast-living, racy couple. Her performance in this role was highly relished by Pepys:

> but so great performance of a comical part was never, I believe, in this
> world before as Nell doth this, both as a mad girle and then, most and
> best of all, when she comes in like a young gallant; and hath the
> motions and carriage of a spark the most that ever I saw any man have.
> It makes me, I confess, admire her.[4]

Nell was also popular for dancing her famous jig as an epilogue to round off performances, although Pepys was of the opinion that Moll Davis of the Duke's Company was a better dancer. Moll was also one of the King's mistresses, and gave birth to a daughter, the fourteenth, and last, of the King's illegitimate children, with Nell's two sons Charles and James ranking seventh and eighth. Nell returned briefly to the stage after the birth of her eldest son to act in Dryden's *The Conquest of Granada*, before retiring for good from the stage in 1671. She had retained the King's affections so effectively for seventeen years that on his death in 1685 he had been planning to make her a Countess. In her relations with the King she was fortunate in having been able, for the most part, to follow the wise counsel of her friend the Earl of Rochester, who had advised her to 'live in Peace with all the World, and easily with the King', to 'Cherish his Love where-ever it inclines, and be assur'd you can't commit greater Folly than pretending to be jealous', and to 'Make Sport when you can, at other times help it'.[5]

1. *Diary of Samuel Pepys*, vol. 1, p. 224.

2. *Ibid.*, vol. 8, p. 193.

3. Judith Milhous and Robert D. Hume, *A Register of English Theatrical Documents 1660–1737*, vol. 1, document 862 (p. 169).

4. *Diary of Samuel Pepys*, vol. 8, p. 91.

5. Philip H. Highfill (et al.), *A Biographical Dictionary of Actors... 1660–1800*, vol. 6, p. 466.

Leslie Hurry's costume design for Cymbeline (1949)

The *Guardian* marked the passing of artist and stage designer Leslie Hurry with an obituary headed 'The master of phantasmagoria'.[1] Hurry (1909–1978) regarded himself as an artist rather than a designer, and his work, which commentators linked to Surrealism and to the English Neo-Romanticism of the 1930s, was known for its dreamlike images and what his obituarist called its 'brooding eeriness'. It was immediately recognisable in the theatre. Having been persuaded by Robert Helpmann to design the latter's 1942 ballet *Hamlet*, Hurry had a thirty-year career as a designer of plays, opera and ballet. Although he did design contemporary drama, it was the classics of the British stage – particularly the works of Shakespeare and his contemporaries – that were most suited to Hurry's imagination. Using a distinctive colour palette dominated by dull reds, yellows, greys and muddy greens, he created elaborate costumes and oversized architectural settings which managed to be simultaneously vast and claustrophobic.

Robert Helpmann's partner, the director Michael Benthall (1919–1974), met Hurry when Helpmann was planning his *Hamlet* ballet, and worked with the designer on Shakespeare's *Hamlet* for the Old Vic Company (1944) and *Turandot* at Covent Garden (1947). Benthall first directed at the Shakespeare Memorial Theatre in 1947, and brought Hurry to Stratford in 1949 to design *Cymbeline*. Productions of the play had not been plentiful (Benthall was only the sixth director to present it at Stratford), but it had been staged there only three years earlier, directed by Nugent Monck. Monck's version – pretty, romanticised, unexciting – was a typical product of mid-1940s Stratford, when the Memorial Theatre was essentially a regional repertory theatre, employing young and largely unknown actors and playing to local audiences. When Anthony Quayle took charge in 1948 he began a new era, raising the theatre's profile with well-known players and directors, and increasing the budget to allow a more lavish approach to design. *Cymbeline*, as visualised by Benthall and Hurry, was a good example of the new pictorial Stratford style.

In 1948, Benthall had complained that the magic of the theatre was being destroyed 'by the simplification of Shakespearean settings and the emphasis on curtains and rostrums'.[2] This was, he thought, a mistake: 'because the ear is interested, there is no reason why the eye should be bored.'[3] Though Benthall's opinions were to change – at the Old Vic in 1956 he directed another *Cymbeline* on a bare stage – in 1949 he devised a production on an operatic scale, set in a fantastical primitive world of 'barbaric splendour'.[4] King Cymbeline inhabited a vast palace of impossible architecture, with soaring arches receding into the far distance at an exaggerated perspective. The stage was peopled with attendants and extras. In the text, Cymbeline makes his first entrance with an unspecified number of lords. In Benthall's production, he was accompanied by his Queen and stepson, plus a dwarf servant of the Queen, four gentlemen, four lords, two servants, five ladies, and Doctor Cornelius.[5]

This costume design for Cymbeline, with its elegant, sinuous figure enveloped by a flowing cloak, is characteristic of Hurry's work. It is annotated in the spidery, and often illegible, handwriting which fellow designer Tanya Moiseiwitsch described as 'made up of horizontal lines and grace-notes'.[6] Fortunately, Hurry worked closely with the makers. Judy White, a member of the Stratford wardrobe department in 1949, recalled that, despite his impressive reputation, he was the first to admit that he needed her team 'to interpret and help with his sometimes very difficult designs'.[7] The note on this design is difficult to read, but there is a reference to Cymbeline's cloak which is to be painted with highlights of gold. Costume designs are vital evidence for the theatre historian but they do not always represent what was seen on the stage. Production photographs show Leon Quartermaine's King wearing a cloak of plain cloth, though the rest of the costume is as drawn by Hurry. In performance it was the Queen who wore the richly patterned glittering cloak.

1. Dale Harris, *Guardian*, 23 November 1978.

2. Michael Benthall, 'Shakespeare in the Theatre', p. 140.

3. *Ibid.*

4. W.A. Darlington, *Daily Telegraph*, 21 May 1949.

5. Prompt book for the production: Shakespeare Centre, Stratford-upon-Avon, O.S.71.21/1949C.

6. *Leslie Hurry: A Painter for the Stage*, exhibition catalogue.

7. *Ibid.*

Gold bracelet presented to Kate Terry by her fiancé (1867)

This opulent gold bracelet, in its royal-blue velvet-covered presentation case lined with cream satin and green velvet, was given by the wealthy haberdasher and silk merchant Arthur Lewis (1824–1901) to his fiancée Kate Terry in 1867, when she retired from the stage to marry him. Wearing bracelets was very fashionable generally then, but the added symbolism of ownership that it represented could not have been lost on Kate, being engraved on either side of the clasp with Posthumus's 'manacle of love' speech to Imogen, from Act One of Shakespeare's *Cymbeline*:

> And, sweetest, fairest,
> As I my poor self did exchange for you,
> To your so infinite loss, so in our trifles
> I still win of you. For my sake wear this;
> It is a manacle of love; I'll place it
> Upon this fairest prisoner.

(1.1.118–23)

The bracelet was specially commissioned by Lewis to fit the long list of all Kate's roles, with the dates she played them, that is painstakingly engraved on the inner surface, prefaced with the date of her birthday, 21 April 1844. Every role is listed, from the earliest in 1847 as Boy in *Children in the Wood* to the title role of *Dora* in 1867. The bracelet is made in five curving hollow sections joined with concealed hinges; it has a safety chain, and the top features a laurel wreath in translucent green enamel, sprinkled with tiny diamonds, encircling a locket compartment. Its lid, set with their entwined initials in diamonds, opens to reveal a coloured miniature photograph of Kate , and the engraved inscription: 'To Kate Terry on her retirement from the stage Oct 5th 1867. From him for whom she leaves it.'[1]

By 1867 Kate Terry (1844–1924), the eldest daughter of the strolling actors Ben Terry and Sarah Ballard, was an established leading lady on the London stage, a great success with a string of major parts to her name, and yet she was only twenty-three. Like many children from an acting family, she started her career as a child, with a walk-on part at the age of three. After her first role in Charles Kean's company, aged eight, as Prince Arthur in the 1852 production of *King John*, she stayed with Kean's company at London's Princess's Theatre, playing Ariel to his Prospero in *The Tempest* in 1857, and Cordelia to his King Lear in 1858, when she was only fourteen. In 1864, she played Ophelia to Charles Fechter's Hamlet at the Lyceum Theatre, impressing the critic of *The Times* with her 'natural, unaffected pathos' in the mad scene.[2] As another commentator later wrote of her performance:

> No doubt Kate Terry contributed largely to Fechter's Lyceum successes. She could not only act, but she so threw herself into her characters that she could *listen* to those who acted with her, and let her audiences not only see, but believe that she was listening with all her heart and soul. The exercise of this rarely displayed histrionic gift was invaluable in the beautiful love-scenes of Fechter.[3]

Elizabeth Murray Kate Terry married the forty-three-year-old Arthur James Lewis in London on 18 October 1867, just thirteen days after her final performance at the Prince's Theatre, Manchester, in Tom Taylor's *Plot and Passion*. The bangle is a curious paradox because the carefully engraved list of all her roles and dates is a testament to the pride and respect that Lewis had for her career. Yet by marrying her, Lewis wanted to make Kate his respectable wife, to elevate her from the perceived shady world of the stage and the suspect life of an actress, which he nevertheless so obviously celebrates with this gift.

Had Kate Terry not retired for marriage and motherhood it is arguable that she would have equalled or even surpassed the fame of her elder sister, the great Ellen Terry, and must have regarded her famous sister's stellar career with a mixture of pride and regret. She remained fond of the theatre all her life, reciting speeches from Shakespeare and other dramatists to their four girls, the eldest of whom, Kate Terry Lewis (1868–1958), was the mother of the great Shakespearean actor John Gielgud (1904–2000). Gielgud gave his grandmother's bracelet to the actress Irene Worth, who in turn bequeathed it to the Theatre Collections of the V&A.

1. Photography by the London photographers Window & Bridge.

2. *The Times*, 26 May 1864.

3. T. Edgar Pemberton, *Ellen Terry and Her Sisters*, p. 103.

66 Your master is not there, who was indeed the
riches of it...**99**
Cymbeline (3.4)

99

Henry Wallis, *Shakespeare's House, Stratford-upon-Avon* (c. 1854), with additions by Edwin Landseer (1866)

Painted by Henry Wallis (1830–1916), most famous for his picture *The Death of Chatterton* in Tate Britain, the original version of this painting of Shakespeare's birthplace hung in John Forster's dining room for twelve years after its completion in 1854. It was observed there by Edwin Landseer, who often remarked that he would like to make his own addition to the painting as a token of his friendship with Forster. It was his idea to add the waiting dog, an addition which greatly delighted Forster.[1]

Forster (1812–1876) was Chairman of the London Committee of the Royal Shakespearean Club, which helped to secure the acquisition of the birthplace for the nation. The Corporation of Stratford-upon-Avon, home of the nation's most famous dramatist, had succeeded in banning the performance of plays from 1602 until 1746, when a travelling company of players staged a production of *Othello* in the Town Hall with such success that the company stayed on for a further five months. Lovers of Shakespeare before then had made the town a place of pilgrimage, and in 1708 the actor Thomas Betterton, then in his seventies, visited Stratford to research materials on Shakespeare's life for inclusion in Rowe's 1709 edition of Shakespeare's works. He was the first investigator to search the town records for information about Shakespeare's family, although unfortunately his inexperience in archival research led to some errors in the edition, with Shakespeare recorded as having three, instead of two, daughters.[2] In response to the growing stream of visitors, the Reverend John Ward, who was Vicar of Stratford from 1662 to 1681, made a note to himself to 'Remember to peruse Shakespeare's plays, and bee versed in them, that I may not bee ignorant in that matter', but the Reverend Francis Gastrell, who owned New Place, the large house purchased by Shakespeare in 1597, had become so annoyed by the stream of visitors and requests to see the mulberry tree in the garden supposedly planted by Shakespeare, that he had the tree cut down in 1756.[3] His action aroused the fury of local residents, who broke the windows of New Place, but a watchmaker, Thomas Sharp, saw a business opportunity and, having bought the mulberry timber, carved it into souvenirs such as small boxes and spoons for sale to tourists. It has been doubted whether the wood from the tree could possibly have made all the items claimed to be carved from it, although the watchmaker testified on his deathbed that all the souvenirs he sold were authentic.[4] Gastrell then fell into dispute with Stratford Corporation because he objected to paying full rates on New Place, when he only lived in the property for part of the year. He became enraged when the Corporation refused to reduce the rates and had the property razed to the ground in 1759, earning himself a most ignominious place in the history of Shakespeare scholarship.[5]

A copy of this picture hangs on the first floor of the birthplace in the location where it was painted, which has remained largely unchanged. Shakespeare's father John is recorded as owning the property in 1552, when it was divided into two, the living quarters at the western end where Shakespeare was born and the adjoining premises used for his father's business as a glover and wool dealer. From 1793 to 1820 the house was lived in by a Mrs Hornby, who guided visitors around the property, showing them a dubious collection of Shakespearean relics. She is described by Washington Irving, who visited in 1815, as 'a garrulous old lady in a frosty red face, lighted up by a cold blue anxious eye, and garnished with artificial locks of flaxen hair, curling from under an exceeding dirty cap'. He was shown Shakespeare's 'tobacco-box; which proves that he was a rival smoker of Sir Walter Raleigh; the sword also with which he played Hamlet; and the identical lantern with which Friar Lawrence discovered Romeo and Juliet at the tomb!' There was an 'ample supply of Shakespeare's mulberry-tree', which Irving suspected of having 'extraordinary powers of self-multiplication'.[6] Wallis's picture dates from the time when the property was poorly maintained; it was offered for sale at auction in 1847 and purchased for the nation with a Trust formed to ensure its preservation.

1. Ronald Parkinson, *Catalogue of British Oil Paintings 1820–1860*, pp. 292–4.

2. S. Schoenbaum, *Shakespeare's Lives* (1991), p. 87.

3. Christian Deelman, *The Great Shakespeare Jubilee*, p. 34.

4. *Ibid.*, pp. 52–3.

5. Johanne M. Stochholm, *Garrick's Folly*, pp. 4–5.

6. Levi Fox, *The Borough Town of Stratford-upon-Avon*, p. 153.

Paul Catherall, limited-edition print of the front elevation of the rebuilt Royal Shakespeare Theatre, Stratford-upon-Avon (2010)

Described by director Peter Hall as 'a very handsome Art Deco building' which 'had very little to do with play-acting', the 1932 Shakespeare Memorial Theatre's stage and auditorium had proved problematic from the start.[1] The two state-of-the-art rolling stages for scene changes never worked satisfactorily and there was insufficient room in the wings. The stage lifts were not deep enough for tall scenery and could not be raised to their full height because the proscenium arch cut off the sight lines from the balcony seats. These seats were so far from the stage that, when he sat in them as a schoolboy, actor Tim Pigott-Smith thought that 'you had to be small to be an actor because the stage was so far away.'[2] The distance from the proscenium to the front stalls meant that audiences found it hard to hear the performance and, in 1944, the orchestra stalls were floored over to bring the audience closer to the stage. Further programmes of alteration to the stage and auditorium took place in the succeeding decades, but Peter Hall came to the conclusion that it was a hopeless task: 'we never got it right and the reason we never got it right was because you couldn't get it right.'[3] He decided as early as 1958 that the only solution was to demolish the building.

This was also the conclusion reached by Adrian Noble, who had been appointed Artistic Director and Chief Executive of the RSC in 1990. His vision was to create a new theatre, either on the site of the demolished Memorial Theatre or on that of the Arden Hotel opposite, which would be a flexible space combining the advantages offered by the thrust stage of a close relationship with the audience, and the technical versatility of a proscenium theatre. His plans proved hugely controversial and became linked in the public imagination with a 'Shakespeare Village' or suspected 'theme park' on the banks of the River Avon. Adrian Noble was left with no option but to resign, and the matter was summed up by the RSC Chair of Governors, Sir Christopher Bland:

Adrian's plan for Stratford was fatally flawed and had no chance of success. It involved the demolition of one Grade II* listed building, the first designed by a woman architect, and the Arden Hotel, part of which was also listed. English Heritage's opposition made a lengthy and expensive planning enquiry inevitable, with a successful outcome unlikely.[4]

The problem with radically changing the existing theatre was that the proscenium arch was integral to the structure. Adrian Noble's successor, Michael Boyd, discovered that a thrust stage with surrounding seating for 1,030 could be built within the walls of the existing auditorium and this proved to be a breakthrough in making a new theatre achievable. Plans were drawn up to include new dressing rooms, a riverside walk, and an observation tower linked by glass walkways to the main theatre. A seven-metre basement was constructed under the stage so that graves and dungeons could be created, and there were a further eighteen metres above the stage: 'more than enough for a couple of Bohemias or Elsinores, not to mention Illyria, Athens and a wood nearby and the entire Forest of Arden'.[5] At a late stage of the design process, the top floor of the building was doubled in height with floor-to-ceiling windows, and a canopy roof floated over the entire building to give it a new profile. The £112.8 million project was completed in 2010. *King Lear* and *Romeo and Juliet* were the first plays to be performed on the new stage in February 2011.

Printmaker and illustrator Paul Catherall is well known for his linocuts of architectural subjects. Here he simplifies the theatre exterior into blocks of colour to create a strong, stylised image of the transformed building, with a glimpse of the spire of Holy Trinity Church beyond.

1. David Ward, *Transformation*, p. 10.

2. *Ibid.*, p. 100.

3. *Ibid.*, p. 10.

4. *Ibid.*, p. 23.

5. *Ibid.*, p. 112.

List of Objects

This list gives a brief description of each object and its V&A reference number. Unless specified, the dimensions are height (for sculptures and three-dimensional artworks) and height x width (for paintings, prints and drawings). The author's name follows the object details. All the contributors are members of the V&A's Theatre and Performance department.

1. *Mr. William Shakespeares Comedies, Histories, & Tragedies* (the First Folio) (1623). Engraving (by Martin Droeshout) and letterpress. Printed by Isaac Jaggard and Edward Blount, London. 34cm (height), (V&A Jones Collection L.1392–1882). BEVERLEY HART

2. Matthias Merian, *View of London* (1638). Etching. 26cm x 73.4cm (V&A S.1113–1982). JAMES FOWLER

3. François Boitard, illustration of *The Tempest, The Works of Mr. William Shakespear*, ed. Nicholas Rowe, 9 vols (London, 1709), 1, opp. p. 1. Book: 22.4cm (height). Illustration: 18.2cm x 10.2cm (V&A DYCE. 8940/1). JAMES FOWLER

4. Loudon Sainthill, preliminary set design for *Pericles*, Shakespeare Memorial Theatre, Stratford-upon-Avon (1958). Pencil, pastel, and gouache on paper. 46cm x 64.5cm (V&A S.2414–1986). JANET BIRKETT

5. Still from the National Video Archive of Performance recording of *The Big Life*, written by Paul Sirett; music by Paul Joseph, at the Apollo Theatre (22 June 2005). Videorecording, 3 cameras, 136 min (V&A VIDEO 05/07/A3/9000). SOPHIE REYNOLDS

6. Anon., *The Duke's Theatre, in Dorset Gardens* (*c.* 1671). Engraving published for the *Encyclopædia Londinensis* (1825). 22.3cm x 29.2cm (V&A S.2351–2009). JAMES FOWLER

7. Russell & Sons, photograph of William Poel's production of *Measure for Measure*, Royalty Theatre, London (1893), (V&A THM/40/2/13/4 William Poel Archive). JANET BIRKETT

8. Agatha Walker, figurine of Dorothy Green as Mistress Ford in *The Merry Wives of Windsor*, Lyric Theatre, Hammersmith, 1923 (1924). Moulded plaster, covered in wax and hand coloured. 36.9cm (V&A S.323–1980). JANET BIRKETT

9. David Scott, *Queen Elizabeth Viewing the Performance of the 'Merry Wives of Windsor' in the Globe Theatre* (1840). Oil on canvas. 185cm x 275cm (V&A S.511–1985). JAMES FOWLER

10. Francis Wheatley, *Interior of the Shakespeare Gallery, Pall Mall* (1790). Pen and ink, and watercolour on paper. 45cm x 61.7cm (V&A 1719–1871). JAMES FOWLER

11. Costume worn by Henry Irving as Benedick in *Much Ado About Nothing*, Lyceum Theatre (1882). Silk, silver braid, pearl beads, and net (V&A S.2761:1 to 2–2010). VERONICA ISAAC

12. Jean-Louis Fesch, *David Garrick as Benedick in 'Much Ado About Nothing'*, Theatre Royal, Drury Lane (*c.* 1770). Watercolour, Indian ink and gold paint on vellum. 24.5cm x 20.5cm (V&A S.446–1979). BEVERLEY HART

13. J.W. Debenham, photograph of *Love's Labour's Lost*, directed by Tyrone Guthrie, Old Vic (1936). The photograph shows (left to right): Rosamund Greenwood (Katharine), Margaretta Scott (Rosaline), Katharine Page (Maria), Rachel Kempson (Princess of France), Alec Guinness (Boyet), Michael Redgrave (King of Navarre), James Hoyle (Dumain), Owen Jones (Longaville), Alec Clunes (Berowne), (V&A Theatre and Performance Department Photographic Collection). JANET BIRKETT

14. François Boitard, illustration of *A Midsummer Night's Dream, The Works of Mr. William Shakespear*, ed. Nicholas Rowe, 9 vols (London, 1709), 2, p. 464. Book: 22.1cm (height). Illustration: 17cm x 10cm (V&A DYCE. 8940/2). JAMES FOWLER

15. Sally Jacobs, reconstruction (2000) of her original set model for *A Midsummer Night's Dream* (1970). Cardboard, polyboard and paper model with photocopied and painted figures, wire, and feathers. 48cm (height) x 74cm (width) x 44cm (depth), (V&A S.706–2001). KATE DORNEY

16. Title page for the piano répétiteur (rehearsal score) by Georges Jacobi for the ballet *Titania*, Alhambra Theatre, London (1895). Manuscript, ink and pencil on music manuscript paper bound as a volume. 30.4cm x 24cm (pages), (V&A THM/140 Georges Jacobi Archive). JANE PRITCHARD

17. Houston Rogers, photograph of Anthony Dowell and Antoinette Sibley as Oberon and Titania in Frederick Ashton's *The Dream*, created for The Royal Ballet (1964), (V&A THM/245 Houston Rogers Archive). JANE PRITCHARD

18. Norman Wilkinson, costume designed for Lillah McCarthy as Helena in *A Midsummer Night's Dream*, Savoy Theatre (1914). Painted crêpe-de-chine, fringe, and beads (V&A S.1355&A–1984). JANET BIRKETT

19. Oliver Messel, crown designed for Vivien Leigh as Titania in *A Midsummer Night's Dream*, Old Vic (1937). Made by Thérèse Clement. Wire, velvet, ribbon, organdie, gauze, cord, cellophane, sequins, rhinestones, imitation pearls, and masking tape. 16.5cm (height), (V&A S.491–2006). JANET BIRKETT

20. Guy Green, Charles Macklin in the character of Shylock (*c.* 1780). Tin-glazed earthenware tile with transfer print. 12.7cm x 12.7cm (V&A CIRC.87–1922). JAMES FOWLER

21. Property bond, Lyceum Theatre, used by Henry Irving as Shylock in *The Merchant of Venice* (1879). Sewn vellum and cotton. 28.4cm x 45cm (V&A S.815–1981). JAMES FOWLER

22. Ticket for Shakespeare Jubilee, Stratford-upon-Avon (1769). Printed paper ticket with manuscript additions and applied red wax seal. 13.9cm x 16.5cm (V&A S.1055–2010). BEVERLEY HART

23. Charles Knight, *Dorothy Jordan as Rosalind in 'As You Like It'*, engraving after Henry Bunbury (1795). 40.8cm x 53.9cm (V&A S.1023–1995). JAMES FOWLER

24. Nick Ormerod, costume design for Audrey in *As You Like It* (1991). Pencil and crayon on paper. 29.6cm x 19.3cm (V&A S.210–1999). KATE DORNEY

25. John Ellys, Hester Booth (née Santlow) in the role of a Harlequin Lady (*c.* 1725). Oil on canvas. 122cm x 89cm (V&A S.668–1989). JAMES FOWLER

26. Siegmund Hildesheimer & Co., scrap depicting Madge Kendal and William Henry Kendal as Rosalind and Orlando in *As You Like It*, St James's Theatre, London, 24 January 1885 (*c.* 1890). Chromolithograph. 14.6cm x 12.4cm (V&A S.61–2008). CATHERINE HAILL

27. Elisabeth Dalton, costume design for Katherina in the ballet of *The Taming of the Shrew*, choreographed by John Cranko (1969). Watercolour, pencil and pen and ink on paper. 62cm x 44.6cm (V&A S.268–1984). JANE PRITCHARD

28. Unidentified photographer, Chris Castor as the Widow, *The Taming of the Shrew*, Royal Court Theatre (1928), (V&A THM/179 Barry Jackson Photograph Collection). CLAIRE HUDSON

29. Ginni Moo-Young, poster for Trevor Nunn's production of *All's Well That Ends Well*, Royal Shakespeare Company, Stratford-upon-Avon (1981). Silkscreen printing. 76.8cm x 50.5cm (V&A S.28–1983). JANET BIRKETT

30. The Great Bed of Ware (*c.* 1590). British, oak, carved, inlaid and painted. 2.67 metres (height) x 3.26 metres (width) x 3.38 metres (depth), (V&A W.47:1 to 28–1931). JANET BIRKETT

31. Gilbert Sommerlad, caricature of Roger Livesey as Sir Toby Belch, *Twelfth Night*, Old Vic Company (1950). Pencil and watercolour on paper. 17.8cm x 12.6cm (V&A S.131:119–2002). JANET BIRKETT

32. Ebenezer Landells after H.K. Browne, illustration of Mrs Jarley's caravan of waxworks, Charles Dickens, *The Old Curiosity Shop* (London: Chapman and Hall, 1867), opp. p.85. Book: 19cm (height), (V&A FORSTER 2401). JAMES FOWLER

33. Douglas H. Jeffery, photograph of Judi Dench as Perdita and David Bailie as Florizel, *The Winter's Tale*, directed by Trevor Nunn, Royal

Shakespeare Company (1969), (THM/374/1/2926 Douglas H. Jeffery Archive). JANET BIRKETT

34. Sarah Siddons, self-portrait in sculpture (*c.* 1790). Plaster. 61cm (V&A S.86–1978). JAMES FOWLER

35. Michael Rysbrack, portrait bust of Shakespeare (*c.* 1730). Terracotta. 57cm (V&A A.6–1924). JAMES FOWLER

36. Still from the National Video Archive of Performance recording of *Cardenio* at the Swan Theatre, Stratford-upon-Avon, adapted and directed by Gregory Doran for the Royal Shakespeare Company, with additional material by Antonio Álamo (9 July 2011). Videorecording, 4 cameras, 156 min (V&A VIDEO 11/11/A/9001–2). BEVERLEY HART

37. Charles Buchel, *Herbert Beerbohm Tree as King John* (1900). Oil on canvas. 218.4 cm x 147.3 cm (V&A S.332–1989). JANET BIRKETT

38. Audrey Cruddas, costume design for King John and Queen Elinor in *King John*, Shakespeare Memorial Theatre, Stratford-upon-Avon (1957). Watercolour and gold and silver paint on paper. 66.5cm x 49cm (S.318–2011). JANET BIRKETT

39. Angus McBean, photograph of Paul Scofield as Richard II at the Lyric Theatre, Hammersmith (1952), (V&A THM/53/2 H.M. Tennent Archive). CLAIRE HUDSON

40. Kevin Spacey as Richard II at the Old Vic, photographed by Graham Brandon for the V&A Performance Documentation Programme (2005). CLAIRE HUDSON

41. Tim Goodchild, tabard designed for Ian McKellen in *Richard II*, Prospect Theatre Company (1968). Brocade, net, felt, raffia, imitation leather, lamé, glass, metal, gold paint, and polythene (V&A S.853–1981). KATE DORNEY

42. Anon., frontispiece for Francis Kirkman, *The Wits, or, Sport upon Sport* (London, 1662; reprinted 1809). 33.2cm x 24.7cm (V&A S.313–1997). JAMES FOWLER

43. Roger Furse, design for Falstaff's 'fat-suit', Old Vic (1945). Pencil on paper. 39.3cm x 56.7cm (V&A S.138–2001). KATE DORNEY

44. Martin Laroche, photograph of Charles Kean as Henry V (1859), (V&A S.139:11–2007). CLAIRE HUDSON

45. Frank Salisbury, *Richard Burton as Henry V* (*c.* 1956). Oil on canvas. 150cm x 125cm (V&A S.32–1998). JAMES FOWLER

46. Lisel Haas, photograph of *King Henry VI, Part Three*, directed by Douglas Seale, Birmingham Repertory Company (1953), (V&A THM/164 Lisel Haas Archive). The photograph shows (foreground, centre) Alan Bridges (Edward IV) and Rosalind Boxall (Queen Margaret), and behind King Edward (left to right) Bernard Hepton (bearded, Earl of Warwick), Alfred Burke (George, Duke of Clarence), and Edgar Wreford (Richard, Duke of Gloucester). Behind Margaret are (background) Jack May (Henry VI) and (foreground) John Greenwood (Prince Edward). JANET BIRKETT

47. Feliks Topolski, drawing of Alan Howard as Henry VI and Helen Mirren as Margaret of Anjou in *Henry VI, Part Two*, Royal Shakespeare Theatre, Stratford-upon-Avon (1977). Felt-tip pen and crayon on paper. 45.5cm x 30.2cm (S.34–1979). JANET BIRKETT

48. Caroline Watson, *The Death of Cardinal Beaufort*, engraving (1792) after Joshua Reynolds's painting (1789). 58cm x 41cm (V&A DYCE. 2944). JAMES FOWLER

49. Ankle boots, worn by Henry Irving as Richard III, Lyceum Theatre (1877). Crimson suede, glass jewels and metallic gold braid; lace fastening at centre front, finished with metal aiglets (V&A S.2754:6 to 7–2010). VERONICA ISAAC

50. Doris Zinkeisen, costume designed for Laurence Olivier as Richard III, Old Vic Company at the New Theatre, London (1944). Made by B.J. Simmons & Co. Velvet, cotton, and rabbit fur (V&A S.824:1 to 2–1997). JANET BIRKETT

51. Charles Grignion, *Mr. Garrick in the Character of Richard III.* Engraving (1746) after William Hogarth's painting (1745). 48cm x 61.8cm (V&A S.40–2009). JAMES FOWLER

52. Philippe Jacques de Loutherbourg, sketch for David Garrick's production of *Richard III* (*c.* 1775). Pen and ink and wash. 22.8cm x 30.8cm (V&A S.1471–1986). JAMES FOWLER

53. Tinsel print of Edmund Kean as Richard and John Cooper as Richmond in *Richard III*; printed by W.S. Johnson between 1846 and 1860. Hand-coloured etching, decorated with fabric, leather, and metallic foil, possibly by H.J. Webb (*c.* 1920). 26.5cm x 31.4cm (V&A E.114–1969). CATHERINE HAILL

54. Playbill advertising *Richard III* and *Harlequin Tom Moody, or, Old Towler, the Huntsman and the Goddess Diana*, Astley's Amphitheatre, for the Benefit of William Cooke, 30 January 1860. Woodcuts by W. Earle, printed by Brickhill & Greenwood (1860). 74.3cm x 24.4cm (S.3801–2013). CATHERINE HAILL

55. William Heath, *The Rival Richards, or, Sheakspear in danger*. Hand-coloured etching, published by William McCleary, Dublin (*c.* 1814). 23.7cm x 35.7cm (V&A S.2533–2009). CATHERINE HAILL

56. Bust of Shakespeare advertising Flowers Ales (mid-twentieth century). Painted and varnished papier mâché. 26.5cm (V&A S.2494–1986). JAMES FOWLER

57. Henry Dawe, *Henry Harris as Cardinal Wolsey in 'Henry VIII'*, engraving after John Greenhill's portrait (1664), published by W.J. White (1820). 34.4cm x 24.6cm (V&A S.4398–2009). JAMES FOWLER

58. Henry Fuseli, *Queen Katharine's Dream*, detail (*c.* 1789). Oil on canvas. 138.4cm x 102.9cm (V&A 1386–1869). JAMES FOWLER

59. Louis François Roubiliac, model for a statue of Shakespeare (1757). Terracotta. 42.2cm (32–1867). JAMES FOWLER

60. Still from the National Video Archive of Performance recording of the puppet play *Venus and Adonis*, performed by the Little Angel Theatre and the Royal Shakespeare Company, directed by Gregory Doran. Recorded at the Little Angel Theatre (3 November 2004). Videorecording, 2 cameras, 60 min (V&A VIDEO 04/12/A/9000). JAMES FOWLER

61. Houston Rogers, photograph of (left to right) Paul Rogers as Pandarus, Wendy Hiller as Helen, and Ronald Allen as Paris in *Troilus and Cressida*, directed by Tyrone Guthrie, Old Vic (1956), (V&A THM/245 Houston Rogers Archive). JANET BIRKETT

62. Thomas Lawrence, *John Philip Kemble as Coriolanus* (after 1798). Oil on canvas. 74.9cm x 45.7cm (V&A DYCE.73). JAMES FOWLER

63. Motley (Margaret Harris), set design for *Coriolanus*, Shakespeare Memorial Theatre, Stratford-upon-Avon (1952). Watercolour and gouache on paper. 39cm x 48cm (V&A S.2371–1986). JANET BIRKETT

64. *Sketch of Stratford Jubilee Booth or Amphitheatre*, published by *The Gentleman's Magazine* (1769). Engraving. 14.6cm x 24cm (V&A S.657–2010). JAMES FOWLER

65. Costume designed by Ezio Frigerio and Franca Squarciapino for Rudolf Nureyev as Romeo in his production of the ballet *Romeo and Juliet*, London Festival Ballet (1977). Silk, silk velvet, braid, paint, and sequins (V&A S.728–1985). JANE PRITCHARD

66. Dame Laura Knight, drawing of Gwen Ffrangcon-Davies as Juliet, backstage at the Regent Theatre, London (1924). Pencil, watercolour, charcoal, and pen and ink on paper. 36.2cm x 25.6cm (V&A S.1–1992). JAMES FOWLER

67. Edward Gordon Craig, sketch for a set design for *Romeo and Juliet* (1891). Watercolour and Chinese white on paper, mounted on a page from a diary dated Easter Day, Sunday 2 April [1893]. 5.6cm x 8.3cm (sketch), 13.3cm x 10.2cm (diary page), (E.24–1971). JAMES FOWLER

68. Benjamin Wilson, *Mr. Garrick and Miss Bellamy in the Characters of Romeo and Juliet* (1753). Oil on canvas. 63.5cm x 76.3cm (V&A S.1452–1986). JAMES FOWLER

69. François-Antoine Conscience ('Francis'), *Charles Kemble and Harriet Smithson as Romeo and Juliet, Théâtre de l'Odeon, Paris* (1827). Lithograph. 36.9cm x 28.6cm (V&A S.2326–2009). JAMES FOWLER

70. Nicholas Georgiadis, preliminary set design for Kenneth MacMillan's ballet *Romeo and Juliet* (c. 1964). Watercolour on paper. 55.2cm x 75.2cm (V&A S.1903–1986). JANE PRITCHARD

71. 'J.B.', *The Theatrical Caesar! Or Cassius and Casca in Debate*, London (1804). Hand-coloured etching, published by S.W. Fores. 35.6cm x 28.2cm (V&A S.126–2009). CATHERINE HAILL

72. Ernst Stern, illustration from *Shakespeare's The Tragedie of Julius Caesar. Newly Printed from the First Folio of 1623* (London: Ernest Benn, 1925). Book: 32.5cm (height). Illustration: 13cm

x 16.3cm (V&A Theatre and Performance Department Library).
JAMES FOWLER

73. Still from the National Video Archive of Performance recording of *Julius Caesar* at the Donmar Warehouse, directed by Phyllida Lloyd (22 January 2013). Videorecording, 5 cameras, 125 min (V&A VIDEO 13/02/A/9000). SOPHIE REYNOLDS

74. William Dawes, *The Downfall of Shakespeare Represented on a Modern Stage* (1765). Oil on canvas. 69.8cm x 90.8cm (V&A S.501–2006). JAMES FOWLER

75. Anon, *Brutus and the Ghost of Caesar before Philippi* (*c.* 1715). Mezzotint published by Pierce Tempest. 41.2cm x 29.4cm (V&A S.169–2010). JAMES FOWLER

76. Silvester Harding, *The Spirit of Shakspere appearing to his Detracters* (*c.* 1796). Hand-coloured etching. 24.8cm x 31.7cm (V&A S.2722–2009). BEVERLEY HART

77. François Boitard, illustration of *Macbeth, The Works of Mr. William Shakespear*, ed. Nicholas Rowe, 9 vols (London, 1709), 7, p. 2298. Book: 22.4cm (height). Illustration: 16.8cm x 10cm (V&A DYCE. 8940/7). JAMES FOWLER

78. Ruskin Spear, study for a portrait of Laurence Olivier as Macbeth (1955). Oil on panel. 57cm x 46cm (V&A S.198–1992). JAMES FOWLER

79. George Clint, study for a portrait of Edmund Kean as Sir Giles Overreach in *A New Way to Pay Old Debts* (1820). Oil on canvas. 28cm x 22.9cm (V&A DYCE.79). JAMES FOWLER

80. Presentation sword and scabbard given to Edmund Kean, November 1819. Sword with basket hilt, the hilt decorated with medallions of jewelled thistles and lined in red velvet, the grip covered with shagreen, with scabbard of suede with engraved silver mounts. British, early nineteenth century. Sword: 101cm (blade: 84cm); Scabbard: 86cm. Total length: 103cm (S.63:1 to 2–1981). JANET BIRKETT

81. Window & Grove, photograph of Ellen Terry as Lady Macbeth (1889), (V&A S.133:429–2007). CLAIRE HUDSON

82.   Lafayette Studio, London, photograph of Sarah Bernhardt as Hamlet (1899), (V&A Theatre and Performance Department Photographic Collection). CLAIRE HUDSON

83.   William Telbin, preliminary set design for *Hamlet*, Lyceum Theatre, London (1864). Watercolour and gouache on paper. 16.2cm x 21.6cm (V&A E.261–1925). CATHERINE HAILL

84.   Lez Brotherston, costume design for *Rosencrantz and Guildenstern Are Dead* by Tom Stoppard, National Theatre (1995). Pencil, pen and ink, crayon, and watercolour on paper. 30.5cm x 40.5cm (V&A S.337–2002). SARAH BELANGER

85.   François Boitard, illustration of *Hamlet*, *The Works of Mr. William Shakespear*, ed. Nicholas Rowe, 9 vols (London, 1709), 7, opp. p. 2365. Book: 22.4cm (height). Illustration: 16.7cm x 10cm (V&A DYCE. 8940/7). JAMES FOWLER

86.   Ronald Searle, costume designs for 'Hamlet Goes Hollywood' (1944). Pen and ink, watercolour, and crayon on paper. 18cm x 21cm (V&A S.416–1978). KATE DORNEY

87.   Skull from *Hamlet*, directed by Richard Eyre, Royal Court Theatre, London (1980). Human bone (V&A S.151–2007). KATE DORNEY

88.   Leslie Hurry, headdress for the Gravedigger in Robert Helpmann's *Hamlet*, Sadler's Wells Ballet (1942). Made by Hugh Skillen. Papier-mâché, plastic, and paint. 26cm (height), (V&A S.656–1981). JANE PRITCHARD

89.   George and Isaac Cruikshank, *The O.P. and N.P. Spectacles*. Hand-coloured engravings (1809). 35.5cm x 23.4cm ('The O.P. Spectacles', V&A S.4776–2009), 36.1cm x 25cm ('The N.P. Spectacles', V&A S.4777–2009). JAMES FOWLER

90.   Isamu Noguchi, costume design for Gloucester in *King Lear*, Shakespeare Memorial Theatre Company (1955). Paper collage with pencil, watercolour, and wire. 25cm x 20cm (V&A CIRC.69–1960). JANET BIRKETT

91.   Roger Furse, costume design for John Gielgud as King Lear, Old Vic (1940). Watercolour and pencil on paper. 56cm x 38cm (S.2147–1986). JANET BIRKETT

92. Unidentified photographer, Paul Robeson and Peggy Ashcroft as Othello and Desdemona, Savoy Theatre (1930), (V&A Theatre and Performance Department Photographic Collection). JAMES FOWLER

93. Anon., *Ira Aldridge as Othello* (*c.* 1848). Oil on canvas. 42.8cm x 34.4cm (V&A S.1129–1986). JAMES FOWLER

94. W. Vincent, *Mrs Bracegirdle as Semernia, the Indian Queen, in 'The Widow Ranter' by Aphra Behn* (*c.* 1690), engraving from a mezzotint by J. Smith. 14.5cm x 9.8cm (V&A S.1500–2012). JAMES FOWLER

95. Ronald Cobb, costume design, inspired by *Antony and Cleopatra*, for the Eve Club, London (1970s). Pencil, watercolour, gouache, gold paint, and glitter on card. 50.8cm x 38cm (V&A S.712–1996). KATE DORNEY

96. Gerard Valck, portrait of Eleanor (Nell) Gwyn, engraving after S. Cooper (*c.* 1670). 16.1cm x 11.9cm (V&A E.998–1960). JAMES FOWLER

97. Leslie Hurry, costume design for King Cymbeline in *Cymbeline*, Shakespeare Memorial Theatre, Stratford-upon-Avon (1949). Watercolour and ink on paper. 58cm x 45cm (S.2215–1986). JANET BIRKETT

98. Bracelet presented to Kate Terry by her fiancé Arthur James Lewis (1867). Gold, enamel, and diamonds, with photograph by Window & Bridge. 7.5cm (maximum width) x 4.5cm (depth), (V&A S.55–2003). CATHERINE HAILL

99. Henry Wallis, *Shakespeare's House, Stratford-upon-Avon* (*c.* 1854), with additions by Edwin Landseer (1866). Oil on canvas. 65.5cm x 49.5cm (V&A F.38). JAMES FOWLER

100. Paul Catherall, limited edition print of the front elevation of the rebuilt Royal Shakespeare Theatre, Stratford-upon-Avon (2010). No.48 of 100. Linocut. 57cm x 76cm (S.3800–2013). JAMES FOWLER

Bibliography

Richard D. Altick, *The Shows of London: a Panoramic History of Exhibitions, 1600–1862* (Cambridge, Massachusetts, and London: Belknap Press, Harvard University Press, 1978)

Geoffrey Ashton and Iain Mackintosh, ed., *Royal Opera House Retrospective 1732–1982: 250 Years of Actors, Singers, Dancers, Managers and Musicians of Covent Garden Seen through the Eye of the Artist*, Exhibition Catalogue (London: Royal Opera House, 1982)

Geoffrey Ashton, 'The Boydell Shakespeare Gallery: Before and After', in *The Painted Word: British History Painting: 1750-1830*, ed. Peter Cannon-Brookes, Exhibition Catalogue (Woodbridge; Rochester, New York: Boydell Press for the Heim Gallery, London, 1991), pp. 37–43

Geoffrey Ashton, *Catalogue of Paintings at the Theatre Museum, London*, ed. James Fowler (London: Victoria and Albert Museum, in association with the Society for Theatre Research, 1992)

Emmett L. Avery and Arthur H. Scouten, *The London Stage 1660–1700: A Critical Introduction* (Carbondale: Southern Illinois University Press, 1968)

Emmett L. Avery, *The London Stage: Part 2: 1700–1729: A Critical Introduction*, 2 vols (Carbondale: Southern Illinois University Press, 1960)

Malcolm Baker, *Figured in Marble: The Making and Viewing of Eighteenth-Century Sculpture* (London: V&A Publications, 2000)

322

George Bradford Bartlett and W. Gurney Benham, *Mrs Jarley's Far-Famed Collection of Waxworks, with full directions for their Arrangement, Positions, Movements, Costumes, and Properties.* (London and New York: Samuel French, [1889])

Jonathan Bate, 'Shakespearean Allusion in English Caricature in the Age of Gillray', *Journal of the Warburg and Courtauld Institutes* 49 (1986), 196–210

Jonathan Bate and Russell Jackson, ed., *Shakespeare: An Illustrated Stage History* (Oxford: Oxford University Press, 1996)

Sally Beauman, *The Royal Shakespeare Company: A History of Ten Decades* (Oxford: Oxford University Press, 1982)

Aphra Behn, *Five Plays*, selected and introduced by Maureen Duffy (London: Methuen, 1990)

Michael Benthall, 'Shakespeare in the Theatre', in *Orpheus: A Symposium of the Arts*, ed. John Lehmann (London: John Lehmann, 1949), vol. 2, pp. 137–43

Berlioz and the Romantic Imagination: An Exhibition Organized by the Arts Council and the Victoria and Albert Museum, ed. Elizabeth Davison (London: Arts Council, 1969)

The Memoirs of Hector Berlioz Member of the French Institute, trans. and ed. David Cairns (1969; reprinted London: Allen Lane, 1999)

Michael Billington, *Peggy Ashcroft* (London: John Murray, 1988; reprinted 1990)

Michael R. Booth, *Victorian Spectacular Theatre 1850–1910* (London: Routledge & Kegan Paul, 1981)

The Boydell Shakespeare Prints, with an introduction by A.E. Santaniello (New York: Arno Press, 1979)

Peter Brook, *Threads of Time: A Memoir* (London: Methuen, 1998)

Judith Buchanan, *Shakespeare on Silent Film: An Excellent Dumb Discourse* (Cambridge: Cambridge University Press, 2009)

Hal Burton, ed., *Acting in the Sixties* (London: BBC Publications, 1970)

David Cairns, *Berlioz: Volume One: The Making of an Artist, 1803–1832* (1989; reprinted London: Sphere Books, 1991)

[John P. Cavanagh,] *The Drama Delineated: A Source Collection of Original Drawings of the French 18th-Century Stage* (Romsey: Motley Books, [1981])

E.K. Chambers, *The Elizabethan Stage*, 4 vols (1923; reprinted Oxford: Clarendon Press, 1945)

Mary Clarke, *Shakespeare at the Old Vic: 1955–6* (London: A. & C. Black, 1956)

Mary Clarke and Clement Crisp, *Making a Ballet* (London: Studio Vista, 1974)

Charles B. Cochran, *The Secrets of a Showman* (London: W. Heinemann, 1925)

Samuel Taylor Coleridge, *Specimens of the Table Talk of the late Samuel Taylor Coleridge*, ed. H.N. Coleridge, 2 vols (London: John Murray, 1835)

Plays by George Colman the Younger and Thomas Morton, ed. Barry Sutcliffe (Cambridge: Cambridge University Press, 1983)

Francis Aspry Congreve, *Authentic Memoirs of the Late Mr Charles Macklin, Comedian* (London: J. Barker, 1798)

Dutton Cook, *Nights at the Play: A View of the English Stage*, 2 vols (London: Chatto and Windus, 1883)

Paul Cope, *Let Paul Robeson Sing! A Celebration of the Life of Paul Robeson* (London: Paul Robeson Cymru Committee / Bevan Foundation / Theatre Museum, 2001)

Edward Gordon Craig, *Ellen Terry and Her Secret Self* (London: Sampson Lowe, Marston & Co., 1931)

Jonathan Croall, *Gielgud: A Theatrical Life* (London: Methuen, 2000)

Jonathan Croall, *John Gielgud: Matinee Idol to Movie Star* (London: Methuen Drama, 2011)

John Wilson Croker, *Familiar Epistles to Frederick J—-S, Esq.: on the Present State of the Irish Stage* (Dublin: J. Barlow, 1804)

Thomas Davies, *Memoirs of the Life of David Garrick, Esq., Interspersed with Characters and Anecdotes of his Theatrical Contemporaries*, 2 vols (London: 'Printed for the author, and sold at his shop in Great Russell-Street, Covent-Garden', 1780)

Barry Day, *This Wooden 'O': Shakespeare's Globe Reborn* (London: Oberon, in association with the Shakespeare Globe Trust, 1996; reprinted 1997)

Christian Deelman, *The Great Shakespeare Jubilee* (London: Michael Joseph, 1964)

Diana de Marly, *Costume on the Stage, 1600–1940* (London: Batsford, 1982)

Bernard Denvir, *The Eighteenth Century: Art, Design, and Society 1689–1789* (London: Longman, 1983)

Charles Dickens, *The Old Curiosity Shop* (1841), ed. Norman Page (London: Penguin, 2000)

Gregory Doran, *Shakespeare's Lost Play: In Search of 'Cardenio'* (London: Nick Hern Books, 2012)

John Downes, *Roscius Anglicanus*, ed. Judith Milhous and Robert D. Hume (London: Society for Theatre Research, 1987)

Martin Bauml Duberman, *Paul Robeson* (1989; London: Pan, 1991)

The Reminiscences of Alexander Dyce, ed. Richard J. Schrader (Columbus: Ohio State University Press, 1972)

Philip Edwards (et al.), ed., *The Revels History of Drama in English Drama. Vol. 4: 1613–1660* (London: Methuen, 1981)

George Farquhar, *The Recruiting Officer*, New Mermaid edition, ed. John Ross (London: Ernest Benn, 1973)

Raymund FitzSimons, *Edmund Kean: Fire from Heaven* (London: Hamish Hamilton, 1976)

R.A. Foakes, *Illustrations of the English Stage 1580–1642* (London: Scolar Press, 1973)

Brian Fothergill, *Mrs Jordan: Portrait of an Actress* (London: Faber and Faber, 1965)

Richard Foulkes, 'Charles Kean's King Richard II: A Pre-Raphaelite Drama', in Foulkes, ed. Shakespeare and the Victorian Stage, pp. 39–55

James Fowler, 'David Scott's Queen Elizabeth Viewing the Performance of 'The Merry Wives of Windsor' in the Globe Theatre (1840)', in Shakespeare and the Victorian Stage, ed. Richard Foulkes, pp. 23–38

James Fowler, 'Picturing Romeo and Juliet', Shakespeare Survey 49 (1996), 111–30

James Fowler, 'Hester Santlow: Harlequin Lady', in World of Baroque Theatre: A Compilation of Essays from the Cesky Krumlov Conferences 2007, 2008, and 2009, ed. Jiri Blaha and Pavel Slavko (Cesky Krumlov, 2010), pp. 47–52

Levi Fox, The Borough Town of Stratford-upon-Avon (Stratford-upon-Avon: Corporation of Stratford-upon-Avon, 1953)

The Letters of David Garrick, ed. David M. Little and George M. Kahrl, 3 vols (London: Oxford University Press, 1963)

The Private Correspondence of David Garrick with the Most Celebrated Persons of his Time, ed. James Boaden, vol.1 (Cambridge: Cambridge University Press, 2013)

Evgenia Georgiadis, Nicholas Georgiadis: Paintings, Stage Designs (1955–2001) (Athens: Olkos, 2004)

John Gielgud, Stage Directions (London: Heinemann, 1963)

John Gielgud, with John Miller, Shakespeare: Hit or Miss? (London: Sidgwick & Jackson, 1991)

Gielgud's Letters, ed. Richard Mangan (London: Weidenfeld & Nicolson, 2004)

Moira Goff, The Incomparable Hester Santlow: A Dancer-Actress on the Georgian Stage (Aldershot: Ashgate, 2007)

Robert Gottlieb, Sarah: The Life of Sarah Bernhardt (New Haven and London: Yale University Press, 2010)

W.W. Greg, The Shakespeare First Folio: Its Bibliographical and Textual History (Oxford: Clarendon Press, 1955)

John Gross, *Shylock: Four Hundred Years in the Life of a Legend* (Chatto & Windus: London, 1992)

Rupert Gunnis, *Dictionary of British Sculptors, 1660–1851* (1951; London: The Abbey Library, 1968)

Andrew Gurr, *Playgoing in Shakespeare's London* (Cambridge: Cambridge University Press, 1987)

Catherine Haill, *Theatre Posters* (London: HMSO, 1983)

Peter Hall's Diaries: The Story of a Dramatic Battle, ed. John Goodwin (London: Hamish Hamilton, 1981)

Robin Hamlyn, 'The Shakespeare Galleries of John Boydell and James Woodmason', in Jane Martineau (et al.), *Shakespeare in Art*, pp. 97–113

Joseph Harker, *Studio and Stage* (London: Nisbet & Co., 1924)

Ronald Harwood, ed., *A Night at the Theatre* (London: Methuen, 1982)

F.W. Hawkins, *The Life of Edmund Kean. From Published and Original Sources*, 2 vols (London: Tinsley Brothers, 1869)

William Hazlitt, *Characters of Shakespeare's Plays* (London: C.H. Reynell, 1817)

William Hazlitt, *A View of the English Stage* (London: Robert Stodart, 1818)

Philip H. Highfill, Jr., Kalman A. Burnim, and Edward A. Langhans, *A Biographical Dictionary of Actors, Actresses, Musicians, Dancers, Managers, & other Stage Personnel in London, 1660–1800*, 16 vols (Carbondale: Southern Illinois University Press, 1973–93)

Harold Newcomb Hillebrand, *Edmund Kean* (New York: Columbia University Press, 1933)

Alan Hughes, *Henry Irving, Shakespearean* (Cambridge: Cambridge University Press, 1981)

Robert D. Hume, ed., *The London Theatre World, 1600–1800* (Carbondale, Southern Illinois University Press, 1980)

Hugh Hunt, *Old Vic Prefaces: Shakespeare and the Producer* (London: Routledge & Kegan Paul, 1954)

Leslie Hurry: *A Painter for the Stage*, catalogue to accompany the touring exhibition of the same name (Stratford, Ontario: The Gallery, 1982)

Leslie Hurry, *Settings & Costumes for Sadler's Wells Ballets*, ed. Lilian Browse, with an introduction by Cyril W. Beaumont, (London: Faber and Faber, 1946)

Barry Jackson, 'On Producing *Henry VI*', *Shakespeare Survey* 6 (1953), 49–52

Gerald Jacobs, *Judi Dench: A Great Deal of Laughter* (London: Futura, 1986)

Ben Jonson, *Epicœne, or The Silent Woman*, New Mermaid edition, ed. R.V. Holdsworth (London: Ernest Benn, 1979).

Rüdiger Joppien, *Philippe Jacques de Loutherbourg, RA, 1740–1812*, Exhibition Catalogue (London: Greater London Council, 1973)

Jeffrey Kahan, *The Cult of Kean* (Aldershot: Ashgate, 2006)

T.C. Kemp, 'Acting Shakespeare: Modern Tendencies in Playing and Production', *Shakespeare Survey* 7 (1954), 121–7

T.C. Kemp and J.C. Trewin, *The Stratford Festival: A History of the Shakespeare Memorial Theatre* (Birmingham: Cornish Brothers, 1953)

Rachel Kempson, *A Family and its Fortunes* (London: Duckworth, 1986)

Count Harry Kessler, *The Diaries of a Cosmopolitan 1918–1937*, trans. and ed. Charles Kessler (1971; reprinted London: Phoenix, 2000)

Laura Knight, *Oil Paint and Grease Paint: Autobiography of Laura Knight* (London: Ivor Nicholson & Watson, 1936)

Laura Knight, *The Magic of a Line: The Autobiography of Laura Knight D.B.E., R.A.* (London: William Kimber, 1965)

Philippa Langley and Michael Jones, *The King's Grave: The Search for Richard III* (London: John Murray, 2013)

Janet Leeper, *Edward Gordon Craig: Designs for the Theatre* (Harmondsworth: Penguin, 1948)

Mervyn Levy, *Ruskin Spear* (London: Weidenfeld and Nicolson, 1985)

George Henry Lewes, *On Actors and the Art of Acting* (London: Smith, Elder & Co.,1875)

Paddy Lyons and Fidelis Morgan, ed., *Female Playwrights of the Restoration: Five Comedies*, Everyman's Library (London: Dent 1991)

Iain Mackintosh and Geoffrey Ashton, *Thirty Different Likenesses: David Garrick in Portrait and Performance* (Buxton Museum and Art Gallery, 1981)

Iain Mackintosh, 'Deciphering *The Downfall of Shakespeare Represented on a* Modern *Stage* of 1765', *Theatre Notebook* 62 (2008), 20–58

Charles Macklin, *Four Comedies*, ed. J.O. Bartley (London: Sidgwick & Jackson, 1968)

Roger Manvell, *Ellen Terry: A Biography* (London: Heinemann, 1968)

Roger Manvell, *Sarah Siddons: Portrait of an Actress* (London: Heinemann, 1970)

Herbert Marshall and Mildred Stock, *Ira Aldridge: The Negro Tragedian* (London: Rockliff, 1958)

Jane Martineau et al., *Shakespeare in Art*, Dulwich Picture Gallery, London, in collaboration with Ferrari Arte Spa, Palazzo dei Diamanti (London: Merrell, 2003)

Judith Milhous and Robert D. Hume, ed., *A Register of English Theatrical Documents, 1660–1737*, 2 vols (Carbondale: Southern Illinois University Press, 1991)

John Miller, *Ralph Richardson: The Authorized Biography* (London: Sidgwick & Jackson, 1995)

John Miller, *Judi Dench: With a Crack in her Voice* (rev. ed.; London: Orion, 2002)

Michael Mullin, *Design By Motley*, pamphlet to accompany the touring exhibition of the same name (Urbana-Champaign: University of Illinois, 1988)

George Nash, *Edward Gordon Craig* (London: Victoria and Albert Museum, 1967)

Allardyce Nicoll, *The Garrick Stage: Theatres and Audience in the Eighteenth Century*, ed. Sybil Rosenfield (Manchester: Manchester University Press, 1980)

Garry O'Connor, *Ralph Richardson: An Actor's Life* (London: Coronet, 1983)

Garry O'Connor, ed., *Olivier: In Celebration* (London: Hodder & Stoughton, 1987)

George C.D. Odell, *Shakespeare from Betterton to Irving*, 2 vols (London: Constable and Company, 1921)

Laurence Olivier, *On Acting* (London: Weidenfeld and Nicolson, 1986)

Tarquin Olivier, *My Father Laurence Oliver* (London: Headline Book Publishing, 1992)

Walter Pape and Frederick Burwick, ed., *The Boydell Shakespeare Gallery* (Bottrop, Essen: Peter Pomp, 1996)

Ronald Parkinson, *Catalogue of British Oil Paintings 1820–1860* (London: HMSO for Victoria and Albert Museum, 1990)

T. Edgar Pemberton, *Ellen Terry and Her Sisters* (London, C.A. Pearson, 1902)

John Pemble, *Shakespeare Goes to Paris: How the Bard Conquered France* (London: Continuum, 2005)

Nicholas Penny, ed., *Reynolds* (London: Royal Academy of Arts in association with Weidenfeld and Nicolson, 1986)

The Diary of Samuel Pepys: A New and Complete Transcription, ed. Robert Latham and William Matthews, 11 vols (London: Bell, 1970–83)

John Percival, *Theatre in my Blood: A Biography of John Cranko* (London: Herbert Press 1983)

Giles Playfair, *The Flash of Lightning: A Portrait of Edmund Kean* (London: Wiliam Kimber, 1983)

Giles Playfair, *The Prodigy: A Study of the Strange Life of Master Betty* (London: Secker & Warburg, 1967)

Marian J. Pringle, *The Theatres of Stratford-upon-Avon, 1875–1992: An Architectural History* (Stratford-upon-Avon: Stratford-upon-Avon Society, 1994)

Michael Redgrave, *In My Mind's Eye* (London: Weidenfeld and Nicolson, 1983)

Aileen Ribeiro, 'Costuming the Part: A Discourse Fashion and Fiction in the Image of the Actress in England, 1776–1812', in Robyn Asleson, ed., *Notorious Muse: The Actress in British Art and Culture, 1776–1812*, Yale Studies in British Art 11 (New Haven, Connecticut, and London: Yale University Press, 2003)

Tony Richardson, *Long Distance Runner: A Memoir* (London: Faber, 1993)

J.W. Robinson, ed., *Theatrical Street Ballads: Some Nineteenth-Century Street Ballads about the Theatre* (London: Society for Theatre Research, 1971)

Ingrid Roscoe, 'The Monument to the Memory of Shakespeare', *Journal of the Church Monuments Society* 9 (1994), 72–82

Martial Rose, *Forever Juliet: The Life and Letters of Gwen Ffrangcon-Davies, 1891–1992* (Dereham: Larks Press, 2003)

George Rowell, *Queen Victoria Goes to the Theatre* (London: Paul Elek, 1978)

S. Schoenbaum, *Shakespeare's Lives* (Oxford: Clarendon Press, 1970; new edition, Oxford: Clarendon Press, 1991)

Clement Scott, *From 'The Bells' to 'King Arthur': A Critical Record of the First-Night Productions at the Lyceum Theatre from 1871 to 1895* (London: John Macqueen, 1896)

Walter Scott, *Introductions, and Notes and Illustrations, to the Novels, Tales, and Romances of the Author of Waverley*, 3 vols, (Edinburgh: Robert Cadell, 1833)

Ronald Searle, *To the Kwai and Back: War Drawings 1939–1945* (London: Collins, in association with the Imperial War Museum, 1986)

The Works of Mr William Shakespear, ed. Nicholas Rowe, 9 vols (London 1709)

The Complete Works of William Shakespeare, ed. Peter Alexander (revised edition, Glasgow: HarperCollins, 2006)

Shakespeare's Play of King Henry the Fifth: Arranged for representation at the Princess's Theatre, with Historical and Explanatory Notes by Charles Kean, FSA (London, John K. Chapman and Co., 1859)

William Shakespeare and others, *The Merry Conceited Humours of Bottom the Weaver: 1661* (London: Cornmarket Press, 1970)

Romeo and Juliet: A Tragedy, by Shakespeare, Theatre-Royal, Drury-Lane, Regulated from the Prompt-book (London: 'Printed for John Bell', 1774)

William Shakespeare and others, *The Tempest, or, The Enchanted Island: A Comedy* (London 1676)

The Correspondence of the Right Honourable Sir John Sinclair, Bart. with reminiscences of the most distinguished characters who have appeared in Great Britain, and in foreign countries, during the last fifty years, 2 vols (London: Henry Colburn and Richard Bentley, 1831)

Roger Southern, ed., *Birmingham Repertory Theatre, 1913–1971* (Birmingham: Birmingham Repertory Theatre, 1971)

George Speaight, *The History of the English Puppet Theatre* (1955; 2nd ed., London: Robert Hale, 1990)

Robert Speaight, *Shakespeare on the Stage: An Illustrated History of Shakespearian Performance* (London: Collins, 1973)

Elizabeth Sprigge, *Sybil Thorndike Casson* (London: Gollancz, 1971)

Constantin Stanislavsky, *My Life in Art*, trans. J.J. Robbins (London: Geoffrey Bles, 1924)

Ernst Stern, *My Life, My Stage*, trans. Edward Fitzgerald (London: Gollancz, 1951)

Johanne M. Stochholm, *Garrick's Folly: The Shakespeare Jubilee of 1769 at Stratford and Drury Lane* (London: Methuen, 1964)

Tom Stoppard, *Rosencrantz and Guildenstern Are Dead* (London: Faber, 1968)

Kim C. Sturgess, *Shakespeare and the American Nation* (Cambridge: Cambridge University Press, 2004)

Ellen Terry, *The Story of My Life* (London: Hutchinson, 1908)

J.C. Trewin, *The Birmingham Repertory Theatre, 1913–63* (London: Barrie and Rockliff, 1963)

Gerd Unverfehrt, 'John Boydell's Shakespeare Gallery in Gillray's Caricatures', in *The Boydell Shakespeare Gallery*, ed. Walter Pape and Frederick Burwick, pp. 161–74

Hans van Lemmen, *Tiles: A Collector's Guide* (London: Souvenir Press, 1979)

George Vandenhoff, *Dramatic Reminiscences; or, Actors and Actresses in England and America* (London: Thomas W. Cooper & Co., 1860)

George Villiers, *The Rehearsal*, ed. Edward Arber (London: Constable and Co., 1919)

David Ward, *Transformation: Shakespeare's New Theatre* (Stratford-upon-Avon: RSC, 2011)

The Dramatic Works of John Webster, ed. William Hazlitt, 4 vols (London: John Russell Smith, 1857).

Timothy Wilcox, *Laura Knight at the Theatre: Paintings and Drawings of the Ballet and the Stage* (London: Unicorn Press, 2008)

Tate Wilkinson, *The Wandering Patentee, or, A History of the Yorkshire Theatres from 1770 to the present time*, 4 vols (York: Wilson, Spence, and Mawman, 1795)

Audrey Williamson, *Old Vic Drama: A Twelve Years' Study of Plays and Players* (London: Rockliff, 1948)

Franco Zeffirelli, *Zeffirelli: The Autobiography of Franco Zeffirelli* (London: Weidenfeld and Nicolson, 1986)